BE YOUR OWN
HEADHUNTER
ONLINE

BE YOUR OWN HEADHUNTER ONLINE

Get the Job You Want Using the Information Superhighway

Pam Dixon

Sylvia Tiersten

Random House

Trademarks

A number of entered words in which we have reason to believe have trademark, service mark, or other proprietary rights may exist, and have been designated as such by use of initial capitalization. However, no attempt has been made to designate as trademarks or service marks all personal computer words or terms in which proprietary rights might exist. The inclusion, exclusion, or definition of a word or term is not intended to affect, or to express any judgment on, the validity or legal status of any proprietary right which may be claimed in that word or term.

New York   Toronto   London   Sydney   Auckland

Contents

CHAPTER 1

v

CHAPTER 2

ONLINE WORKING STRATEGIES   34

CHAPTER 3

POSTING YOUR RESUME ONLINE   72

CHAPTER 4

NETWORKING ON THE NEW FRONTIER   106

CHAPTER 5

WORLD WIDE WEB: THE JOB SEEKER'S GOLD MINE   140

CHAPTER 6

INFORMATION AT YOUR FINGERTIPS 196

CHAPTER 7

WHERE THE JOBS ARE   252

Appendix A: Getting Yourself Online   317

Appendix B: Alphabetical Address and Country Code Lists   355

Appendix C: Resources   367

Preface

To get the maximum benefit from *Be Your Own Headhunter Online: Get the Job You Want Using the Information Superhighway*, it is important to understand both how the current workplace evolved and where it is headed. As someone who has been involved in recruiting and employment for over a quarter-century, I hope to provide you with an informative perspective that will help you to anticipate and take advantage of changes in this new terrain as you map your career.

In 1970, the world was very different from today. Color TV was only found in the homes of the well-to-do. Video recorders were unheard-of. The largest selling imported car was the Volkswagen Beetle; a "Honda" was strictly a motorcycle. Personal computers did not exist. The Internet was but one year old, the province of academics and researchers.

It's hard to pinpoint when that world faded away and today's began to emerge. We are learning, however, that the only constant in the world is change. The '90s saw intense pressure on costs, as competitors from other parts of Asia as well as Japan offered quality at low prices to consumers worldwide.

This is the world we live in today. One where high quality is merely the price of entry into a market; it must be matched with competitive pricing and attentive customer service. Companies are squeezed between the expense of delivering quality and support and selling at a low price. As the quest to reduce costs continues, employers look at the cost of labor—often the highest component in the price of just about anything—as a place to cut.

This need to cut labor costs has dramatically changed the relationship between employers and employees, both current and prospective. For the current employee, there is no guarantee of a gold watch after years of service. You are expected to demonstrate your worth, your "added value" in the current parlance, everyday. Otherwise, your position—even your entire department—might be eliminated in the name of cost efficiency. This scenario applies to virtually every industry, from retailing to high tech, health care to finance.

As a prospective employee, it is incumbent upon you to constantly prepare yourself for the job market as it is today through learning and keeping your eye on the companies in your industry for opportunity. Many human resources executives agree that the challenge for you is to plan and execute your own, individual career path instead of one plotted out by your employer. Indeed, your path may take you away from your current employer to a new one.

This is where *Be Your Own Headhunter Online: Get the Job You Want Using the Information Superhighway* comes in. Using the tools and resources described in this book, you will be able to maintain your readiness no matter what may come. If the worst happens, you'll have the ability to find another opportunity quickly using traditional methods as well as the advanced ones described herein. And, through continual monitoring of the labor market by browsing Web sites, checking newsgroups and bulletin boards, you may be able to spot opportunities more quickly that accelerate your advancement and growth. Either way, reading this book will be tremendously valuable.

Bernard S. Hodes
Founder, President, & CEO
Bernard Hodes Advertising, Inc., New York*
April 1995

---

* Bernard Hodes Advertising is the world's largest firm specializing in recruitment advertising and employee communication. Founded in 1970, the Agency has offices on four continents and host the World Wide Web server CareerMosaic™.

Acknowledgments

Although our names are the only ones printed on the cover of this book, by no means did this book get published by our efforts alone. We gratefully acknowledge the contributions of our project editor, Janice Borzendowski, who edited this manuscript with authority and style. We also thank Lauralee Reinke for her sensitive and superb formatting and design. We are also indebted to James Nocito for creating the inspired cover and inside illustrations for this book.

Our agent, Margot Maley of Waterside Productions, has been a beacon of light for us, always encouraging us along the way.

And special thanks to Tracy Smith, Editorial Director at Random House Electronic Publishing. Before the Internet became a household word, she had the foresight to see the job search and career applications of online services.

Many other individuals contributed hours of their time and expertise to help us with this project. Michael Rowe at E-Span, William Warren at the Online Career Center, several technical wizards at Netscape, Tim Gibbon and others at Career Mosaic, and John Anderson.

Also, thanks to the technical writers and experts who assisted us. Thanks especially to Dave Dixon for his many helpful manuscript suggestions, to Laurie Valadez for her support, and to Ivor and Lola MacFarlane for providing research assistance.

Introduction

In an era of downsizing and global competition, savvy workers have at least two jobs: their present gig, and searching for the next one. This is true of entrepreneurs who prospect for new clients, corporate employees who've endured multiple downsizings, and would-be career switchers. It's also true of 20-somethings and recent college graduates who tend to work part-time, overtime, or shift between jobs while keeping their long-term career options open. It's hard to think of anyone today who shouldn't be looking over his or her shoulder for the next trend, the next business opportunity, or the next flurry of corporate pink slips.

Be Your Own Headhunter Online: Get the Job You Want Using the Information Superhighway addresses the concerns of everyone who's living and working in today's tough job market. It's a job seeker's manual for the digital frontier and the international job marketplace that's been spawned in part on the information superhighway. This book tells you how the Internet, commercial online services, and the Web can help you find a job, expand your network of contacts online, and track leading-edge opportunities all over the world.

The Internet, which delivers tomorrow's information today, is a potent job search tool. International in scope, the Internet is bursting with information about jobs, careers, relocation, and topics ranging from computers to commodities to cryonics. Classic books on job hunting emphasize transferable work skills and the importance of networking. While these strategies are still important, no job seeker in today's competitive environment can afford to overlook the increasing importance of networking and job hunting in cyberspace.

The electronic job searching and networking skills that were considered a luxury—a sort of additional "leg up"—as recently as a year ago are now professional necessities. Gone are the days of just picking up a Sunday paper and finding your dream job advertised. Gone also are the days of expecting your executive recruiter to be the only one to have the exclusive "inside track." Now, many employers essentially sidestep the recruiters by advertising jobs online. Also, more and more companies are hiring "Internet surfers" and "electronic information specialists" to cruise cyberspace looking for good candidates. Clearly, employers expect job seekers to know the rules of the electronic road.

And what about those recruiters? They're now busy using the Internet to help people find jobs nationwide and worldwide. By reading this book, you can learn their online secrets and be your own headhunter—we'll show you all of the inside tricks and give you a head start on your job search.

You may be concerned that it's only people working in technical or scientific professions who will benefit from a book like this. Not true! As we've already mentioned, online job seeking skills are a must for everyone. We've seen thousands of jobs online that have nothing to do with computers or science. In addition to many thousands of positions for engineers and computer types, we've also seen positions for photographers, janitors, make-up artists, graphic designers, writers, chefs, managers, CEOs, CFOs, librarians, salespeople, teachers, insurance specialists, produce brokers, organists, doctors, nurses, accountants, financial planners, attorneys, legal assistants, landscape architects, secretaries, and many more—all online.

When we asked employers why they were advertising positions online, many responded that they want someone who stays up to date, even if the position didn't necessarily require computer skills. Many employers are now advertising positions *only* online, especially in technical professions. Computer animators, computer game creators, computer systems analysts, and many engineers and scientists will find the best jobs in their professions only online. Indeed, in any profession where a computer skill is involved, it's increasingly likely that the job will be announced online.

We want to encourage you, no matter what your level of computer expertise is, to get plugged in and to tap into the job market that is blossoming in cyberspace. Everyday, culture skews more and more toward electronic commerce. More often, positions are routinely announced online; companies put their electronic claim-stake in the ground via a home page on the Web, and many individuals are as a matter of course posting their electronic resumes and "home pages." Don't get left behind! There's an electronic world just waiting for you. All you have to do is use this book as your guide, turn on your computer, and use your modem to hop online. You'll find that your dream job may not be such a far-fetched figment of your imagination after all.

In this book, we'll show you the "how to" in plain English. We discuss, in reader-friendly language, how to use the Internet, commercial online services, and the Web for the purpose of finding a job or exploring new career options. We provide specific tips and strategies for job seekers of all stripes: from recent college graduates to career-switchers, from climbers of the corporate ladder to part-timers or those looking for a new full-time job.

If you've never been online before, you'll be happy to know that we've avoided technobabble wherever possible. We've simplified and streamlined the information for you, giving you insider tips along the way.

This book is divided into three parts. In the first part, we give you the must-have online job searching skills you need, including strategies for finding a job through commercial online services, instructions on how to create and post your electronic resume, online networking do's, don'ts, and how-tos, a guide to using the World Wide Web in your job search, a look at how to write your own home page, career and job resources, and Internet search tactics. In the second part of the book, you'll find an extensive listing of where to look online to find a job and to post your resume. And, finally, you'll find an appendix section that includes information about getting online as well as more resources for you to tap into.

Throughout the text, you will notice five icons:

When we use a technical term, look for this icon to point you to "translations."

Look for time-saving tips for the online "road" here. These tips are online tricks we've picked up during our researching.

This icon identifies additional information about the current discussion.

This icon highlights tips for how you can save money using online features.

This icon alerts you to and helps you avoid the inevitable electronic "potholes" along the information superhighway.

This icon, used in Chapters 6 and 7 signals an electronic site that is especially worth exploring, either for quantity or quality of jobs offered.

We want to emphasize that this is not a book about the Internet per se. Internet books are hitting the bookstores faster than you can say "information superhighway," and these typically discuss how to subscribe to the Internet, how to transfer files, and how to accomplish myriad technical tasks.

Unlike these Internet books, we've included just enough information to get you up and running on your job search without giving you an overload of details, because we know you're more interested in finding a job than becoming and Internet expert. Therefore, we discuss such things as electronic resumes and electronic networking and finding jobs online. When you need to know specific online skills to access information about these career/job search topics, we of course take the time to tell you what you need to know.

1

GETTING STARTED

Getting Started

Job hunting: It's always been considered the toughest job you'll ever have. Probably more advice—free and otherwise—has been dispensed regarding what you have to do to land the job of your dreams—or any job, for that matter. And now, to make the job hunting process more complex, you've heard that many—if not most—of the "good" jobs in your field are being advertised on that mysterious information superhighway—for which *you* have no driver's license. Not to worry. This book provides all the information you need to get the job you want using online technology, whether you're out of work and need a job *now*, are just "shopping around," or are dreaming of a whole new career and just want to see what's available.

Be Your Own Headhunter Online is divided into three sections: The first section is a primer on navigating online networks with the specific purpose of finding a job. Even if you haven't been online before, or don't own a modem yet, you'll find advice for working through the entire process from setting up to gaining online expertise. (You'll also find definitions of some of the most commonly used terms that have become part of the "technobabble" resulting from all the new online services and features.) If you're already online, or consider yourself an expert, you'll discover that this book is a treasure trove of valuable online job resources as well as specialized information about using the World Wide Web in your job search.

The second section of the book contains a list of online job data banks and job lists, resume banks, and valuable job resource information. Although the daily, explosive growth of online job services makes any attempt to write a definitive list an impossible task, this list will nevertheless serve as an excellent starting point and reference for further explorations. The list also includes information about how you can find the most up-to-date information available about jobs via the Internet.

The third and final portion of the book is composed of appendices that contain detailed technical information, names of helpful software products, resource addresses, and other reference materials to guide you in your online job search.

If you are new to the Internet, commercial online services and other online areas, going online to find a job may seem intimidating to you at first, like traveling in a foreign country whose language you don't speak. But once you've been online for a week, know the pertinent phrases and where the best places are to stop, you'll relax and start "enjoying the scenery." In fact, you may come to enjoy it so much that you stay online long after you've found a job.

In the simplest terms, the Internet is a network of interconnected computers. An estimated 25 million people worldwide access the Internet.

The reason the online world, or *cyberspace*, has become so pleasant to travel in is that, other than the rich resources available for job seekers, it has also become very easy to access and navigate. Companies such as CompuServe, America Online, GEnie, Delphi, Mosaic, Netscape, and others are working nonstop to make online technology intuitive and accessible to everyone. (Ten or eleven years ago, you practically had to be a computer expert just to access the Internet.)

LET'S TALK NUMBERS

According to the most recent figures, the Internet, the World Wide Web, and other computer networks are growing at an astonishing rate of 80 percent each year. In the past three years, the number of jobs offered online has burgeoned, to the point where the idea of job hunting via online technology seems to be growing faster than the Internet itself. This rate of growth, unfortunately, makes it difficult to pin down exact figures of how many jobs are online. Mike Rowe, vice president of marketing of E-Span, a large electronic job database, says his corner of the online job world is expanding wildly. In just one calendar year, E-Span's business increased by 400 percent, with no signs of letting up anytime soon. E-Span is not the exception to the rule, by any means. All online areas appear to be growing at this rate or faster. The following are some broad, *conservative* estimates:

* Commercial online services, with all of their forums, online help wanted ads, and career services such as E-Span, boast an estimated 6,000 new jobs *per month*.

* Usenet, freenets, and community nets—between online jobs offered and job leads discovered through networking—boast an estimated 10,000 jobs *per month*.

 In this book *networking* refers to the process of going online to make personal and professional contacts with other people. Networking can also refer to the process of looking for information online. This is in contrast to *networked*, which refers to a system that has hooks to other systems. When you dial one number, you can access hundreds of other computer networks. The Internet is an example of a computer network. A non-networked computer system means that when you dial the computer with your modem, you can access only that particular computer. Some bulletin boards and databases are examples of non-networked computers.

* The Online Career Center (a database on the Internet where employers can place help wanted ads and review

resumes; and where job seekers can find employment opportunities and place their own resumes online) offers 8,000 jobs *per month.*

♦ Non-networked online employment boards offer an estimated 2,000 jobs *per month.*

♦ The federal government offers an estimated 3,000 jobs *per month* online.

♦ Universities offer an estimated 1,000 jobs *per month* online.

♦ Other Internet job areas and lists account for about 3,000 jobs *per month* offered online.

♦ The World Wide Web, through such career areas as Career Mosaic and The Monster Board, account for about 100 jobs *per month,* not including the jobs received by job seekers with their resumes on the Web who have gotten jobs.

 The World Wide Web is a computer network that links information through key concepts. It is searchable via a graphical point-and-click interface, making it user-friendly.

As you can see, there are thousands of jobs listed online, and by the time you read this book, there will be more. Job listings are updated or *refreshed* at varying rates; E-Span updates its jobs twice a week, for example, and the Online Career Center refreshes jobs once a month.

WHERE TO FIND ONLINE JOBS

Online jobs can be found on a variety of networked and non-networked services. This means that you can find some of the jobs grouped in one place, such as on the Internet. Or, you can find job listings on a dial-up bulletin board that is not connected to any other online area, such as the Career Link bulletin board, located in Phoenix, Arizona. Career Link posts 450 new jobs every week, a portion of which you can see in Figure 1.1.

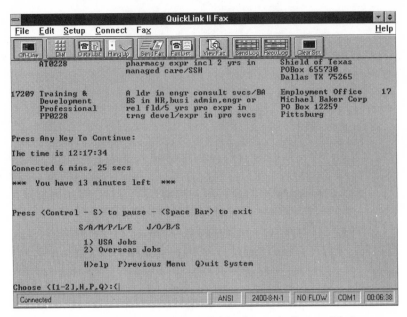

Figure 1.1 A sampling of jobs available through Career Link.

Here are the online job hotspots:

♦ Commercial online services such as Prodigy or GEnie. You can find job listings such as E-Span, highly targeted, profession-specific jobs on forums or bulletin boards, and you can find jobs through networking on these services.

♦ Usenet. Usenet contains many actual job listings as well as areas in which job seekers can actively network and find inside job leads and useful contacts. Usenet also offers many places for job seekers to place their resumes online.

 Usenet, also called *network news*, is a network available on every continent. It features thousands of discussion areas where ideas can be exchanged from advice on childrearing to job listings. About 3 million people accessed Usenet in 1993.

♦ The Internet. The Internet is home to several dozen top jobs resources, including the Online Career Center, Federal Government job listings, ArtJob, Bionet Employ-

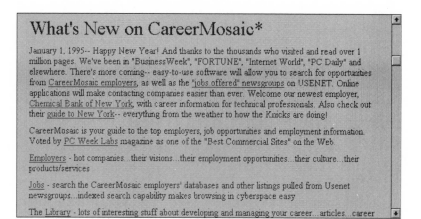

What's New on CareerMosaic*

January 1, 1995-- Happy New Year! And thanks to the thousands who visited and read over 1 million pages. We've been in "BusinessWeek", "FORTUNE", "Internet World", "PC Daily" and elsewhere. There's more coming-- easy-to-use software will allow you to search for opportunities from CareerMosaic employers, as well as the "jobs offered" newsgroups on USENET. Online applications will make contacting companies easier than ever. Welcome our newest employer, Chemical Bank of New York, with career information for technical professionals. Also check out their guide to New York-- everything from the weather to how the Knicks are doing!

CareerMosaic is your guide to the top employers, job opportunities and employment information. Voted by PC Week Labs magazine as one of the "Best Commercial Sites" on the Web.

Employers - hot companies...their visions...their employment opportunities...their culture...their products/services

Jobs - search the CareerMosaic employers' databases and other listings pulled from Usenet newsgroups...indexed search capability makes browsing in cyberspace easy

The Library - lots of interesting stuff about developing and managing your career...articles...career

Figure 1.2 A snapshot of Career Mosaic, available on the World Wide Web

ment, GIS Jobs Clearinghouse, the International Career Employment Network, and many more.

♦ The World Wide Web. The World Wide Web, also known as the Web, W3, or WWW, is home to exciting career areas such as the Interactive Employment Network, Career Mosaic, The Monster Board, and more. As you can see in Figure 1.2, the career resources on the Web have the advantage of a user-friendly interface. The Web is also a place where job seekers can place their home page or multimedia resume. This offers job seekers a whole new dimension in self-marketing. (See Chapter 5, "World Wide Web," for a complete discussion.)

♦ Dial-up employment bulletin boards. There are scores of dial-up bulletin boards across the country, and some of them are dedicated to jobs and employment. If you live near one of these employment boards, you can dial up and find local jobs that may not be on the Internet or commercial networks. Also, if you want to find a job in another geographic area, these are good places to look for jobs.

A dial-up bulletin board is one type of online service. Bulletin boards (BBSs), can be a good way of getting started in the online world because of their user-friendly interfaces.

♦ Specialty databases, such as alumni, professional association, and college databases that offer jobs to selected groups of people are also good jobs resources. These databases are typically non-networked.

ONLINE JOB CATEGORIES

Every kind of job imaginable is listed online. You'll find jobs for writers, teachers, attorneys, doctors, nurses, biologists, all manner of scientists and researchers, computer specialists, janitors, managers, sales reps, national account managers, publishers, artists, designers, safety analysts, stockbrokers, financial planners—you name it. Figure 1.3 shows a sample job list from just one of the hundreds available online.

But be aware: Not every job is included in every online area. The kind or type of job you will find online depends entirely on where and how you go about looking for a job. That's why this book provides specific information to help you find the best places to look for your dream job and the best methods to use while looking.

In Chapter 7, "Where the Jobs Are," you'll find a list of hundreds of places to look for jobs, and you'll see what kinds of jobs are offered in each online area. For example, if you look at *ba.jobs.offered* in Usenet (see Figure 1.3), you'll discover a list of about 800 jobs, many, though not all, of which are hi-tech related (digital librarian, technical sales, computer systems analyst). If you look at the Metropolitan Tucson Electronic Communications Network, (Tucson's community net), a por-

```
Sat, 24 Dec 1994 22:44:49       ba.jobs.offered          Thread   59 of  808
Lines 22                    Graphic Artist/Designer         No responses
dce@netcom.com  David Elliott at NETCOM On-line Communication Services (408 261

Books That Work, a peninsula multimedia company seeks graphic
artist/designer.  Ideally this person can work in many different styles
and adapt his or her skills to a variety of multimedia issues. An
"idea" person with strong design skills, this graphic artist can start
at the design stage and work with a software production team to create
a product with vision and artistic integrity. Must be able to
communicate ideas quickly in sketches.

Responsibilities  could include  general art direction, illustrations,
user interface design, animation and storyboarding, screen layout and
design, and management of freelance artists. Adobe Photoshop skills
mandatory.  Bonus points for Adobe Illustrator, scanning experience and
Macromedia Director experience. We offer benefits and stock options.
Please send variety of work samples on disk or paper, a SASE and resume

    <n>=set current to n, TAB=next unread, /=search pattern, ^K)ill/select,
       a)uthor search, B)ody search, c)atchup, f)ollowup, K=mark read,
       !=pipe, m)ail, o=print, q)uit, r)eply mail, s)ave, t)ag, w=post

                                           --More--(85%) [1244/1450]
```

Figure 1.3 Sample job listing from *ba.jobs.offered*.

```
                                                                    28%
                      Week of July 19, 1993
The following positions are currently open for application:
                          OPEN COMPETITIVE
Position:                        Salary:            Closing Date:
Latent Print Examiner (Subject to on-  $2,623/Month  August 13, 1993
call status)

Police Dispatcher (Minimum of 50 wpm  $10.75/Hour    July 26, 1993
net)

Police Service Operator (Minimum of  $10.24/Hour     July 26, 1993
45 wpm net)

Director of Environmental Management  $45,500-        July 23, 1993
                                      $73,700/Annually
qqqqqqqqqqqqqqqqqqqqqqqqqqqqqqqqqqqqqqqqqqqqqqqqqqqqqqqqqqqqqqqqqqqqqq
[PageDown: <SPACE>] [Help: ?] [Return to Menu: u]
```

Figure 1.4 A sampler of jobs from Metropolitan Tucson Electronic Communications Network

tion of which you can see in Figure 1.4, you find primarily nontechnical jobs (police officer, landscape designer, teacher). Obviously, you'll want to spend some time studying the list to make the best use of your online time.

A *community net*, or community network, is a network based in one geographic area like a town or a city. Community nets typically offer low-cost access to the Internet. When a community net access is free, it's called a *freenet*.

If you are in a profession that isn't usually listed in help wanted ads (like musicians who often find work by word of mouth), don't short-change yourself by thinking there's nothing for you online. Employers, too, network online, and the best way to keep abreast of what's happening in your field is to regularly interact online.

ONLINE VS. TRADITIONAL JOB SEARCHING

Much of what you do in an online job search is the same as in a traditional job search: You network, prepare and send resumes, plan for interviews, and check job leads. What distinguishes an online job search from a traditional job search, and what has some people talking about *paradigm shifts*, is the way you accomplish these goals. The following sections give a brief comparison.

Global Reach

An online job search allows you to make contacts all over the world with very little effort. For those of you who are looking for a job in another country, this is a real plus. This is especially important if you have a very narrowly defined specialty with few peers in your local area, or if you are trying to gather leading-edge information about trends in your profession. And once you do find a job in another state or country, there's no better way to smooth a relocation than via online networking.

For $10.00 to $50.00, online networking can do for you in one month what would otherwise take thousands of dollars in plane tickets and at least a month of travel to accomplish. (See the Chapter 4, "Networking," for details on how to network online.)

Speed

An online job search can progress very quickly. Instead of waiting for monthly or weekly networking meetings, you can join existing and continuous network gatherings. Instead of waiting for the Sunday papers to browse job advertisements, you can look through hundreds of new jobs *every day*. And rather than waiting for a job opening at one of your target companies (that is, companies you know you want to work for), you can submit electronic resumes (a resume that is stored electronically, either online or in a database) to *all* of them and know that it will be included and searched in their resume databases.

The faster you make key contacts, get your resume to the right people, and find job leads that are right for you, the better your odds are of quickly finding the right fit with a job. The online job searching medium has the ability to speed up your job search significantly, especially if you combine it with traditional job searching efforts.

In some professions, any kind of job search is going to require a long-term approach. If you're a highly trained specialist, such as a nuclear engineer, going online to find a job is a fantastic

**idea, as there is a higher probability of finding the right employ-
ers. But it's still going to take some time. Online employment
services are a great boon to job hunters, but be realistic about
your expectations, depending on what you do for a living.**

Access to Inside Information, Top Experts, and Peers

Unless you're a powerful player in your field and get invited to
the "right" parties, an online job search is the ideal way to get
in contact with top experts and peers in your field. Some of the
world's top scientists, financiers, thinkers, employers, and even
government leaders are online regularly. And a side benefit is
that the online medium tends to break down traditional
boundaries of position and geography. If you're a journalist
living in Seattle and want to make an appointment to talk to
the top editor of a London newspaper about the possibility of
working there, you can hop online and develop the equivalent
conversation. (The secrets to doing this type of interacting are
covered in Chapter 4, "Networking.")

In addition, thanks to *sig files*, the signatures people put with
their names on email, you can easily find people who work in
your target company or target profession. Developing a contact
with an inside person is as easy as starting a conversation with a
person standing next to you. Figure 1.5 shows a sample of a
signature file at the end of an email message.

Cost

Once you learn some online skills and are able to focus your
online job search, online job searching can be very efficient
and probably you will spend less money on an online job
search than you would on a regular job search. Think of it this
way: For about $10.00 in postage stamps, $20.00 in good sta-
tionary and envelopes, and the cost of printing or photocopy-
ing, you can mail out about 30 resumes. But for the same
$10.00 to pay for a commercial online account for one month
and the price of this book, you can send your resume to *hundreds* of companies and inside contacts, post your resume

```
Private Customer Dept
Harmonia Mundi USA
hmusa@netcom.com
310-478-1311, ext 119
Fax: 310-996-1389
```

Figure 1.5 A typical signature file, automatically placed at the end of an email message

where it will be seen by *tens of thousands* of people, and browse jobs accessible only online. The bottom line? Instead of 30 people seeing your resume, it'll be 30,000—and for less money. Now that's a bargain. (You'll find other money-saving tips throughout this book that will help you keep your online costs in line with your budget.)

Focus

Knowing what you want, and how you want to go about achieving your goals, and not getting distracted is what it means to have "focus." Needless to say, in a job search, focus is important. But online or off, this part of the job search is up to you. If you're unfocused in a traditional job search, you'll probably have the same difficulty online. Unfortunately, online technology does not offer a cure for this. But, Chapter 2, "Online Working Strategies," offers suggestions to help you with this aspect of job hunting. No matter what kind of job you're looking for, there are techniques that will help you to keep your job goals clear and in view at all times.

Your Online Personality

If you are a wonderful schmoozer and can charm anyone and everyone no matter what the situation, you may be worried that your sparkling personality will flatten out over the online wires. Well, rest assured that your personality is just as important in an online search as it is in a traditional search. You'll be amazed at how much comes through about a person just through email, live chats, and other online contacts. If you're good with people now, then you'll be great online.

A *live chat* is when you communicate online in real time—as you type, the other person is reading what you're writing as you're writing it.

If, on the other hand, you are a shy, withdrawn type who cringes at the idea of networking, don't worry, because you too will benefit from being online. Online job searches give you more time to plan what you're going to say. You may never be effusive, but you will be able to get your message across clearly and precisely to the people you are trying to reach and impress.

If you have access to the World Wide Web, you can incorporate even more of a personal factor into your job search if you wish. Using the Web, you can add photos of yourself, a video of your projects, or audio snippets of your voice into your resume. As you can see in Figure 1.6, you can personalize everything you do to a much greater extent than is possible with just a text resume. If you sent a paper resume into a multinational or large national company, not much of you can emerge other than your skill sets and work experience. If, however, you list a Web resume address that people can look at for more information, potential employers can get a much better feel for the real you.

In your job search, you should learn about all the tools that are at your disposal, but don't feel you have to use them all. Definitely learn how to use online technology to look for a job, but don't stop doing what worked for you before you discovered online job searching. For instance, are you a member of a trade association? Don't start missing those meetings because you've become infatuated with your new online peers. Keep up online, but keep up your offline contacts, too.

Have you heard about a job at a company with fewer than 10 employees? Send your paper resume to them—don't expect that, all of a sudden, everyone will come up to your level of

Figure 1.6 A sample home page from the Web

technology. This is a real temptation, after you see how great online job searching can be.

Conversely, are you hanging onto techniques that no longer work for you? Are you going to breakfast meetings that yield no contacts—ever? Spend that time instead developing new on-line contacts. Or, are you spending time online checking job listings that never have jobs in your profession? Switch lists—explore new online areas, and get more aggressive about finding places online where people are involved in your profession.

And don't overlook the possibility of combining online and offline worlds. For example, how about arranging a public "virtual cafe" meeting with some of your online peers? (See Chapter 4, "Networking," for more information on doing this.) The bottom line is that you should arm yourself with every technique that works for you, and go after the job you really want.

WHAT YOU NEED TO GET STARTED

Okay, you're convinced that an online job search is worth the effort. Now what? Well, let's deal first with the bad news. It's impossible to access the wealth of online resources unless you can get online, and to get online, you'll need equipment, an account, and some knowledge. The good news is that online access has improved dramatically in the past five years, to the point that you will have little difficulty finding a suitable online account. And you shouldn't have to spend a fortune to get online. Read on to find out how you can get yourself up and running.

Equipment

There's no way around it: You will need a computer and a modem to access the online world. If you already have a computer and a modem, great. Skip to the next section about accounts. If you are currently a student at a college or a university, you should have access to a computer and a modem through your school. If you don't, check with the placement office or the computer lab for details about how you can get access.

If you bought this book because you want to get online, but you don't have the equipment yet, you may have more options than you realize. Of course, you can use a friend's or a relative's equipment, or you can buy your own. But you may also want to check out some other possibilities first.

Many areas of the country now have community networks or freenets, some of which offer free or low-cost online computer use through public libraries or other community sites. Check Appendix A, "Getting Yourself Online," to see if you are lucky enough to live in one of these communities. If you do, then you may be able to forestall purchasing equipment until after you've found a job and can better afford it.

Types of Online Accounts

Once you're set up with a computer and a modem, you'll need an account. Again, if you're a college or university student, you probably already have an online account, and a pretty good one at that. If you don't, definitely check with your college placement office, computer lab, or one of your professors to see about getting an Internet account. If you're not a student or if you will be graduating shortly, you still have lots of options, described in the following sections.

Local Bulletin Boards with Links to the Internet

Once upon a time, a local bulletin board meant a small place you could dial up and meet people from your local area, but that was the extent of the access. Now, many local bulletin boards are connecting partially to the Internet and other computer networks such as Usenet. For this reason, a local BBS may be a good opportunity for you to explore the Internet or Usenet at a low cost and with a user-friendly interface.

Bulletin boards are a good first step and alternative option, but because local bulletin boards tend to come and go more rapidly than other services and because bulletin board systems usually don't offer complete Internet access, they will not serve as the best long-term option for you in your job search.

To find out if you live in an area with a networked local BBS, call your local computer society if there is one. Or check the national magazine *Online Access* for its periodic listings of bulletin boards. While you're at the bookstore or market, also check around for local computer publications. For example, in San Diego, there is a local publication called *Computer Edge* that lists all of the regional bulletin boards. Purchasing a copy of this magazine makes finding the elusive BBSs infinitely easier.

Freenets and Community Nets

As already mentioned, a community net or freenet is a computer system that is made publicly available either free or for very low cost. The service isn't always perfect, because the goals of a freenet are to provide network access to everyone or to as many people as possible. Freenets and community nets rely heavily on grants and volunteers, so don't be surprised if you have a limit to how much time you can spend using their resources.

Nevertheless, if you live near a community net or freenet, by all means take advantage of it. There are some exceptionally well-designed freenets that will ease you onto the Internet through a simple menuing system. Also, a freenet will give you the opportunity to explore the Internet without getting nervous about cost. And not least of all, most freenets have their own job lists that you can browse.

Check Appendix A, "Getting Yourself Online," to see if you live in an area with a community net or a freenet. This would mean a very quick and inexpensive solution to your account needs. If you don't see your area listed, don't despair—your area may be in the process of organizing a freenet. Call your local computer society or local government to check on developments in your area.

 FTP stands for *file transfer protocol*. It refers to a tool that you can use to move or transfer a file from one computer to another. Typically, you will want to transfer a file from a remote computer to your machine. How you actually transfer the files depends on the type of Internet connection or account you have.

Commercial Online Service Providers

Strictly speaking, any account you purchase is commercial. Nevertheless, the term *commercial online service* in most cases refers to a company that offers online access to a host system for a fee. The host system usually contains a basic database plus access to others—again, for a fee.

America Online, CompuServe, eWorld, GEnie, and Prodigy are currently the most popular examples of this type of service. You can purchase an account, log on, and access job and general reference resources. You'll find magazine databases, discussion groups, online encyclopedias, and even job and resume banks.

In addition, there are other online services available or about to become available. With all of these choices, which one do you choose? It's unlikely that you'll want to purchase more than one account initially, so where should you start? Each service has a distinct "personality." A service's personality is more or less determined by a combination of its database offerings, ease of use, and the general nature of its users.

Of all the services, CompuServe has the strongest business slant. It has many professional forums where you can chat with peers, and provides access to many more professional databases than other service. The Online Career Center, for example, is a super job resource just recently made available to CompuServe members.

Prodigy, until recently, was considered the most useful to children and families. But now, Prodigy is offering access to the World Wide Web through a very easy-to-use graphical interface. This has changed Prodigy's position of importance for you. If you are completely new to online technology, (and in your heart are secretly afraid to get online) Prodigy just may offer you the simplicity you need to overcome your jitters. Just be aware that the main thing you'll get with Prodigy is Web access. You won't find CompuServe's professional environment.

If you are looking for a cozy, friendly networking area, you may want to try GEnie. GEnie is the most difficult service to classify, other than to say that GEnie's members are great networkers and have a strong reputation for being helpful and loyal.

Macintosh users will do well to try eWorld. This service is designed well, in that it is sleek and easy to use. It also boasts a very strong career area. What stands out about eWorld for the job seeker is the current strength of its experts available for networking.

America Online is another mainstream service. There is a moderately strong career section, and there are some valuable professional networking forums.

As of this writing, several new online services are emerging, chief among them Microsoft Network. Microsoft is keeping its plans under wraps, however, so very little is known about the way this service will shape up. One thing we do know is that there will be a career area.

When you sign up for a commercial online service, be sure to ask about Internet access. To do this, call the service's toll-free number, and ask a sales representative, "What kind of Internet access does your service provide?" Currently, most of the commercial online service providers offer access to Usenet news—a very valuable service that you'll use many times as you network for a job. As we've already mentioned, Prodigy offers Web access, which means that you also have access to the Internet.

Within a year or so, look for the commercial online service landscape to change dramatically. You'll see just about all of the commercial services providing Web and Internet access.

What would a book about online technology be without an exception or two? At this writing, there are two commercial online service providers that offer everything the other commercial online service providers offer, plus full Internet access. They are Delphi and BIX. When you purchase an account with either of these commercial services, you will be able to telnet, gopher, and FTP, and more—the hallmarks of Internet access.

But even before these companies implement Web access, one of the benefits of purchasing a commercial online account is that if you are new to cyberspace, these services make your first visits a lot easier and less confusing. Part of what you are paying for is an easy interface, and all of these services deliver just that. Another benefit of joining at least one commercial service is that, even if you have a great Internet account somewhere else, there are networking opportunities available commercially that are not available anywhere else.

Cyberspace is a generic—and overused—term for all things having to do with the online world or with the growing global network of interlinked computers.

For example, on CompuServe, you can find discussion groups unavailable anywhere else, including on the Internet. There are also very experienced career experts on some of these services who will really take time to help you in your job search. One such person, a top-flight career counselor, is Susan Basset, who goes online with eWorld every day for live chats with people who want career guidance. Basset has conducted live practice interviews with candidates, helped candidates find jobs resources, helped job seekers find contacts, and more. For contact phone numbers, check out Appendix A, "Getting Yourself Online."

Commercial Internet Accounts

As recent as ten years ago, if you weren't an academic, a university researcher, or a scientist working for certain agencies, you would have had an incredibly difficult time getting onto the Internet. Now, most cities in North America and throughout the world have at least one enterprising business owner who is offering Internet access to the public for a fee. Usually, accounts cost about $20 to $30 a month. Some charge a flat fee; others have a pay-by-the-hour arrangement. To purchase an Internet account, look at the list of Internet providers in Appendix A, "Getting Yourself Online." Choose a provider near your geographic area, and simply call him or her up. Say you are interested in purchasing an account, and ask for details. If you have questions about which computer, modem, software, and so on to use, the account provider will be able to tell you those that will work with that system.

As you will immediately discover when you go to purchase an account, you'll be faced with a decision: to SLIP or not to SLIP. SLIP or PPP accounts, as they are commonly called, will allow you, as a home user, to access the resources of the World Wide Web and the Internet. A non-SLIP account will allow you to access the Internet.

SLIP stands for *serial line Internet protocol.* PPP stands for *point-to-point protocol.* Both allow people to use regular telephone lines (versus high-speed lines) to run Internet software or other programs on their own computers. If you have a SLIP or PPP connection, you can run software such as Mosaic Netscape on your machine. You also can interface directly with other machines on the Internet, which greatly simplifies the process of transferring files.

Because this is a book about finding a job online and not a book about researching online, it's safe to say that if you can get Web access, by all means do. (Even two years ago, advising someone to access the Web would have been like advising someone to buy a Cadillac when an economy car would've done the job. But now, the only thing growing faster than the Internet is the World Wide Web, and it's an important job tool.) It's worth the extra $5 or so a month that you'll pay. Currently, there are job resources available on the Web that aren't available anywhere else—and more come online *every day.*

The drawback of Internet and SLIP accounts is that finding help is more difficult. In fact, you'll be pretty much on your own, except of course for the Internet and Web advice you find in books and online. But the advantage of having an Internet/WWW account is that you will have access to very compelling job resources that you will find nowhere else—at least, not currently. For more information on the World Wide Web, read Chapter 5, "World Wide Web." For more detailed information about SLIP and Internet accounts plus account providers, refer to Appendix A, "Getting Yourself Online."

Account Summary

By now, you are either feeling overwhelmed by your choices or are getting your checkbook out now, wondering how many accounts you're going to purchase. In either case, here are some tips to help you choose an account that's right for you:

♦ If you have never been online before, consider starting with a commercial online account such as CompuServe or GEnie. When you've become comfortable with the resources on one of these services, then venture over to the Internet or the Web.

♦ If you already have a commercial online account, consider adding an Internet or SLIP account to your repertoire. The less technical you are, the more you should consider purchasing a SLIP account—its user-friendly interface makes navigation much easier.

♦ If you are very short on funds, research BBSs with links to Usenet and email capacities. If you can't afford an online account at all, there is still a great deal you can accomplish in your online job search through email.

Obviously, you can't just turn on your computer, log on to an account, and presto! be an online job expert. You're going to need some very specific knowledge about where to and how to go online. But if you read this book, you're going to be well on your way to being your own expert.

Take time to read this book very carefully, especially the practical chapters "Online Working Strategies," "Posting Your Resume Online," "Networking," "World Wide Web," and the jobs list, "Where the Jobs Are." The information in these chapters will give you all of the information you need to fully and capably conduct your online job search, even if you're new to cyberspace.

═══ STEP-BY-STEP ONLINE JOB SEARCHING

The steps in an online job search are simple, and they closely parallel those you would follow to find a job using traditional job search methods.

1. Set up a computer, a modem and an account.

2. Prepare your electronic resume (explained in Chapter 3, "Posting Your Resume Online"). Clarify your career goals, set your sights on a target company and job, and focus on a specialty area within your profession. Read the lists of job resources and ways to harness the power of online services.

3. Get online. After you read the portions of this book that apply to you, go online and really "work" the Net. Check all of the job listings that apply to you. Put your electronic resume online in many different areas. Get on discussion groups and expand your network. When you finally land an interview, prepare for your interview with time-saving and powerful online tools. And keep learning and exploring new areas.

4. Be diligent. After you get online, develop a presence, work your job search plan, and stick with it. Don't just put your resume up on a board and then forget about it. Tell people your resume is there, check on your resume, and keep looking for more places to send it. Check the job listings you've targeted every week and send out your resume to jobs that look interesting to you. If you haven't landed a job in a month, don't stop. Keep looking, and keep your name in front of people and your ear to the network ground.

5. Follow up—rigorously. Once you're online, you'll discover that you will develop many contacts quickly. Keep a dialog going with these people. If someone sends you a message or a job lead, take the time to follow up immediately. When you hear about a possible job lead, send a quick email to the contact address. The online job hunt can move very quickly, so you need to, too.

6. Don't eliminate traditional job search techniques. Once you're comfortable looking online for jobs and have become efficient at it, add traditional elements to your job search. Just because online job searching is a fantastic tool doesn't mean that you should forgo other methods to find a job. Keep checking the paper for ads, keep going to professional meetings, and keep lunching with your professional peers.

HOW TO USE THIS BOOK

This book consists of chapters designed to help you through every step of the online job search process. You'll find practical, detailed information about electronic resumes, Web pages, online networking, how to navigate and really work the online world, and troubleshooting advice. Depending on your level of expertise, the following are recommended plans of action.

Novice—You're Brand New to the Online World

If you are brand new to the online world, be patient with yourself. If you find yourself in "information overload," take a break. Give yourself some time to adjust to the language and concepts of online job searching. Here's a suggested plan of action for you:

♦ Read the chapters in this order: Chapters 2, 3, and 4.

♦ Next read the appendices of the book to fill in any gaps in your knowledge, especially "Getting Yourself Online."

♦ Choose a commercial or Internet account and sign up.

♦ When you log on to your account for the first time, leave a message for the *sysop* (the system operator, who manages a portion of a computer network such as a forum) introducing yourself and telling him or her you're looking for a job online. Ask for suggestions (you're sure to get some).

♦ Take advantage of the online practice areas to practice uploading and emailing.

♦ Once you've become comfortable with the commercial service, put your electronic resume together using Chapter 3.

♦ Using Chapter 3 again, upload your resume to one target board and enter a forum discussion, using Chapter 4 on networking as a guide.

♦ Take some time to read the "Where the Jobs Are" and the "World Wide Web" chapters.

♦ Expand your job search to include emailing your resume to the Online Career Center, and using keyword searches on your commercial account. Continue to explore and investigate, and keep learning.

♦ In a month, you're probably going to be at an intermediate level, so look into utilizing Usenet from your commercial service; you may also want to check into getting an Internet account.

You're on your way!

Intermediate—You Have a Commercial Account or an Internet Account, and You Feel Comfortable Online

It's very important that you, as an intermediate online navigator, hone your online skills carefully. The biggest pitfall you may face is that, because you're comfortable with cyberspace, you may have become superficially familiar with several of its features, but never thoroughly explored any specific areas. When you're looking for a job, it's imperative that you conduct in-depth research, so here are some suggestions to help you take advantage of your existing skills base:

♦ Read all of Chapters 1 and 2 carefully and thoroughly before you go charging through the alluring job list. You will discover key working methods and tips that will make you faster, more knowledgeable, and more efficient online.

♦ If you're hazy about any point of FTPing, posting, or uploading, take time to practice those skills now. Read the appendices, and go to your account and do some test runs.

♦ Prepare your electronic resume and upload it to your account.

♦ Check the job list for more options, and begin systematically exploring them. Make sure you have a plan, and keep exploring new territory and learning more skills.

♦ Learn about the Web, and take time to investigate getting a Web resume up.

Experienced—You've Been on Commercial Online Accounts, the Internet, and the Web

You online cruise with the greatest of ease, and have no difficulty FTPing, searching ARCHIE, WAIS, getting on Listserves, and you're all set to begin your job search *now*. Here are the steps you should take:

♦ Prepare an electronic resume, using the style tips outlined in Chapter 3, "Posting Your Resume Online."

♦ Study the job listings to see where you have the best possibility of finding a job for your profession, and make a plan of attack.

♦ Make sure you take advantage of the World Wide Web: Put up a home page and add all of the bells and whistles appropriate to your profession.(See Chapter 5, "World Wide Web.")

♦ After your resume is in front of a lot of people, concentrate on networking. Conscientiously work Usenet, forums, and bulletin boards.

♦ Spend time browsing the Net for new opportunities that are hidden deep in a gopher or that are embedded on the Web in an obscure place. Give yourself an hour or two a week just to pull out all of your searching tricks and techniques to uncover ideas, trends, and information—all relevant, of course, to your job search or profession.

TROUBLESHOOTING

As wonderful as the online world is, it isn't utopia. Rather, think of the online world as a sort of electronic parallel universe, and remember that you'll be confronted with many of the same difficulties that occur in the "real world." The media, as you're no doubt aware, has left no stone unturned in depicting the online world as populated with techies, con artists, lonely and desperate "outsiders," and sexual deviants. Further, the online world is made to seem like a drug, and once on it, you will become "addicted," and spend all your time—and money—online.

The reality, like the real world, is that, yeah the bad guys are out there, but most of the people online are honest, hard-working, interesting, and helpful, most of whom are willing to share their time and expertise with you. And, yes, you may find yourself spending a lot of time online initially, as you learn about it, struggle with it, and determine what it can do for you. But you'll find that the benefits of being online are worth the hassles and the frustrations you'll inevitably face. This section discusses some of the more common areas of concern, along with advice for handling these situations.

Troublespots

I'll Spend Too Much Money Without Even Realizing It

It's a myth that if you go online, you will lose your shirt in phone bills and other online charges. This causes great consternation among people new to the online medium—especially those looking for work! People are often so nervous about money, they barely get anything done online because they always have their eye on the clock, or they're unsure of which actions will cause an extra online charge on their account. If this describes you, here are some suggested solutions.

Solution #1: If you are on a commercial online service, use a navigator. Navigators, briefly, make it possible to decrease your online time. Refer to Appendix C, "Resources," for more information

Solution #2: Dial up at night. On some systems, nighttime rates are lower than daytime rates. Some services even cut their rates in half for nighttime users, simply to encourage a more even distribution of network traffic. Check with your account provider for details.

Solution #3: Follow the "first month" rule. It's usually the first month that's the most expensive for new users. They go wild and search every for-pay database, read all of the forum messages in real-time, and send oodles of email everywhere. The phone bill comes, and the reality of what they've done hits them. To avoid falling into this trap, acknowledge—but don't give into—the temptation to do it all at once. Pace yourself. If you signed up on a commercial online service like America Online, haunt all of the member support services for the first month. (They're usually free.) Read all of the information that you can find about using the service. When you really need to find some information or access a service, ask customer support first about all of the billing charges, or check yourself. Figure 1.7 shows a sample customer support area.

Go easy the first month. Wait for your phone bill, and check to see how much your bank or credit card balance has been tapped for services rendered. Have you stayed well within your

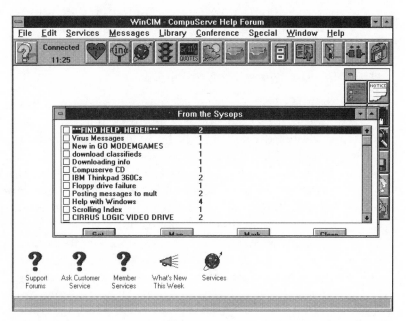

Figure 1.7 A customer support forum for online subscribers to CompuServe

budget? Then you should add one or two forays the next month. If you exceeded your budget, try and analyze where you are spending your money, and see if you can get more efficient. Ask for help. Call your commercial service's toll-free number and ask for customer service. Then ask the customer representative for information about navigation software. Navigation software is a type of computer program that automates the tasks of sending and reading email and posting messages. For example, GEnie users can purchase Aladdin, which enables them to write email and messages to bulletin boards offline, and then tell the Aladdin program to post them later. Aladdin can accomplish the task in a minute or two, whereas you might have taken 10 or more minutes. Most commercial service providers have this software available or built into their online systems. Appendix C, "Resources," has more information on these programs.

Solution #4: Realize that on the Internet, time is money.   If you have signed up for a dial-up Internet account, then you will be charged by the hour, not by the databases you access. You have the freedom to do whatever you want online without worrying about surcharges or extra fees. Just set a timer.

If I Go Online, I'll Get Addicted

People who have never been online are sometimes concerned that like television or a computer game, they will become so enraptured that they will be unable to monitor the time they spend using all the services and features. Actually, this type of addiction rarely occurs. Most people tend to get the information they want or need, and then, like taking a coffee break, spend a little time looking around at hobby interests or fantasy vacation areas; then they get offline.

If, however, you are prone to going overboard, read Chapter 2 on "Online Working Strategies" to get tips on efficiency and time-saving work habits. Focus on your job search, and don't let anything else get in your way. It will take all of your online time to find a job—you'll be networking, browsing job lists, preparing for interviews, and researching. Direct your zeal at making progress in your job search.

I'm Spending All This Time Learning to Use the Online Services—I Need A Job Now!

Unfortunately, it does take time to learn any new skill. Just remember, though, once you learn to use the online employment services, you'll have access to many more job possibilities than if you stick to traditional job searching methods. In addition, these new skills will probably come in handy in your new job. Most organizations are already—or will be soon—using online services to conduct business.

Fortunately, the commercial online services are becoming so easy to use that you'll be a pro in no time. In addition, you can make use of Web browsers, software such as Mosaic Netscape that creates a graphical point-and-click interface for the World Wide Web. (See Chapter 5 on the "World Wide Web" for a discussion of Web browsers.) You may have a much easier time going online than you think.

I'm Worried about My Privacy

There's no doubt about it, you'll want to be very careful online. Before you post a message to a bulletin board, be aware that whatever you post on a commercial online service forum or roundtable has a potential audience of about 1 million; whatever you post on Usenet has an estimated audience of about 3 million; if you post information on the Internet itself, it has an estimated audience of about 20 million. The following are some guidelines to follow before you post anything online.

If you are thinking about posting a cherished trade secret or revealing something very personal, consider the risks very carefully. Once posted on a bulletin board, that "secret" is in the public domain. *Even posting a message on a bulletin board puts that material in the public domain.*

Make a note of anything to which you want to retain specific copyright, and include a notice of copyright, as shown in Figure 1.8. Note that this discussion excludes email. Email is for

> Right to download and store or output the materials in CareerMosaic is granted for your personal use only, and materials may not be reproduced in any edited form. Any other reproduction or editing by any means mechanical or electronic without the express written permission of Bernard Hodes Advertising, Inc., is strictly prohibited.
>
> (c) Copyright, 1995, Bernard Hodes Advertising, Inc. *CareerMosaic is a trademark of Bernard Hodes Advertising, Inc. All rights reserved.

Figure 1.8 A sample posting with a copyright notice included

the most part private—with a few caveats. (For details read the upcoming section on email.)

What if My Current Boss Sees My Resume Online?

If you want to go online to jobhunt, but think that your current boss might see it and jeopardize your position, consider the following solutions.

Solution #1: Post your resume only on anonymous job banks. There are job banks that post resumes without names, thus protecting your privacy problems. Job Bank USA is one of these types of banks. (See the "Resources" appendix for more details.) Unfortunately, these job banks typically charge you a fee of $25.00 to $100.00 for their services.

Solution #2: Post your resume online all of the time. Many professionals avoid this problem by maintaining a constant presence online—that is, their resumes are online all the time, which precludes someone in management *suddenly* seeing it and assuming you've become dissatisfied with your current position.

Solution #3: Conduct most of your job search activities through email. Email is, for the most part, considered to be private information. The contents of email are currently considered to be copyrighted by the author of the email, since you are sending a message to an individual, not posting it to the world at large.

You can send resumes, correspond, respond to online job advertisements, network, and even research through email. You won't be able to reap all of the potential benefits of online technology by limiting your use to email, but you still dramatically increase your chances of getting a job you want.

If you write email at work using your company's computer and account, watch out. In this situation, your employer does have the right to browse your email if you've created it at work with company materials.

Solution #4: Encrypt your email and/or resume. If you are *very* concerned about privacy, you can use any number of software encryption products to ensure that only the people you designate can read your materials. (The "Resources" appendix tells more about encryption software.) Very few people encrypt their resumes, but it certainly can be done. Only you can be the judge of the level of privacy you require.

What Are the Chances of "Catching" a Computer Virus?

You've no doubt heard rumors about computer viruses that infect computers and ruin them forever. Most people never encounter viruses. If you are using an online service account, you can almost count on not seeing a virus. In the unlikely case that a computer virus initially gets by the sysops, you would receive ample warning about it.

One way to protect yourself from an email virus is to be aware of what common email address extensions look like. The most common are .com, .edu, .net, .gov, .org, .mil, .ca (a country code for Canada). If you see mail that has an unusual extension and it's from someone you don't know, don't retrieve it. Either delete it or contact your sysop and ask about it.

CONCLUSION

The goal of this chapter was to whet your appetite to all the job possibilities just ripe for the picking off the online services. Hopefully, it also convinced even the most serious Luddite out there that this technology can help to better humankind—in this case *you*, in your search for a new or better job. But there's lots more to learn, and a lot to do, so read on.

ONLINE WORKING STRATEGIES

Online Working Strategies

You've heard people say in a sarcastic tone, "You don't have to be a rocket scientist to know how to do that." Well, ten years ago, you pretty much *did* have to be a rocket scientist to know how to use the online services to find a job. Fortunately, all that's changed. Today, the explosive growth of commercial online services, the Internet, and other online repositories makes it possible for professionals in most areas to find jobs via the electronic superhighway. People from every career area—finance, medicine, graphic arts, sales, journalism, computer science, law, and more—are discovering that there are plum job opportunities waiting to be discovered in cyberspace.

Early in the development of online technology, online jobs were hidden in obscure niches of the Internet, and the methods of discovery were equally obscure. Now, thanks to the Internet, commercial online services, bulletin boards, and the like, it's safe to say that you *don't* have to be a rocket scientist to find a job online.

The Internet, always a good job resource for scientists, has expanded rapidly within the last few years to become a prime resource for almost anyone who's looking for a job. Abundant job lists filled with high-level opportunities and attractive, keyword-searchable databases are attracting an increasingly mainstream audience to the Internet. As mentioned, along with the Internet offerings, every major commercial online service, including America Online, CompuServe, Delphi, GEnie, Prodigy, and Microsoft Network, hosts large career sections. Most include hundreds of actual job leads along with helpful career information such as tips on how to interview, write resumes, and get online help from experts.

If you are a novice online navigator, you've picked a good time to begin; if you're an old hand, then you know how much simpler online navigation has become in recent years. The burgeoning availability of jobs and other compelling information in every corner of the online world has hundreds of thousands of people jumping online. To make online job searching and online navigation easier for the average person, point-and-click graphical interfaces are becoming commonplace, and online technology is finally becoming user-friendly (see Figure 2.1). For several years now, commercial online services like America Online have been offering smooth Mi-

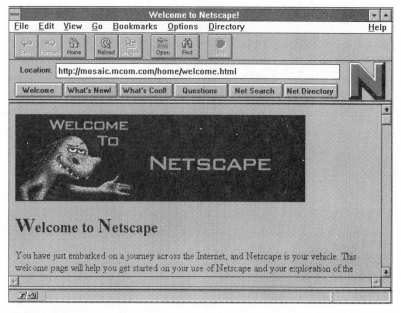

Figure 2.1 A sample of Netscape, a graphical interface that makes navigating the Internet a snap

crosoft Windows, Macintosh, and DOS-based interfaces that make navigation through their systems quite simple. And now the Internet, once infamously difficult to navigate and hook up to, is being demystified as commercial services offer inexpensive access and easy interfaces to all or parts of it. And easiest of all, Web browsers, like Mosaic, Netscape, and Cello, are software packages that give World Wide Web users a friendly interface. Graphical Web browsers like these can be used to access the Internet through SLIP and PPP accounts. (Chapter 5 has more on the World Wide Web.)

It is conceivable—even likely—that in the next three to five years, all online services will be interconnected with a unified graphical interface. This means that users will be able to log on to CompuServe, for example, and access every portion of CompuServe, the Internet, and the World Wide Web, all while using the same account and an easy-to-use interface. Currently, CompuServe allows subscribers user-friendly access to Usenet along with user-friendly FTP access to the Internet.

Nevertheless, even when this unified interface arrives, it's still going to be important to know how to manage and synthesize the huge quantity of information available to you. All of the rich online information and communications technology in the world will mean nothing to you unless you can use these electronic tools to accomplish what you want.

Specifically, when you go online to find a job, it's easy to get lost in all of the data that multiplies daily in the online world. That's why this chapter gives you all of the tools you need to get the most out of Internet databases and jobs lists, commercial online services, and other online areas. Using these tips, you'll save money and time online, and you'll be able to focus your electronic job search more productively.

If you are a novice, read this chapter carefully. You'll find broad techniques that will help you across a variety of interfaces and databases. Instructions on how to acquire information from the Internet and commercial databases is included in Chapters 5 and 6. If you are an experienced electronic researcher, you may want to browse this chapter quickly, as it never hurts to have as many online weapons in your arsenal as possible.

USING COMMERCIAL ONLINE SERVICES FOR JOB SEARCHING

Commercial online services have expended tremendous efforts to make an online job search easy. There are libraries of career resources, job lists, discussion boards filled with potential contacts, and opportunities for live online chats. The upcoming sections detail how you can take advantage of all these services have to offer.

The Lowdown on Commercial Online Databases

On online databases, information is organized, stored in a computer, and then made accessible via modem. These databases can be updated as often as the person managing the computer system desires—weekly, daily, or even hourly.

One example of such a database is E-Span, a database of job listings offered through CompuServe, Prodigy and America Online, as shown in Figure 2.2. According to Michael Rowe, E-Span's marketing director, the thousands of available jobs are completely updated twice every week. If you logged onto CompuServe, checked E-Span on Monday and then again on Wednesday, you would find that the database was set up the

Figure 2.2 E-Span's menu of offerings, as shown from CompuServe

same way, but that the content would be completely different. The lucrative opportunity offered on Monday might have been filled and removed from the system, or five new positions in your area of expertise could have been added.

Tips for Getting the Most from Online Commercial Services

Of course, the benefit of accessing online databases that are constantly updated is that the information is always current. The down side of that is the effort it takes to keep up with new information, and sort through that which doesn't necessarily apply to you. Read through the following tips. They will help keep you—and your pocketbook—in good order as you navigate these data repositories.

Tip #1: Find and use keywords and key phrases, and keep looking for more. Commercial services have made their databases keyword-searchable. This means that when you log onto a service, you will find a "go to" or "move to" prompt available from some point in the menu. If you type in a word, the computer will look up your word and find the services that match it and list them for you. For example, let's say that you've just graduated from law school. You're probably used to accessing the Internet from campus, so you know all about the jobs available online. To widen your net and stay connected to the online world, you decide to purchase a basic account with GEnie.

After you've logged on to your new GEnie account, you find yourself at GEnie's menu navigator. Looking down the list of services, as shown in Figure 2.3, you could click on Career/Professional Services immediately, or Online and then choose the menu item Move to page/keyword, and type in the keywords *job* or *career*. Either way, you'll end up at the Career/Professional Services area.

Once in the career area, looking down the alphabetical list, you would immediately discover areas directly of interest to you including Dr. Job, E-Span Job Search, the Law Roundtable, the Business Resource Directory, the Dialog Database Center, along with many other topically focused roundtables not directly related to your particular job search (see Figure 2.4).

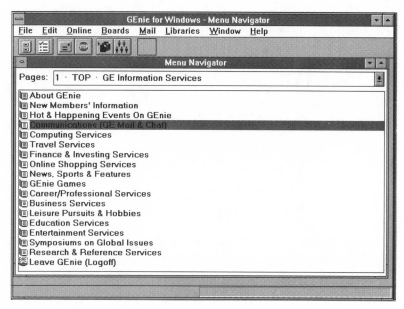

Figure 2.3 GEnie's opening menu

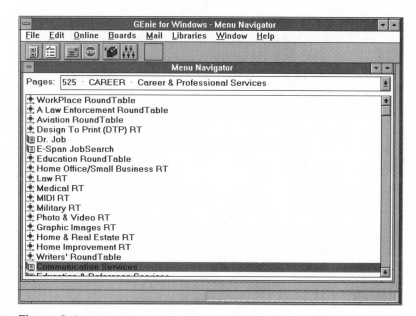

Figure 2.4 GEnie's career menu

```
        BUSINESS RESOURCE DIRECTORY

  1. Search database
  2. Control menu

  Enter #, <Q>uit, <H>elp?^Q1

  Query?^Qresume
       1439 documents found

           Browse/Retrieval options

  1. Title display
  2. Refine query
  3. Search database
  4. Environment display

  Enter #, <P>revious, <H>elp, <Q>uit?^Q'
```

Figure 2.5 A sample keyword search in
GEnie's Business Resource Directory

After finding these resources, you would then enter the
specific resources you're interested in and begin searching for
jobs or job help related to you. If you needed to write your first
resume and wanted advice, you could enter the Dr. Job database and find helpful articles. If you then clicked on and
entered the Business Resource Directory, you could type in a
keyword, such as *resume,* and discover a plethora of advice you
could then download from that directory. To see the results of
a sample search, see Figure 2.5.

GEnie is not unusual in its setup—keyword searches are a
common way of accessing information contained in commercial online databases. So, if you haven't already, compile a list
of keywords that relate directly to the job you are looking for. If
you aren't sure what constitutes a good keyword, start with the
obvious and then check a thesaurus and try various combina-
tions of terms. For instance, for the newly graduated law student, appropriate keywords would be *law, legal, attorney,
legislation, jobs, career,* and *careers.* For a teacher looking for a job
as a sixth grade classroom instructor, appropriate words would
be *education, teacher, teaching, elementary education, children, jobs,*
and *careers.*

As you research jobs online, keep notes on other keywords
you notice being applied to your career area. If you notice a
new term being applied to your target job, add it to your
keyword list. Keywords, like slang, tend to change with use and

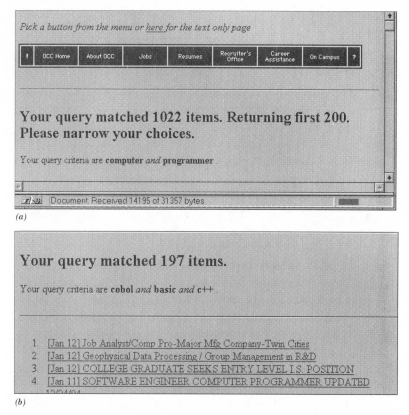

Figures 2.6a and b A comparison of Online Career Center keyword searches in GEnie

with time. For example, employers don't use the keyword *pro-grammer* to find resumes of computer programmers anymore because too many job seekers use it generically and it doesn't narrow a search well, as you can see from the lists in Figure 2.6a. Instead, employers use words designating specific programming languages such as C++, COBOL, or BASIC. The more specific and focused results can be viewed in Figure 2.6b.

There's no fixed list of keywords to look up for your profession, so common sense and common usage are your best guide to what is current and what will work for your career area. Browse recent online resumes from other job seekers in your career area and note the keywords they've used. Also, tune into the specialized publications in your target career area—online or in print—for buzzwords and descriptive terms. There's no penalty for trying out lots of keywords!

Tip #2: Take advantage of "read me" files. Another trick with databases is to print out the *read me* or information section, leave the database, go to another you're interested in, and repeat the process. Then once you're offline, you can read through the information about each database at your leisure. This not only makes the information *portable*, it also saves money.

Suppose you have an account with America Online and you want to find out how to access the jobs available in E-Span. Simply print out the files, as shown in Figure 2.7, save them, and read them later. When you later go online to search for jobs, you can have the information right in front of you as a guide.

If you're going online to retrieve a company profile from an expensive commercial database like Dialog, you'll especially want to familiarize yourself with the help files. Dialog has its own set of commands, and you'll want to know exactly what to ask for and how to ask for it while you're ringing up the online tab. If you're particularly nervous about accessing a particular database, you can always write down every step you'll take by studying the help files, including which keywords you're going to use or what information you're going to ask for.

For example, let's say you've seen a job opening with a company in Detroit, Michigan. You're interested in the job but, because you live in Florida, you aren't privy to the latest information about the company. You decide to double check a

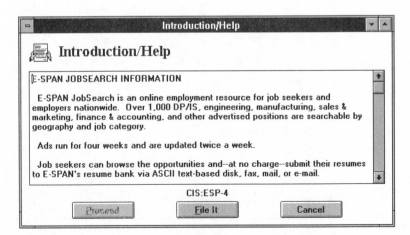

Figure 2.7 A portion of E-Span's help files

newspaper database for any recent articles that mention the company's name. But *before* you go online, here are the questions you should get answers to:

♦ Which service offers the database? (Read help files.)

♦ How does the service charge—by the amount of time you're on, or by the number of *hits*? (Read help files.)

♦ What are the commands that I must invoke to access information? (Read help files.)

♦ What keyword(s) should I be searching for?

♦ How many tries should I make before I log off?

Tip #3: Have an Online Strategy. Before you go online, jot down some notes about your online search. Ask yourself:

♦ Why are you going online and what do you want to accomplish? Are you going online to network or to look at job listings?

♦ Do you want to search for information about a company that you want to work for in the near future?

♦ When do you want to go online?

♦ How often do you want to check in?

♦ How much can you afford to spend for your online job search?

♦ How do plan to document your online time so that you can deduct your expenses from your income taxes?

After you've answered all of these questions, set a regular schedule, and give yourself specific online tasks. Keep a detailed notebook. Treat your online job search just as systematically and as seriously as you would treat a job search using conventional means, and keep close tabs on your costs. Work steadily toward that goal both offline and online.

We recommend that you set a specific day to check online classified advertisements, perhaps every Monday night. Be methodical and thorough, checking through all of the keywords that you've been noticing and writing down.

Perhaps Wednesday night would be a good night to catch up on reading job-focused bulletin board discussions and to email to your new online peers. On the weekend, you could browse for information about your (hopefully) new company, your new location if necessary, and so on. The point is, have a plan, and stick to it.

John Blakely, director of Software Engineering for Magnet Interactive Studios looked online for a job for more than a year. Even though he already had a good job, he decided he would make an effort to find his "dream" job. Because he was an America Online subscriber, Blakely decided to make a habit of checking E-Span every week. Each time he noticed a great job offer in his area, Blakely applied. After a year, he found the right fit, and now says he is in employment nirvana as a designer of computer games. He's even been promoted. And when he has to hire new engineers, guess where he looks for candidates? Right, online.

Tip #4: Don't be afraid to ask for help.   Part of what you pay for when you subscribe to a commercial service is technical support. So by all means, take full advantage of any offers of assistance. For instance, before you begin using your valuable time and money scouting out databases on your own, email a query to the member assistance section (every for-pay service has one) and ask for a list of all job-related services on the system. Also ask for names and email addresses of the system operators (sysops) who can help you target your job search more effectively. Janet Attard is a good example. At the time of this writing, she's the sysop for GEnie's career area, and knows every available file and can offer very specific advice to job seekers. She also has a staff of content area experts to help her, so she can point new users directly to people who can offer sound career advice. She also is in a position to know of a file or a job lead that a new member couldn't find because of a keyword discrepancy or a filing error.

Never be embarrassed to ask for help! Sysops are founts of information—remember, that's what they're paid for. Concentrate on your job search, and let the sysops help you find what you need. As you can see from Figure 2.8, Attard sends a greeting and explanation to each person who visits her area. People wanting more information need only to send her a follow-up email note.

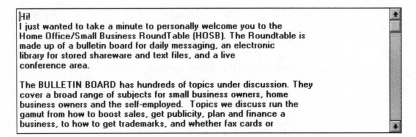

Hi!
I just wanted to take a minute to personally welcome you to the
Home Office/Small Business RoundTable (HOSB). The Roundtable is
made up of a bulletin board for daily messaging, an electronic
library for stored shareware and text files, and a live
conference area.

The BULLETIN BOARD has hundreds of topics under discussion. They
cover a broad range of subjects for small business owners, home
business owners and the self-employed. Topics we discuss run the
gamut from how to boost sales, get publicity, plan and finance a
business, to how to get trademarks, and whether fax cards or

Figure 2.8 Message from Janet Attard, a sysop for GEnie.

Tips for Getting the Most from Discussion Groups

As you explore different online areas, you will quickly discover discussion groups. They are called many different names: On GEnie, online discussion groups are called *roundtables*; in CompuServe, they're called *forums*; and on Usenet they're called *newsgroups*. These groups are ubiquitous on commercial services, and sometimes people have a tendency to overlook anything that's "in their face" all the time. The point here is, don't overlook the online discussion groups.

Discussion groups, such as the one in Figure 2.9, that are focused on a specific professions such as journalism, medicine, law, or photography are one of the best places to find a job other than a job list.

Typically, professionals working in a career area will frequent these boards. Often, they will have positions with companies you'd love to work for. Once you become savvy about how you post, you'll find that bulletin boards will become very powerful networking tools. Here are some practical tips to help you make the most of commercial bulletin boards and discussion groups.

Tip #1: Use keywords to find appropriate discussion groups.
Let's say you've just graduated from college with a communications major. In addition, you've just completed a six-month internship with a hot public relations firm, and you've decided that you definitely want to seek work in the public relations field. But for now, you're working as a temp until you find a position you really want to settle into.

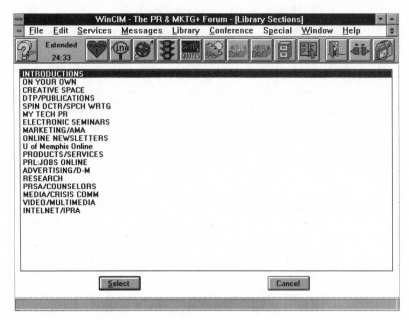

Figure 2.9 CompuServe's PR & Marketing Forum

You decide that you can spend around $50.00 a month on your job search. As a part of that budget, you sign up for a basic account on CompuServe. After reading the information files, you further decide that you can afford to spend a total of four hours every month on the *forums* (CompuServe's bulletin boards).

Instead of wandering around the menus blindly to find the forums best suited for your target career, you would:

1. Go to CompuServe's menu, click on Find, and then type in your keywords (see Figure 2.10). You discover that the most obvious keyword, *public relations*, brings up only one listing: PR & Marketing Forum. That sounds good.

2. Nevertheless, you decide to try more keywords to expand the scope of your search. You try *marketing*. The list of services that comes up, as shown in Figure 2.11, includes Business Database Plus, Business Demographics, Desktop Publishing Forum, PR & Marketing Forum, Entrepreneur's Forum, the UK Professionals Forum, and several other items. It's a veritable gold mine!

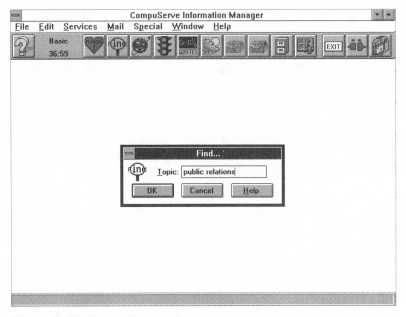

Figure 2.10 CompuServe's Find menu

3. Checking further, (using Find services is part of the basic package and doesn't carry extra charges) you try the keyword *communications*. You discover all sorts of software forums, but you also discover the Telecommunications Forum, something that might be useful for browsing.

At this point in your search, probably the only difficulty you'll have is to decide which forum to visit first.

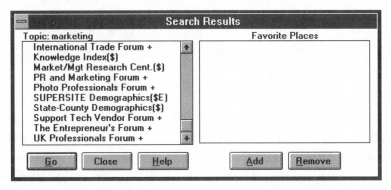

Figure 2.11 Results of using *marketing* as a keyword search

Tip #2: Post focused queries targeted specifically to your job search. By posting focused, intelligent queries on these bulletin boards, you will increase your network dramatically. According to Orville Pearson, senior vice president for Programs and Professional Development of Lee Hecht Harrison, an outplacement firm for high-level executives, approaching online boards with a clear career focus has powerful job-finding potential. "In a typical job search, people will talk with hundreds of people—their 'network'—before they find a position," says Pearson. "If you don't have a network yet, an online bulletin board is a fantastic place to start. Think about it—you have access to experts nationwide, all from your computer terminal."

A good way to approach a discussion is to choose a very specific area of expertise within your profession, and then open a dialog about it. Let's go back to the example of public relations, where a good board to begin posting to is CompuServe's PR & Marketing Forum. The forum, or bulletin board, is divided into two sections: a section where messages are posted and a library section where files are posted. Click on the message section, and you find a section called Introductions. This is the right place to start. This section is shown in Figure 2.12. Notice the title of the forum at the very top of the screen. Here, it's "The PR & MKTG Forum." Next is a menu bar that allows you to navigate the entire CompuServe system.

Below the menu bar are icons that provide shortcuts to the most popular menu items. For example, if you clicked on the Find button (the microscope icon), you would immediately be presented with a blank to fill in with a keyword. You can also get to the find option from the menu by clicking on Services and then on Find. It's just one additional step this way.

Now look at the list under "Introductions," which is the section of the forum we are in. We've highlighted the first message item, "New guy, (freelance)." This is someone who is new to the forum and is introducing himself. The check mark in the box to the left indicates that you want to read the messages. To the right, is the number 7, indicating that there are seven messages in response to the freelancer's original post, or message. Look at the message NEWCOMER. Notice that there is only one response. It's worth comparing the two

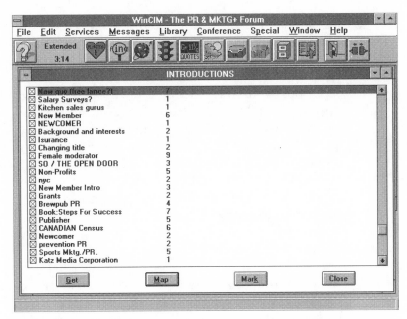

Figure 2.12 The message area of CompuServe's PR & Marketing Forum

messages to see why the freelancer got more responses to his post than the NEWCOMER.

At the bottom of the screen are four buttons: Get, Map, Mark, and Close. If you click on the Get button, you will retrieve the highlighted or checked messages. If you click on the Map button, you will find out when the message was posted (date and time), the size of the message (by number of characters), and who posted the message (the name of the person). If you click on the Mark button, you will mark the message (put a check in the box). The Close button will close the screen. CompuServe's software will do all the retrieving for you—all you have to do is to click and read.

After browsing a few messages in this area, let's assume you're ready to post your carefully crafted first message. It might read something like this: "Hello, I'd like to introduce myself. I have just graduated from xyz University. I majored in communications, and I've just completed an internship. I am interested in working with a midsize, nonprofit organization that specializes in the arts. A research area I'm especially interested in is to determine how small to midsize nonprofits can develop name recognition without a budget to purchase newspaper advertisements." (More information on online networking and writing posts that get high-level responses is included in Chapter 4, "Networking.")

To post your own message, click on the Messages menu option. In the menu that appears, you will find an option to Create Message. Click on this option. A blank screen will be presented to you. Type in your message, and then check off the section of the forum you want it to go to. For this first message, check the box Introductions. Each online service will differ slightly in its specifics of how to post, but you will find all of them to be as simple to navigate as CompuServe.

This type of message will bring you to the attention of professional peers in your target career area and establish your expertise in the minds of readers. It will also help you to gain valuable knowledge about your career niche. By posting messages in this manner, you learn to carefully craft and consider your queries and responses. This is one place you don't have to worry about getting tongue-tied or wearing the wrong outfit.

Tip #3: Browse and post in the resume section.   Commercial bulletin boards, no matter what service they're located on, usually have an area where jobs are listed for that particular profession, and another area where subscribers can upload their resume. Again using CompuServe's PR & Marketing Forum as the example, after you posted your introductory message, you could read the list of topics and discover a special area for online jobs listings called PRL: Jobs Online. Employers who want recruits with computer skills often post opportunities on topical bulletin boards like the PR & Marketing Forum. If you see a job lead you like, you can download the job offer and respond via email or regular mail later.

If, however, you don't see an offer you like, don't immediately log off the board in an effort to save money. Take a few moments to browse the Library section, because filed away there are resumes that other subscribers have uploaded for employers to browse. Read through a few of these resumes (see Figure 2.13) and see how you compare. If you discover that your resume style is outdated or vastly different, take some notes. Analyze what makes a particular online resume stand

PRL:JOBS ONLINE			
Title	Size	Date	Accesses
☐ ▦ Dallas Jobs as of Dec. 22, 1994	15818	12/23/94	52
☐ ▦ VisitGuide marketing opportunities	1711	12/22/94	21
☐ ▤ December, 1994 job openings from	18287	12/22/94	67
☐ ▤ International PR/Media Buying Re	255185	12/16/94	7
☐ ▤ Top lame-duck speechwriter seek	3942	12/14/94	16
☐ ▤ An IT Marketeer Will Travel World	4994	12/14/94	7
☐ ▤ Senior Account Supervisor/New B	791	12/11/94	81
☐ ▤ Several new marketing and marke	2208	12/11/94	167
☐ ▤ B-T-B Tech MarCom Spclst Availa	3595	12/12/94	12
☐ ▤ NETWRK.TXT	9868	12/10/94	44

Figure 2.13 Portions of online resumes from CompuServe's PR & Marketing Forum

out to you, and then craft your resume accordingly. Chances are, if one garners your attention, it probably has the same effect on employers. When you're ready, make a point of uploading your resume to every appropriate bulletin board or forum available to you. (Save your notes on resumes, as we'll be discussing in detail how to prepare your electronic resume in Chapter 3.)

Tip #4: Use navigation software. Navigation software allows you to do a lot of online work *off* line. For example, you can log on and direct the software to download all of your email and bulletin board messages or go to a bulletin board and download all messages covering certain topics.

The software will retrieve the information while you wait and signal you when it's done. Then, you can log off and read everything offline. This type of software can save you quite a bit of money, because it can retrieve material in much less time than you can.

If you're not sure what software to ask for, send an email query to the help section of the particular online service you subscribe to, and ask them what software they have available to make navigation as fast as possible. They'll be able to give you all of the information you need. For example, if you subscribe to Delphi, access the Customer Support area. It is one of the menu options. Click on the Mail option and compose an email message that says something like: "I'm new online, and I am interested in finding out about software that is available to help me save money online. Do you have navigation software that helps users do tasks offline?" As of this writing, Delphi has two navigation products available: D-Lite and Rainbow. For a brief description of other navigation software, refer to Appendix C, "Resources."

Or, as mentioned in Chapter 1, you can also call the service's toll-free number and ask a customer support representative for help.

Live Chats

Live chats, designated times when you can log on to a service and hob-nob in real time—that is, as if you were talking together on the phone or in person—with experts and celebrities, are wonderful for accessing otherwise difficult-to-reach experts. Unless you just moved here from Mars, you no doubt have heard about the *chat* that CompuServe hosted with Vice President Al Gore. Anyone with a subscription to CompuServe was welcome to join in—until the "conference room" became overcrowded. (Yes, overcrowding can occur online, too.)

Chances are, for your job search, you won't have trouble getting in on the live chats you're interested in. If there is a specific question you want to ask an expert about your job search, keep abreast of upcoming live chats.

If you have never participated in a chat before, you may find yourself freezing at the keyboard, or make lots of typos, or just basically find yourself electronically tongue-tied. Unless you're very sure of yourself, it's a good idea to listen to several low-key live chats before you jump in on one that is very important to you.

If you use Microsoft Windows and you have a specific question you want to ask, you can write out your question or questions in a text file using either your Microsoft notepad or your word processing program. Then, keep the text window open and go online. When your time comes to ask a question, you can cut and paste your question from the text window to the online window.

INTERNET JOB SEARCHING

The Internet, as much-discussed as it is, remains a mystery for most people because the Internet is difficult to define (an understatement). Basically, the Internet is a network of more than 45 thousand independent but interlinked computers. In the third quarter of 1994, the Internet grew by 21 percent and it is projected that by the first quarter of 1999, Internet hosts will likely hit 100 million. But as difficult as the Internet is to define, for job seekers it is a must if they want to find some of the richest job hunting resources imaginable.

To find out how to access the jobs riches of the Internet without getting lost in a mire of technical information, read the upcoming sections carefully.

The Only Constant Is Change

The one thing you can count on when it comes to the Internet is that it will change—and rapidly. The best way to handle this is to stay flexible. Don't get stuck looking in just one area of the Internet, and don't expect that everything will always look exactly the same all of the time. If you find that you are getting lost or are not finding exactly the resource you're after, relax. Appreciate the fact that you're learning more about the Internet everyday, and realize that some of the best job "finds" will come as a result of getting lost. Synchronicity and serendipity are wonderful components of an online search and are often underappreciated.

When necessary, reread the navigation sections of this book and the appendices. Then, log on and just browse. Think "big picture." Determine that for 15 minutes, you will just look around and try to get a feel for how information is organized on the Internet. Most people, even the most techno-phobic, find that within about a week of Internet browsing they feel comfortable with the environment they've discovered.

Fill Your Internet Tool Chest

After you've logged onto the Internet, you'll find that there are a number of search tools designed to help you cut through the thickets of network information.

Internet Hotspots

Some resources on the Internet are as easy to search as commercial online databases and are excellent sources for job lists and career help. They are the best places to start as you overcome your trepidation about using this seemingly overwhelming network. No matter how nontechnical you are, as soon as you log on to these resources you'll discover that they are very simple to use. One of these is the Online Career Center. As a starting point for specific job search exploration on the Internet, you can't do any better.

Let's assume, for this example, that you're looking for a job as a financial planner, and you want to use the Online Career Center to search for possibilities. Follow these steps:

1. After you have your modem and software hooked up, purchase an Internet account. Remember, all you have to do to purchase an Internet account is to call one of the contact numbers you'll find in Appendix A. It's as simple as picking up the phone.

2. Once you have access, log on to your account.

3. Type in the electronic address of the Online Career Center.

4. After a few minutes, you'll see an opening menu directing you to the Online Career Center. Choose that option.

5. To look at the jobs available, choose the menu option that says Search Jobs and hit Enter (see Figure 2.14a). From a SLIP account, you would click on the option you wanted. In this case, Resume was chosen (see Figure 2.14b).

6. After a few moments, another menu (like the one in Figure 2.15a or b) will appear on your screen, and you'll be asked to choose how you want to look for jobs. If you're looking for a job in Hawaii, say, choose the Browse Jobs by State option. If you just want the best possible job in your profession no matter where it is, then choose the Keyword option.

You should be able to see by comparing Figures 2.14, 15, and 16 that how you access the Internet greatly impacts what you will see on your screen. And bear in mind that there are subtle differences between almost every online system or account. It's these kinds of subtle differences that make a single description of "how to" accomplish something on the Internet an impossible task. And it's also why it's so important to have an overall idea of how to tackle the information you'll have access to online.

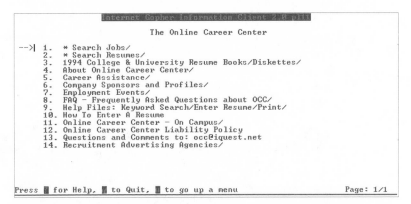

Figure 2.14a The Online Career Center opening menu, as shown from a basic Internet account.

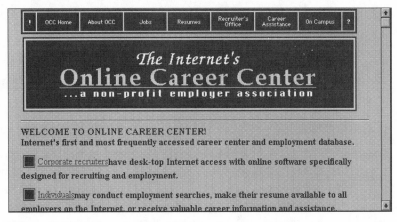

Figure 2.14b The Online Career Center opening menu on the World Wide Web, as shown from a SLIP account running Mosaic, a point-and-click graphical interface.

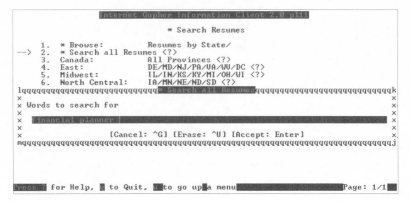

Figure 2.15a Resume search menu of Online Career Center from a basic Internet account, often called a terminal or shell account. (Terminal in this case is short for "terminal emulation," which means that you are connecting in a particular way to a machine that is then directly connected to the Internet.)

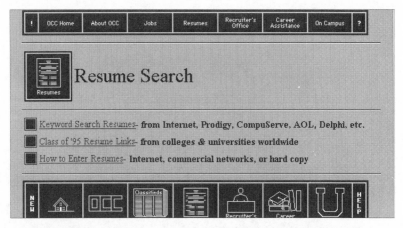

Figure 2.15b Resume search menu of the Online Career Center as seen on the World Wide Web.

7. When you choose the Keyword option, a long fill-in-the-blank will pop up on your screen with a blinking cursor inside. All you have to do is type in your target keywords, which in this case would be *financial planner*, as shown in Figure 2.16a. Other words you might try are *financial* or even *banking* or *bank*. In a few moments, depending on how many jobs or resumes the system has to list, a numbered list will come up on your screen. Figure 2.16b shows what the results of a keyword search for *financial*

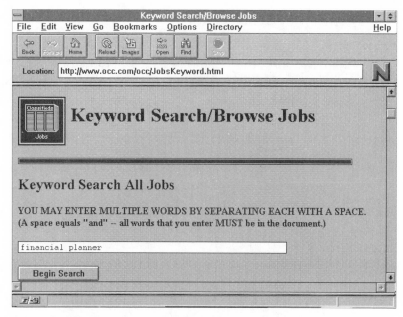

Figure 2.16a Keyword search of Online Career Center

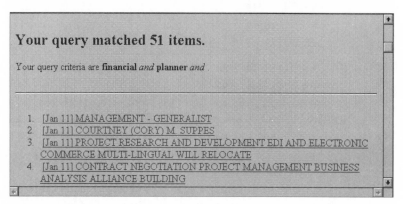

Figure 2.16b Results of keyword search

planner would look like. Now, you can scroll through the jobs and capture or print out the information you want to save.

Once you feel that you have mastered this Internet resource, begin to explore other options. To do this, start browsing more of the Online Career Center's menus, and slowly begin investigating others. Another good way to explore is to try your hand at Usenet, which is discussed at length shortly.

Internet Search Plan

When you are searching on the Internet for job leads, career advice, and other job-related information, don't just hop from database to database as new and interesting topics catch your eye, hoping that somehow you will happen onto a database that will help you in your job hunt. If you approach your Internet job search like this, you will walk away saying, "I found too much information, and I can't use any of it!"

Just as with commercial online searches, a big part of avoiding information overload is to have a plan. This becomes even more important on the Internet, where thousands of enticing databases can distract you from your job search goals. An Internet search plan should include:

♦ A list of databases you want to search, plus their Internet addresses.

♦ A list of job areas you plan to look at on a regular basis, plus the corresponding Internet addresses and a list of keywords.

♦ A time schedule of how you're going to use your time online.

Sooner or later, you will succumb to the urge to unabashedly browse the Internet. You'll find yourself looking at every piece of information that interests you, whether or not it has anything to do with your job search. You'll see a discussion group about David Letterman, and you'll read 350 messages just to hear the latest gossip. If you want to be a television producer, reading the Letterman discussion group might be justifiable. But if you're looking for a job as a biologist, well. . . . Two hours later, you'll wonder where the time went and start calculating how much you'll have to pay for your little "National Enquirer" excursion. But don't be too hard on yourself, because sooner or later it happens to everyone. One word of advice: Try to give into these off-the-subject forays during the least expensive times, such as off-hours.

On the other hand, we do encourage you to use the Internet to explore some area of specialized interest that you've never had time to really look into. Find a way to make your interests help you become a better job candidate, a better interview subject, or look better on a job application. For example, if you're a copywriter who wants to go to work for an advertising firm that specializes in luxury products, then it's legitimate to browse the Internet for information on luxury car discussion groups, boats, fine wines, and classical music. (And, if along the way you find the perfect Burgundy to go with that fancy dinner you're planning for Friday night, hey, that's okay, too. Just don't ever stray so far from your job focus that using the online services becomes a diversion instead of a source of help toward reaching your real goal—the perfect job!)

INTERMEDIATE INTERNET JOB SEARCHING

If you've been on the Internet before and already feel comfortable with navigating and browsing the basic job search areas like the Online Career Center, then you're ready for bigger and better. Let's start with Usenet.

Usenet

One of the more misunderstood resources on the Internet is Usenet. Usenet is simply an area of the Internet where discussion groups are kept, but the way the topics are named throws a surprising number of potential job seekers off track. They see the long, cryptic lists of topics and think, "Who needs something this difficult to read?" The fact is, that odd little title you're thinking about ignoring might just be the doorway to some real job gems. (To see an example of Usenet groups, see Figure 2.17.)

Usenet is now available through most commercial online services, not just the Internet.

If you find that you're one of the people who can barely stand to look at Usenet, set aside 15 minutes every week and promise yourself that, for those 15 minutes, you will choose a Usenet board and read what's on it. For instance, if you're a high school science teacher, you may want to choose a board that relates to your profession, such as *K12.ed.science*. Or, you may want to read up on an area of science that you're planning a unit on. For example, if you were planning a unit on astronomy, you could read *sci.astro* and glean very valuable informa-

Usenet, a "User's Network" created originally by two graduate students Tom Truscott and Jim Ellis, is organized in a hierarchical structure. Each of the 10,000-plus groups are named by subject, geographical area or an organization name, followed by a period and then more information. As the topic becomes more focused, you get more levels of the group name. Keep in mind that some groups are local, and some are national\international.

Here are a few examples:

misc.jobs.misc = miscellaneous hierarchy, subect of jobs, miscellaneous jobs
misc.jobs.contract = miscellaneous hierarchy, subject of jobs, contractual jobs
sdnet.jobs = San Diego hierarchy, jobs. (This is an example of a local hierarchy, that is, one available usually only to Usenet users in the surrounding area. Some Internet providers, however, do offer access to all such newsgroups.)
sci.astro = science hierarchy, subject of astronomy
sci.bio = science hierarchy, subject of biology
alt.journalism = alternative hierarchy, subject of journalism
biz.jobs.offered = business hierarchy, subject of jobs, jobs being offered

Figure 2.17 A list of Usenet discussion groups and the translations

tion, as shown in Figure 2.18. Once you become familiar with Usenet, you'll wonder how you could have thought about trying to find a job without it.

Usenet As a Prime Job Search Resource

The Usenet is a truly spectacular resource for job seekers, and it's relatively easy to access once you understand how it's set up. The structure is simple: It is a long list of more than 8,000 topically based, self-organized content areas. Many of the Usenet content areas are discussion groups where people gather to chat about specific topics. The others are lists of jobs, with some lists having an average of 4,000 jobs posted on them.

Making the most of Usenet is an art, and the following are time-tested tips that will help you become a Usenet master.

74726 Question about the moon.
74727 Magellan Ends Successful Mission
74728 Cassini Makes Excellent Progress in Past Year
74730 Mars Program Planned for Next 10 Years
74731 Pluto Fast Flyby Redefined as Pluto Express
74732 Hubble's '94 Comeback Due in Large Part to WFPC-2
74733 Ulysses Completes First Phase of Study of Sun
74734 End of SP-100 Project Turns into Technology Transfer Success Story
74735 SIR-C/X-SAR Exceeds Expectations
74852 Re: SIR-C/X-SAR Exceeds Expectations
74736 JPL Contributes to UARS Ozone-Depletion Data
74737 JPL GPS Instruments Measure Mountain Movements

Figure 2.18 A sampling of the *sci.astro* board on Usenet

Tip #1: Use Internet bulletin boards in your job search, but before you do, be aware of the differences between most commercial bulletin boards and the Usenet boards. Usenet discussion groups are similar to those on commercial online services in many ways. Both types of discussion areas are topically focused, both allow you to post responses and upload resumes, and both are powerful network-building tools. And both Usenet and commercial boards are available through commercial online services.

But the Usenet, even though it can be reached through the commercial services, is different in one important way: It is home to a highly variable, specialized, unique online culture. If you want to use the Usenet effectively in your job search, we recommend that you "lurk" awhile (read the messages on a Usenet group or bulletin board without posting a message) before you start posting messages. Although it may feel like eavesdropping to keep silent while reading everyone else's thoughts, it's the smart way to approach Usenet. A good rule of thumb is to lurk for a week, then post.

When you're in a hurry to find a job, it may seem like a waste of valuable job hunting time to lurk, but there are thousands of different Usenet discussion groups you can participate in, and every one of them has a different tone. Some are very academic; some are informal. Matching the timbre of the board is critically important to the people who use Usenet regularly, so take the extra time to "learn the board." That way, your networking will be as effective as possible when you're ready to go.

For example, on the Usenet board *alt.journalism*, a discussion sprang up in 1993 about which journalism school was best, or if a degree in journalism was an effective preparation for newspaper reporting. A number of seasoned editors from well-known newspapers weighed in on the subject, arguing all angles of the discussion. Several budding—and very savvy—journalism majors entered the conversation, offering their perspective as students. After over a year of online discussion during which the editors practically wrote a book on how to get a top job in journalism through their posts, these journalism majors had not only gained information about how to find a job, but they had also made some very valuable contacts at high levels.

During this academic-based *alt.journalism* discussion, several other would-be journalists entered the conversation, arguing their points politely but intensely. These people were ignored, because the tone of their messages, while perhaps appropriate on another board, was ill-suited to the friendly, relaxed tone of the other participants. If the newcomers had read the board for a week or two and then posted, they would have been able to target their messages much more effectively.

Tip #2: Learn how to manage those large, nonkeyword-searchable but very compelling Usenet job lists. In addition to being a great place for networking, Usenet is also a fantastic source for job listings. If you've never seen a Usenet job list before, you may find yourself pleasantly surprised by the sheer number of jobs available. But as soon as you start to dig through the long lists, you may find that pleasant feeling fading away as you become overwhelmed by the masses of information, such as shown in Figure 2.19. Avoid the information overload with these two list-wrangling methods:

1. Plan, then scan. Before you ever log on to the Internet with the intent to look at Usenet jobs lists, write down a specific plan of action. Your written plan can be as simple as a list on an index card—it doesn't have to be elaborate to be effective. Your plan should include the exact name of the list you're going to research (*it must be spelled correctly*), a description of what the list contains, the order you're going to search in, and an estimate of how long you're going to be online. It's not a bad idea to write your job target on the card as a reminder. Before you log on, make sure you have a clock or a watch available. Once

```
40638 Network Manager - Los Angeles CA - Internet Provider
40639 ### need OS/2 PM development SOM1/2 for IBM Florida ###
40640 $$$ need WORKPLACE OS microkernel WIRELESS COMM $$$
40641 !!! need WORKPLACE Shell SECURITY and OS/2 interface !!!
40642 NEC's OnLine JobFair
40643 NEC's OnLine JobFair # 2
40644 ISM (BC) Jobs in Asia
40645 Need a BABYSITTER
40646 FEDERAL JOB OPPORTUNITIES
40650 Re: FEDERAL JOB OPPORTUNITIES
40652 Re: FEDERAL JOB OPPORTUNITIES
40653 Re: FEDERAL JOB OPPORTUNITIES
```

Figure 2.19 Some of the 4,000-plus jobs on Usenet *misc.jobs.misc*

you're online, check your time. Then, unless you're logging onto Usenet just to have fun, search Usenet by *group
name*. Searching by group name is available from the
Internet and from the commercial online services. Be
disciplined and use this option—don't just log on and
run down all 10,000 groups, jumping in here and there
every time a subject piques your interest. Before you
realize what's happened, you will have used your budg-
eted time and money without ever getting a chance to
focus on your job search. It's amazing how time flies
when you're browsing Usenet.

2. Use capture files to your advantage. Once you've found
    the list you're interested in, instead of taking the time to
    read everything online, capture the text and wait until
    you're offline to read details. For example, if you are
    working for an accounting firm in Nebraska and the
    winters have simply become too cold and too long for
    you, you might want to access the Usenet list *ba.jobs.offered*
    (Bay area jobs in Northern California).

*To capture text, you will use your communications software, which is
what dials your modem and puts you online. Procomm and Quick Link
II FAX are two examples of communication software. Of course, there
are many varieties of this software available, so the exact steps you have
to take might differ slightly from this. The general steps, however, will be
the same.*

*While you are online, look at the menu above the screen. Find the File
option and click on it. A new menu will come up, with more options.
One of them will say Capture Text or Capture Screen. Choose this option.
After you do, you will be asked what file name you want to give your
capture session. It's a good idea to name your capture files based on what
you are looking at. For ba.area.jobs, you might say: C:\bayjobs.*

*Then, just press Enter, and everything happening on screen will be
saved to your C:\bayjobs file. To stop the capture, go back to the File
menu and click on Capture Text. The capture feature will then be
turned off.*

3. After locating the list, open a capture file and go to the
    top of the *ba.jobs.offered* list. As you see in Figure 2.20, the
    list contains an average of 800 jobs. Scroll as quickly as

```
35861 Games Contractors [C, Games Systems] [Recruiter] 1713
35862 Architect Dev[Real-time,OS,RISC,Chipset config, UNIX, C][Recruiter]1721
35863 Windows Prog[C++, Financial, MFC] [Recruiter] 1738
35864 Windows Progr[MFC/OLE/OXC] 1yr Contract Win95 1752
»35865 2D Animator [Fine Arts background, MAC/Macromedia Director]Recr 1756
35866 Windows Programmers[C++, Win, MFC, 1-3 yrs experience ]Recr 1759
35867 wSr. SW Eng[SNMP, RMON, embedded sys, RT OS, kernel des]Recr 1760
35868 Illustrator for MM[Fine arts background; Temp to Perm]Recruiter 1757
35869 MM Programmer-Contract[Mac, Windows, C] [Recruiter] 1740
35870 Mac Development Jobs
35871 Re: FEDERAL JOB OPPORTUNITIES
35872 Re: FEDERAL JOB OPPORTUNITIES
```

Figure 2.20 The top level of *ba.jobs.offered*, which you should capture and scan later.

you can through the list. After you've scrolled from the top of the list to the bottom, log off; then study the list in detail. If you see seven accounting jobs on the list, note the numbers of those seven jobs. Go back online, access the list, and type in the exact numbers of the jobs you want to see. Capture the job descriptions and then log off again, as shown in Figure 2.21. There are two advantages to working this way: You'll have a record of your job search, and you'll save a lot of money because you're time online is kept to a minimum.

If you are using a SLIP account to access the Usenet, you may have a newsreading program such as Trumpet that allows you to archive the news articles. In this case, you would click on Archive each time you wanted an article or job opening saved.

Because Usenet jobs lists are such a valuable resource, some online resource areas, such as Career Mosaic on the World Wide Web, offer several keyword-searchable Usenet jobs lists. You'll know when you've found a keyword-searchable Usenet list because it will say so. For example, Career Mosaic states clearly, "We have keyword-searchable Usenet lists."

Gophers

Rescued from rodent-dom by the advent of online technology, Gophers have been reborn as powerful Internet organizers. Originally developed at the University of Minnesota, they or-

2D Animator (Fine Arts background, MAC/Macromedia Director)Recr 1756, by Tech
From: tsearch@netcom.com (Tech Search)
Subject: 2D Animator (Fine Arts background, MAC/Macromedia Director)Recr 1756
Date: Thu, 12 Jan 1995 02:48:54 GMT

Location: Marin County Salary: Negotiable   Job 1756
Description: 2D animator needed by Marin-based multimedia company. Fine
arts background a must. Experience with Macintosh, Macromedia Director
required. A good sense of humor and creativity desired. Will work with
CD-ROM titles.

Once we receive your resume, you will be placed in our database. Should we
have a position that fits your skills and background, you will be contacted by
one of our staff.

Please send us your resume ONLY if you have COMMERCIAL experience
of at least 2 YEARS.

Figure 2.21 The job description level of *ba.jobs.offered*

ganize vast amounts of information into menus that you can
easily browse. Even if you are logging on to the Internet for the
first time, you will be able to navigate a gopher with perfect
ease. As you can see in Figure 2.22, you could just keep browsing from menu to menu as you explore the Internet, because
exploring on a Gopher is a matter of just choosing menu
options.

Gopher software handles all commands from you, so instead
of typing an Internet address, you press a menu number, then
Enter, and the gopher software takes you to your desired destination. To be sure, this interface is great, but it's not all Gopher
has to offer job seekers. Two other powerful features of Gopher, the mail utility and the search engines, turn Gopher from

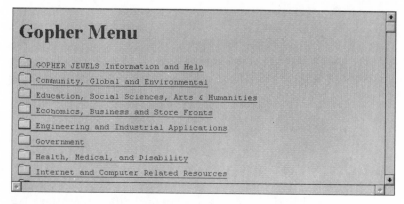

Figure 2.22 A sample Gopher menu

a pleasant but random browsing tool into a real information-grabbing tool.

The main way to utilize Gopher in your job search is to use your keywords to search Veronica, which is an Internet searching tool that allows you to search Gopher menus by keyword. Veronica and Jughead, other gopher searching tools, will be described in more detail later in this book. For now, just be aware that easy-to-use keyword searching tools are available for you when you get on the Internet. If, for example, you are looking for a job as a forensic accountant, you could browse through the Gopher menus, but performing a search is a much more efficient way of finding the specific information you're looking for. To perform a Veronica search, log on to your Internet account, and go to a Gopher. Every Internet account is different, but you will be able to find gopher easily. Most will have a Gopher option right on the opening menu. It's one of the first things you'll see when you log on. All you have to do is choose the menu option that says Gopher and then go to a Veronica option, (it will probably be right on the menu for you). Then choose the menu option that says Search Veronica. A menu will pop onto your screen with a space in which to write the words to want to search for. The cursor automatically blinks inside the space, so all you have to do is type in *forensic accounting*, press Enter, and wait.

After a few minutes, you'll see a list of all your *finds*, or *hits*. Then you can press the menu numbers corresponding to the information you want to see. Let's say that one of the items that you found especially helpful was a file about an association of forensic accountants. At this point, you could press the letter "m" on your computer, which in Gopher is a command to mail the file on your screen to an email address.

Once you press "m," a blank will appear on your screen prompting you for an address to which to mail the file. Type in an email address and press Enter. That's it! The file will be delivered, and you can look at the information at your leisure. Needless to say, mailing files to your email address saves your online time for actual searching.

In Chapter 6 you will find illustrated step-by-step sample Gopher searches using Veronica, along with a sample of how to mail electronic files to yourself or any other email address. You'll also find more information about Gopher commands.

THE WORLD WIDE WEB AND YOUR JOB SEARCH

If you have access to the World Wide Web (the Web), then you'll understand why it will become the way most people access the Internet in the near future. The Web is simple to use, it's attractive, and the possibilities it affords are compelling. If you don't have access to the Web, we want to stress the importance of getting access.

The Web is basically a multimedia method of accessing the Internet. Instead of just retrieving text, Web users can access video, graphics, and sound while online. Anything already on the Internet is accessible via the Web. So, for example, if you have access to the Web, you can still search Gopher menus from it. But what is different about searching gophers from the Web is that instead of looking at a black-and-white screen, if you have a color monitor, you will see the Internet in color. And instead of typing in commands, you can click on menu options with your mouse and navigate through the online world easily.

If you don't have the Web, read Appendix A, "Getting Yourself Online," for the names of Internet account providers near you. Also, Prodigy alone of the commercial online services offers Web access, but expect the others to follow suit in the very near future.

How does all of this affect you and your job search? Obviously, that depends on whether you have Web access or not. Currently, there are at least a hundred job resources available on the Web that are not available anywhere else (and that number is growing rapidly). To find the job opportunities and career areas available on the Web, all you have to do is take your keywords, go to a Web search tool, as shown in Figure 2.23, type in your keywords, and wait for the list of resources to appear on your screen. (Chapter 5 on the World Wide Web has complete details about navigating and searching the World Wide Web.)

Once the list comes up, it's up to you to research and read through every available resource thoroughly. Two Web areas you won't want to miss are Career Mosaic and the Interactive Employment Network.

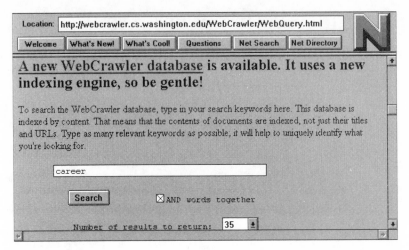

Figure 2.23 The Web Crawler, an effective Web searching tool

≡ BULLETIN BOARDS, COMMUNITY NETS, AND FREENETS

Bulletin boards are generally menu-driven, which means that they are very easy to navigate. In Chapter 7, you'll find the phone numbers for some of the nation's top employment bulletin boards. The tips given earlier describing commercial databases in general apply to bulletin board systems as well. Always read the help files before you start any serious re-searching, and send an email message asking for help if you have any problems.

Some of these bulletin boards will cost you the same as a long distance phone call, so be very careful of how much time you're spending online. Consider calling during off hours to save on phone expenses.

If you are lucky enough to live near either a community net (like the Central Virginia Free-Net, shown in Figure 2.24) or a freenet, then by all means take advantage of it. Like bulletin board systems, community nets and freenets are designed for easy access. The tips given throughout this chapter will serve you well as you roam. Just be aware that community nets and

Welcome to Central Virginia's Free-net!

Central Virginia's Free-Net contains a wealth of information about the people and activities in our community. Please explore! Guests should review the registration procedures under "Free-Net Services."

- CVaNet News, Information and Community Support
- The Help Desk
- Volunteer Information
- Electronic Communications
- Free-Net Services
- SPEAK UP Central Virginia! (NEW)

Figure 2.24 A quick look at a well-organized freenet: The Central Virginia Free-Net.

freenets often have limited resources, so be considerate of network time and purchase a separate account when you're ready. Also, be sure to check for local job listings while you browse.

ON THE ROAD TO A GREAT JOB

The more time you have to practice the search techniques described in this chapter, the more effective your job search will be. Persist in exploring all avenues open to you; don't overlook the obvious, and stay focused on your job search.

When you're looking for jobs online, keep in mind that you'll discover alluring jobs in every corner in the world. Do you see your perfect job in Paris? Don't just fantasize, send an email query, and ask if this is a job that could be arranged as a telecommuting or virtual office position. Keep your mind open to the possibilities that alternative work styles and new office technologies give you.

And finally, if you're new to online jobs searching, be patient with your learning curve and give yourself time to absorb your new skills. And remember that employers value online searching techniques, so none of your work is in vain. In fact, you might just want to add your online searching skills to your resume!

POSTING YOUR RESUME ONLINE

Posting Your Resume Online

In a scene from the long-running smash Broadway hit "A Chorus Line," a row of hopeful dancers hold up their resumes and lament: "Who am I anyway? Am I my resume?" Who of us, when looking for a job, has not felt this same frustration over the fact that so much of our fate depends on a lifeless piece of paper that can only list our accomplishments, but really say nothing about us as people, our work habits, and all the other intangibles that make us good candidates for jobs?

We'd like to be able to say that, thanks to online technology, the resume has gone the way of the dinosaur, but the resume is still a primary means by which employers cull potential job candidates. What *has* changed though, and what this chapter is about, is the form of today's resume, especially for purposes of job searching online. If you're interested enough in online services to be reading this book, then you no doubt have already heard the term *electronic resume*. We're going to use it here, too, but with specific distinctions and refinements.

≡ DEFINITION OF TERMS

At its most elemental, an electronic resume, or e-resume, is one that is stored on a computer system instead of in a filing cabinet or in a pile on someone's desk. It can be a simple ASCII text file, or a multimedia circus filled with video clips, audio, and more. For our purposes, though, electronic resume refers to one that is composed of text only—no graphics or other multimedia extras. The differences are obvious if you look at Figures 3.1(a), 3.1(b), and 3.1(c).

At first glance, it may appear that not only has online technology *not* eliminated the resume process, it's made it more complicated. Actually, what online technology and resume management software have done for resumes is make them more effective job searching vehicles. And you, the job hunter, can't really afford to ignore the changes in resume formatting and distribution, because the impetus for the switch to the electronic format has come from employers.

When employers realized that they could write or purchase software that electronically tracked, sorted, filed, and stored resumes, many large and medium-sized companies began making the switch to electronic systems. This resume tracking software enables employers to search resumes by keyword or phrase, and—depending on the software—the employer can even tell the computer how important a word or phrase is to them. Figure 3.2 shows the process that your resume goes through when it arrives at a company using resume tracking software.

ON THE TRACK

If the idea of a machine evaluating your resume appeals to you even less than the thought of a total stranger doing the same, try to put aside the impersonal aspect of the process and realize that you, as an applicant, have a much better chance of getting the right job with the new changes in how resumes are handled. Why? Because the computer can accurately check for keywords and phrases without getting tired or bored, and a computer isn't biased. And, as long as you have emailed your resume correctly or sent your resume in a scannable format, the computer won't lose your resume.

The idea of performing full-text searches for electronically stored resumes caught on quickly. When the Internet became more accessible and a part of popular culture, Bill Warren of

Andrew David
Box 849
Encinitas, California
92007

Career Objective:

To work as a UNIX systems administrator in a position which is challenging, in a leading-edge environment

Skills:

Expert in the following languages: *C++, Pascal, Embedded SQL, Assembly, Fortran, Basic, and Visual Basic.* I have worked extensively on *UNIX, OS/2, VM, VMS, VOS/Vue*

(a)

Andrew David
Box 849
Encinitas, California
92007

Career Objective:

To work as a UNIX systems administrator in a position which is challenging, in a leading-edge environment

Skills:

Expert in the following languages: C++, Pascal, Embedded SQL, Assembly, Fortran, Basic, and Visual Basic. I have worked extensively on UNIX, OS/2, VM, VMS, VOS/Vue

(b)

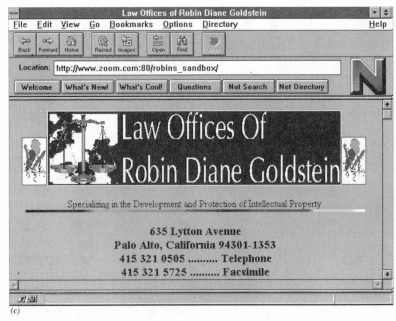

(c)

Figure 3.1 (a) a traditional resume, intended for paper output only, with various font highlights; (b) the same resume for electronic manipulation and storage; note that it is in a "typewriter" font, with no extra attributes; (c) a portion of a multimedia resume, complete with graphics.

Electronic Resume Searching, Step by Step

1. An optical scanner -- a machine about the size of a laser printer -- will capture the image of your printed resume and store it in a bit-mapped, digitized format.

2. The bit-mapped image is then "read" by the optical scanner software, which creates the second form of information -- a resume text in ASCII format. This step converts the image of a printed resume into words that can be recognized by a computer system. If you have emailed an ASCII version of your resume to the system, your resume skips step number one.

3. The last step introduces artificial intelligence (AI) which locates and extracts specific applicant information from within the resume text.

A reminder -- no two resume retrieval systems are identical at step 3. Some systems will search by keyword, others by job titles, others by both, and so on.

Source: Restrac Total Staffing Solutions

Figure 3.2 How resume tracking software works

The Online Career Center and others combined resume-searching technology with online resume banks. As a result, full text-searchable online job and resume databases have experienced rapid growth. Now, employers search not just their in-house data banks, but also online areas for qualified applicants. Employers also list thousands of jobs online. Further,

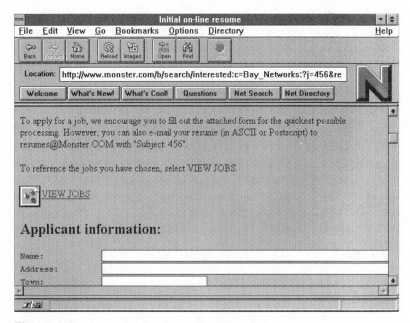

Figure 3.3 An online job application form

many employers use the Internet to network for qualified candidates, as you'll learn in Chapter 4, "Networking."

And already, tens of thousands of job seekers just like you are uploading their resumes to gain visibility around the world. If you're smart you'll join their numbers. The field continues to change: The World Wide Web is impacting the labor market with multimedia resumes and job applications that people can fill out while online, as shown in Figure 3.3.

 Don't throw away that old paper resume, because it still has a place in the job market. It's both smart and necessary to have a good-looking paper resume on hand. Obviously, not every company has resume tracking software yet, and not every employer goes online to find qualified applicants. The point is, don't have only a paper resume. Have an e-resume, too. If you don't, you'll increasingly miss out on plum opportunities offered only online.

CREATING AN EFFECTIVE E-RESUME

Whatever your profession, the first thing you need to know is how to prepare your e-resume, and that's what this chapter is all about. In the following pages, you'll discover detailed instructions that will enable you to take the best from your old resume, rewrite it in language that will get you electronically noticed, format your resume for electronic manipulation, and put your text e-resume online.

Before we get started, a couple of words of warning: There's a lot to learn, so just take it one step at a time, and proceed slowly. Don't try to write your resume and put it online all in one day or in a few hours. Give yourself a few days or a week to digest and complete each step of the process. Once you've gotten your resume written and online, you can take a well-earned break as you watch your resume begin to work for you, getting you noticed in all the right places and for all of the right reasons.

To create a definitive electronic resume, several elements come into play, the writing, the format, the length, and other key elements. Let's break it down.

Writing

The key point to remember about electronic resumes that are going into searchable databases online or off is that text-based e-resumes must be picked up in a computer search before they ever reach human eyes. Consequently, that resume needs to be readable and accessible, not just a hodgepodge of lists and keywords. Compare the electronic resumes in Figures 3.4 and 3.5 for an example of an excellent text-based e-resume, and of one that is less effective.

Don't Verb-alize

Dig out your current resume and peruse it carefully. Chances are, you'll notice you used a preponderance of verbs to highlight your skills and accomplishments. Do you see words like,

---

Sample:
(Name and address here)

Total Quality Management Executive

Keywords: customer support, supervising, TQM, C/SCSC, Certification in Cost/Schedule Control Systems, schedules, GANT/PERT charts, saved, developed, implemented, administered, managed, ACTS, OV/VM, PS/5, Windows, Macintosh, Oracle.

Figure 3.4 An electronic resume that will not be effective because of style problems.

Sample:
(Name and address here)

Total Quality Management Executive

Career Objective: To manage long and short-range space-systems engineering projects as an executive in TQM.

Skills: Expertise in providing reliable and award-winning customer support, ability to supervise up to 500 employees, administer schedules, and implementation of multi-million dollar cost-saving procedures. Skilled in the use of GANT/PERT charts, and have expert knowledge of C/SCSC requirements. Software skills include ACTS, OV/VM, PS/5, Windows, Macintosh, and Oracle. DOD clearance.

Figure 3.5 An electronic resume written using correct formatting and writing style. This resume has the potential of getting chosen by a computer search and of getting favorable attention from the person who will eventually read it.

coordinated, directed, managed, created, negotiated, wrote, instituted, accelerated, and so on? Finding pertinent verbs is definitely an important component in creating a successful paper resume. But for electronic resumes, you'll have to learn to think "nouns," too, because people searching computer databases rarely search for verbs. Your goal is to include industry-specific, descriptive nouns that characterize your skills accurately, and that the people in your field commonly use and look for. For example, instead of saying:

> I am a corporate safety analyst with a bachelor's degree in a related field.

Say:

> I am a corporate safely analyst. I have a bachelor's degree in Engineering from the College of William and Mary.

Instead of saying:

> I have four years of experience in the field.

Say:

> I have four years of experience with OSHA regulations.

In this example, the important keyword is probably *OSHA*. Without it, this resume might never get in front of the right people. Employers typically use as many as 25 *filters* to glean resumes, and some of the most common in today's marketplace are computer skills of any kind, current buzzwords being used in the profession, and educational details

So, do it now: Put your entire resume through the noun test. Look at every section. Ask yourself, "Can I be more specific? What descriptive noun or industry buzzword could I use to describe my skills?" And don't forget to give the Education section of your resume a thorough going-over. You'd be surprised how much weight most employers put on this area. For example, if you wrote:

> Received diploma in 1990 in Architecture, or B.S. Architecture, 1990

you're missing opportunities. Think noun, think specific, think of variations. Here's a sample of a well-presented education section:

High School diploma 1986
Honor Society
GPA 3.9
Extracurricular activities: band, student government president
Undergraduate: College of William and Mary
B.S. Architecture
GPA 3.3
Internship with XYZ Architects

And don't forget to add any awards, special projects, community service, anything that makes you a cut above.

To explore in greater detail how dramatically the right words can affect the success or failure on an e-resume, let's say Joan, a human resources manager at a company with 45 branches across the United States and more than 9,000 employees, has been asked to find 25 qualified applicants for an open position. Before she takes out an ad in a newspaper or contacts a professional recruiter, Joan checks two places: the Online Career Center (OCC) and the in-house resume database.

The expert Joan is seeking is one who will network all of the Western branch offices. Logging on to her computer, Joan accesses the OCC and types in keywords that relate to the position she is helping to fill, which in this case might include words such as TCP/IP, LAN, and Cisco Routers. There are also some specific skills she is looking for, so she'll type those in, too. She might also type in some basic words just to see what comes up. She opens a capture file, saves the resumes that come up, and she logs off. To see the actual results of a search like Joan's, see Figure 3.6.

Joan then goes to her in-house database, which is managed using Restrac software, which allows Joan to evaluate skills. For example, Cisco Routers is very important, so she weighs it heavily. A term like LAN (an acronym for local area network), is more common, so she gives less weight to it so that she can narrow her search.

Based on Joan's evaluations, the computer sifts through all of the resumes on file, even those that were mailed in "over the

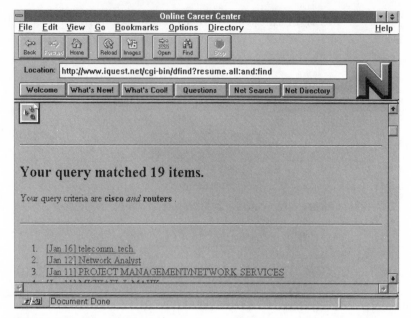

Figure 3.6 Keyword search results from the Online Career Center

transom," that is, not in response to any advertisement or open position. Joan waits until the computer finds the resumes with the most *hits*—word and phrase matches. She picks the top 20, and downloads them.

Now the process again involves the "human touch." Joan prints out all of the resumes, reads them, and further refines her list. She filters out resumes with typos, filled with nothing but lists of keywords, that are poorly written, or are inappropriate. The resumes then go on to the next level of management.

You see the point: Having the right words and phrases in your resume is extremely important. But just as important is how you place the words, because, as you saw, Joan eliminated those resumes that listed keywords, but did not place them effectively and descriptively in context. Initially in an online search, individual words are all important. Thereafter, it's still necessary to be able to express yourself clearly and interestingly, topics discussed in the next sections.

Keep Your Language Current

Browse other online resumes, newspaper ads, and industry-specific publications. Language changes constantly, and these changes impacts the words you choose to describe your skills. No matter how qualified you may be, your language must be up to date to get your top-notch qualifications noticed. Let's go back to the example of the term *computer programmer*, which we discussed earlier in the book. To get noticed online, a computer programmer must type in every language he or she can program. A teacher has to include every subject area and grade in which he or she is experienced. And a sales manager has to add the specific names of the products he or she has worked with along with his or her accomplishments and skills as a manager.

Every profession has buzzwords, and when your are looking for a job online, it's imperative that your familiarize yourself with the pertinent ones in your field. (Figure 3.7 has a sampling of buzzwords to get you thinking, and Figure 3.8 shows some that are relevant to computer programming.) Good places to look for trendy business lingo include the want ads in the *Wall Street Journal* and other major newspapers. Get online and look at the resumes in E-Span, Usenet, and other online areas. (Remember, E-Span is available on CompuServe, America Online, GEnie and eWorld. Usenet is available via most Internet accounts or through America Online and CompuServe.) Read journals and magazines in your profession. And if you live near a university library, take the time to go and read the most recent scholarly publications and association newsletters. Keep a notebook of the words you find; don't trust your memory for this important component of your e-resume.

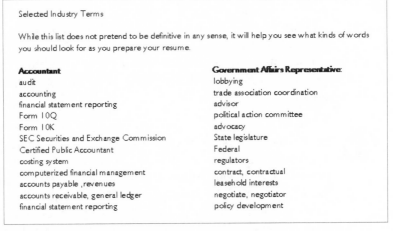

Selected Industry Terms

While this list does not pretend to be definitive in any sense, it will help you see what kinds of words you should look for as you prepare your resume.

Accountant	**Government Affairs Representative:**
audit	lobbying
accounting	trade association coordination
financial statement reporting	advisor
Form 10Q	political action committee
Form 10K	advocacy
SEC Securities and Exchange Commission	State legislature
Certified Public Accountant	Federal
costing system	regulators
computerized financial management	contract, contractual
accounts payable , revenues	leasehold interests
accounts receivable, general ledger	negotiate, negotiator
financial statement reporting	policy development

Figure 3.7 A buzzword sampler

Industry Terms For a Computer Programmer/Analyst

The terms a computer programmer/analyst chooses will vary, depending completely on what kind of languages and platforms the person is familiar with. Here are samples that will give you an idea of the types of words employers search for and what words top programmers are putting in their resumes:

advanced machine programming
IBM Assembler
MVS/ESA
install, installed
Superbase 4
platforms, platform, language, languages
SQL
UNIX
VAX Ultrix, VAX VMS
HP 3000 SPL
mulitimedia software
Wrote, write
C, C++, Fortran, BASIC, COBOL

Figure 3.8 Effective industry terms for a computer programmer

Put keywords in the proper context. Once you have found specific words to describe your skill sets, don't just list them in a block at the beginning or end of your resume. Weave your keywords throughout your introductory paragraph and the body of your resume. You'll still attract the computer's attention, and you'll also appeal to the person who is ultimately going to read your entire resume. This polished, more sophisticated approach is particularly important for high-level professional jobs.

Avoid overusing important words. In most searches, each word counts once, no matter how many times it's used. *Cognitive science* written 20 times in a resume would still garner only one hit. Also, in databases where the computer can only search the text of a resume for one specific word, you have a better chance of having a matchable word in your resume if you use a variety. Use as many different words to describe your skills as possible.

 Be aware of case-sensitivity. Case-sensitivity refers to the responsiveness—or lack thereof—of systems to recognize the difference between upper- and lowercase letters. For example, DOS is not case-sensitive; you can type Dos, DOS, or dos, and all three variations will be recognized. Unfortunately, systems that are case-sensitive do not have this capability, and you

must type the words exactly as they already are used in the system, or they will be useless for searching purposes. So, check and double-check the spelling, capitalization, and punctuation of your industry-specific keywords, and stick with what you see most often.

Other E-Resume Elements

First Impressions

Career Objective. This is an optional element, and many people choose to leave it off their resumes. Before you make a decision, again we recommend that you look online through other resumes in your field. Chances are, if Career Objective is a common element, then it's what's expected and what employers look for, so you probably should include it too.

A Career Objective entry on a resume generally is a sentence or short paragraph that describes exactly what you do and/or what kind of job you want. The value of adding this element in a text-based e-resume is that employers who are browsing online can see very quickly if you're someone they want to interview; it saves them the trouble of reading through an entire resume unnecessarily.

Be sure your Career Objective is focused. As Jan Ackerman, a national recruiter for SHL Systemshouse who hires more than 100 people a year says, "I don't want to have to be someone's career counselor. [People] should know what they want to do. I want to hire the best person for the job."

If you're unsure how to create a good Career Objective, here are some examples to use as guidelines:

For an elementary school teacher:

"I want to teach 4th grade in a self-contained classroom full time."

Not:

"I want to work as an elementary school teacher."

For a computer systems engineer:

"I want to manage system and network configurations for UNIX 4.1.2, SOLARIS 1.2, and SYBASE Relational Database 4.9.2."

Not:

"I want to work as a computer systems engineer."

You get the picture: Be succinct, but be specific and clear.

The introductory paragraph.   If you decide not to include a Career Objective entry on your resume, then the first paragraph of your resume becomes the most important element. Not only does this paragraph introduce you to the person reading your resume, it's your first opportunity to display your *skill sets* to potential employers. Skill sets—words that describe precisely your special attributes as an employee—are what employers usually search for in resume databases.

Skill sets should not be just a listing of keywords that you think might compel the computer to isolate your resume. While it might initially have that effect, the human reading your resume is going to be less than impressed with the absence of those keywords in a cohesive, striking introductory paragraph.

Let's use the same elementary school teacher and computer systems engineer to show effective introductory paragraphs. The teacher:

"I have taught 4th grade for five years. Subject areas of expertise are history, particularly American and European; English literature, especially the Classics; American literature; general mathematics; basic physical education; art, including figure drawing, watercolor, ceramics, and paper sculpture; and science, particularly general biology. My computer skills include knowledge of DOS, MS Word for Windows, Paint, dBASE 1, and numerous classroom management programs. I also have expertise on the Internet and with online tools in the classroom. I have a basic understanding of French and German, enough to teach introductory courses. I also play piano and the recorder, and can teach both at an advanced level."

The computer systems engineer:

> "I have five years of experience in CAD application and engineering workstation management. I am an expert on these platforms: HP700 series; SUN SPARC 1, 2, 5, 10, 20, 1000; SUN Series 4. I am proficient on these UNIX platforms: SGI and DECStations. I am also expert on Macintosh and IBM PC, and the following operating systems: SOLARIS, SUN, Ultrix, DOS, CGOS, and DNIX; also C Shell, Bourne, and Korne. My expertise on specific applications includes CADS4x, STP, SYBASE, Ontos, PPP, MS Word, Excel, MACWRITE, MACPROJECT, Frame, PageMaker, and WordPerfect. I am fluent in C++, Visual Basic, Fortran, COBOL, and Basic."

Length

We've all heard the admonition (it's practically a resume law!) that no resume should be longer than two pages. Well, it isn't always so—not anymore. A better guideline is to make sure you do yourself justice. Someone fresh out of college may be able to describe his or her accomplishments effectively in one or two pages, but no employer really expects someone who's been a professional for ten years to be able to do the same. This is not to say that you should babble endlessly about every detail of your work life, but don't shortchange yourself either because you're afraid you'll be automatically eliminated from contention for a position because your resume runs to three pages. Write tightly and succinctly, but don't leave out any of the good stuff.

Some commercial electronic job banks *do* only want resumes that are no longer than two pages, while others, especially in-house corporate resume databases, allow many more pages. And most Internet resume databases carry resumes averaging two to three pages. A really smart thing to do is create more than one version of your resume—a long and short version—and use whichever is appropriate, based on where you're posting it.

Order of E-Resume Elements

There is no rule for this either, but a safe guideline for organizing the elements in your electronic resume is as follows:

♦ Name and contact address

♦ Career objective or introductory paragraph

♦ Work experience, listed in most-recent to least-recent order

♦ Education, including degrees, certificates and/or licenses, awards, and distinctions

♦ Hobbies (optional)

♦ Reference names and addresses

≡ PREPARING TO GO ONLINE

ASCII Formatting

Once you've written your resume and made the prose sparkle, it's time to prepare it for electronic transfer via email or scanning. To do this, you'll need a computer and a word processing program like WordPerfect, Microsoft Word for Windows, or whichever of the many available programs you prefer. It does not matter which program you choose to write in. What matters is how you save what you write. Each word processing program is different, which usually results in conversion problems across different computer platforms; therefore it is necessary to save your files in a very simple, pared-down format that is almost universal. And that format is ASCII. ASCII is the acronym for American Standard Code for Information Interchange, a character set defined in 1968 to enable computer compatibility among different devices.

In addition to saving files to ASCII, you're going to have to suffer formatting withdrawal. Yes, you'll have to keep yourself from using boldface, italics, and any of those other fancy-schmancy design elements we're all so fond of to show off the high points in our resumes. All those extras translate to garbage during the conversion process unless your uploading your resume to a system running the same program you wrote in. Now, we're not saying not to keep this more fashionable

```
location: colorado west
From : hwusa@occ.com
Subject: CPA
Location: CO 80027

DANIEL D. SCHARF, CPA

  749 Wildrose Way
  Louisville, CO  80027

  AOL: Dkscharf

SUMMARY OF QUALIFICATIONS
  15 years of financial management experience with track record of accomplishmen
ts in company growth, personnel development, and financial responsibility. Resou
rceful hands-on leader with ability to anticipate and resolve problems using mul
tiple paths.

  Financial Management and Administration
  Evaluated and developed recommendations on long-term goals and strategic plans
for multi-million dollar business operations.
  Worked with client management to determine cash management and financing solut

Press <RETURN> to continue,
  <m> to mail, <D> to download, <s> to save, or <p> to print:|
```

Figure 3.9 A resume in ASCII format as it would appear online

resume on hand—you'll of course need it for those circumstances where you have to use a paper resume. We're just saying that if it's going to be uploaded online, keep it simple and save it to ASCII so that it can be viewed online, as shown in Figure 3.9. Figure 3.10 shows what happens when you can't resist using formatting attributes.

Follow these steps to create your ASCII resume:

1. Open a new document in your word processing program.

2. Input your resume—accurately—using a standard typeface like Times or Helvetica.

3. After you're happy with the content, formalize the layout—by this we mean spacing, lists, and so on; remember, no boldfacing, italics, etc.

4. Save the file in ASCII. To save a file in ASCII using a PC, open the File section of your word processing program. Choose the Save As option, and give your file a name when prompted.

   Your program should also allow you to save a file in different formats. For example, WordPerfect for Windows makes it possible to save documents as ASCII (DOS text) or in a variety of other formats, such as Microsoft Word for Windows documents. All you have to do is click on the option you want. Of course, your word processor

```
UffUffUwwɛɛ~ ɛ+ ɛww ɛfwfwfwvwfwfw ɛfwfwfwvwfwfwvwfwfwvwfwfwfwwf0ɛ@Yɛwwfwfɛɛwfwfwfwvwfwfw
U
Uffwfwfwvwfw}fɛUffUffUffwɛ*L]]~ n Ɵyn Ɵ~ n~]#L;;*ɛɛw ɛwvfwwffUffUwwfwfwvwfwfwwf` ɛ`O~
ƟƟnƟƟnƟnnuƟɛnn | Ɵɛnn Ɵnn~]ɛLL;;ɛwffUffUffUffUffUf~ ɛ~ CɛwffUffUffUffUffUffUfwɛ;LjƟ~
nnƟnƟnn Ɵn]]~ Lɛ;ɛfUffUffUffUfUf~ ɛ~ lɛwffUffUffUffUffUffwɛ*]wƟɛnn{Ɵɛnn Ɵynɛ ɟnƟƟ~ n
wfUffUffUfUffU~ fɛwɛɛLnƟ~ nɛƟƟ}nɛ]n]nƟƟ}n~ Ɵ{nɛ;ɛwffUffUffUffUff` ɛ~ FɟffUffUffUffUff
fUffUffUfUffUffU~ fɛw;nuƟ nxƟɛ]ƟnƟn~ Ɵɛnn]nƟnƟƟn{Ɵ|nɛ];ɛwUffUffUffUffP ɛ`;ɟfUffzUɟfUff
D~ U D~UɟffUfɛnsƟ nsƟ}nzƟ nyƟɛnƟnn]L;wUfUffUfUffU~ ɛ~ .ɛwUf}U      DUUDUUffU;aƟ
n}Ɵ
~ fLrƟ nz Ɵɛnn~ Ɵɛ]n~]ɛLL]]~ nɛƟnntƟɛnɛwwUffU}fɛw~ ɛo9ɛffD~ U      DUUfUffUwnmƟ~ n Ɵ
nLL;;L;;L]L]LL~ ;ɛL;;L~ *ɛɛ*ɛ~*ɛL;;L;]nsƟɛ;*ffUffUfw~ fɛ ɛ`MɛfUD~ UɛDUfUffUf;}Ɵɛ]]L;ɛ
ɛɛɛɛɛɛɛɛɛ*ɛ*;*;L]]uƟɛnfUffUfwfwfw ɛ OɛfD~ UɛDffUffUfɛ~ ƟɛL;*ɛɛɛwɛwfwwf~ wɛɛɛɛɛw
;~ Lɛ]Ɵ~ nxƟ
;fUffUffwfwɛɛ R~ UɛDUfUffU~ f3;n]]*ɛɛɛɛɛɛɛɛɛɛɛ*ɛɛ*ɛ*ɛɛɛɛɛɛɛɛɛɛɛ*ɛ**;;LL]]Ɵnn
```

Figure 3.10 A resume created using Quark, viewed on an IBM machine without Quark

will be slightly different, so be sure to check the manual that came with your word processing program for the exact steps you will need to take.

After you've saved the file in ASCII, reopen it. Check for any distortions. Has the spacing become garbled in the translation? Are the paragraphs clearly indented? Is the formatting still as you designed? If there are any problem areas, insert spaces and hard returns as necessary to correct, then repeat the saving/reopening process until all is in good order. Finally, print out a copy for your files.

Macintosh users can save a file in ASCII following very similar steps as PC aficionados. Of course, the steps may vary slightly, depending on the word processing program you are using. In general, however, open the pull-down File menu and choose the Save As option. The Drive Format menu will come up. Click on it, and choose the Text Only option. Then click on the Default Format for file box. The menu will close.

Now you can either click on Save to Current Drive with Current Name, or you can rename your resume by choosing the Save Document As option. When the new menu comes up, fill the new name in the blank. Press Enter. You'll be returned to the Drive Format menu. Click on Save. That's it.

5. Record the file name and path (for example c:\wpdocs \resume, or b:\resume) where you've stored your resume

so that you have it handy later when you're ready to email your resume.

Preparing a Scannable Resume

Although most companies with resume tracking software prefer that you email your resume to them, some companies and electronic job databases do accept paper resumes, as long as they can be scanned into the computer system.

The same steps just discussed apply: Remember, the paper resume, too, will be converted to ASCII, so forgo all fancy formatting, and use a standard typeface. Then:

- Print your resume on a laser or ink-jet printer. Do *not* use a dot matrix printer, because output will not scan successfully.
- Print on only one side of the paper.
- Mail your resume flat, with a protective sheet of cardboard on either side. This ensures a clean scan.

GOING ONLINE WITH YOUR RESUME

Everyone is nervous about uploading his or her resume the first time. But once you've done it and seen how simple it is, and have gotten good results, all your fears will quickly subside. But before we start, let's take a minute to discuss all the hype about the audience for online resumes. Because an estimated 20 to 35 million people are connected to the Internet, some say that your online resume will be viewed by about 20 million people. Actually, while 20 million people may have *access* to your resume, *depending on where you post your resume*, it will be viewed either by hundreds, thousands, or tens of thousands of people; it's impossible to determine.

Resume Hotspots

You will want to upload or send your resume to as many possible places and people as you can. Here are some of the many options available:

- To a commercial online service such as GEnie or Delphi.
- To various portions of the Internet.

- To a dial-up bulletin board system.

- To a company contact address in response to a job lead.

- To your target company—human resource professionals constantly check their in-house electronic databases for applicants.

Emailing Your Resume

The basic steps for emailing a resume are the same no matter which software program you are using, but you'll need to become familiar with your program before you proceed so that you can incorporate any diversions from this list.

1. Retrieve your notation of the path and file name where you earlier stored your ASCII resume.

2. Log on to the account where you'll be mailing the resume.

3. Go into the mail utility or mail area of your account.

4. Choose the option to create a new message.

5. Type in the email address of the person to whom you're mailing your resume, the file name, and any other information required.

6. Either transfer the text of your resume to the message area or, depending on the system you're using, just send the file without transferring text to your screen.

Here are three specific examples of emailing your resume using some common software.

Emailing from a Commercial Online Service

We'll use CompuServe as our example to show you how simple emailing your resume is. If you subscribe to a different commercial online service, your directions for emailing will vary slightly, but the general process will be the same. You'll be prompted for the file name of your resume and the email address to send it to.

For detailed instructions for your particular online service, call the service's toll-free number and talk to a customer service representative. Or you can perform a keyword search on *sending mail* or *mail* and you will find the mail help files for your particular service. (This keyword search will work for CompuServe, too, if you have any additional questions.)

Here is a step-by-step guide to emailing your resume from CompuServe:

1. Log on to CompuServe.

2. Choose the Mail menu option.

3. Choose the Send File option. (This option will send your resume without a cover letter from you. This is the most frequently requested option from employers.)

4. A blank will open on your screen called Recipient list. You will be prompted to fill in the name and email address where you want the file sent.

5. Fill in the Name blank with the contact name, and fill in the Address blank with the correct email address. If you are sending your resume to an Internet email address, type Internet: before the address. For example: **Internet: marmot@cts.com**. If you are sending your resume to a CompuServe address, just type in the CompuServe address.

6. Click on Add, then on OK. You will be taken to a new screen where you'll see the email address and name filled in already. You will also see a blank Subject line to fill in. Type the word resume.

7. In the blank below the Subject line, fill in the *complete* file name of your ASCII resume. To the right of this blank, you will see four options that you can choose from: Text, Binary, GIF, or JPEG. Since you are sending a text—or ASCII—file, choose the Text option.

8. Click on Send Now. Your ASCII resume will be sent immediately.

Posting Your Resume

More than 90 percent of the time, you will email your resume to get it online or in a database. You can email your resume to a company's email address, to the Online Career Center, to

E-Span, and in response to an employer's position announcement.

To determine whether to email or post, be sure to read the announcement at the end of the online job listing where usually the employer tells you how to make contact. Many say "email resumes to..." or "fax your resume to..." In general, however, it is safe to email your resumes to bulletin boards, databases, individuals, and companies.

You will post your resume when you want it to reside on a Usenet resume list. (Remember: When you email, your resume goes to a single address and is usually seen by an individual. When you post, your resume goes to a public site and can be viewed by anyone who "happens by" online.) As with email, there are several ways of posting, depending on the kind of setup you are using.

The good news about posting a resume is that it's very intuitive and simple. The bad news is that the steps for posting are different for each system. There are, however, some general steps for posting, and we'll describe them first. Then we'll give you specific examples.

1. Retrieve the information you noted earlier about the filename and path to which you saved your ASCII resume.

2. Log on to the account you'll be posting from.

3. Enter the area you'll be posting to. For example, if you're on a CompuServe account and you're going to post to Usenet, you would log on to CompuServe and then go to Usenet—not the mailbox. If you were posting from the Internet, you would enter Usenet and not your email utility.

4. Find and follow the posting directions for the area. For example, from CompuServe, posting to Usenet is a matter of going to Usenet, clicking on Post and then typing in your resume (or cutting and pasting your resume, if you have Windows). From the Internet, how you post depends on your account. There is usually a command called Post Message.

That's it—those are the basic steps. Once you've posted a few times, you'll wonder how you ever got along without Usenet and other posting areas. And there's just no better way to gain high visibility—fast.

 We've said if before, but it bears repeating. Don't forget that your resume can be viewed by anyone who is a subscriber to the service or area where you post it. So if you're worried about your boss finding out about your job search, you may want to post only to private bulletin boards or company data-bases.

Posting to Usenet from CompuServe

If you are unsure of your online skills, we strongly recommend that you experiment with posting to Usenet first from either CompuServe or America Online. It is a lot easier for a new user than working your way through some of the other newsreaders available. (A newsreader is a software program, available on-line, that helps you read and post to Usenet.)

The basic steps for posting are as follows: Access and sub-scribe to a newsgroup or groups, type or upload your message, then post your message. Here are the detailed steps.

1. From CompuServe's (again, our sample service) main menu, use the Go feature to reach Usenet Newsgroups. If the name has changed by the time you read this book, you can perform a keyword search using the Find utility. Use the keyword *Usenet*, and choose the option that takes you to Access Usenet Newsgroups. Choose the option by double-clicking or by highlighting and pressing Enter.

2. Choose Subscribe to Newsgroups.

3. A menu will open. To the right, in the Search by Key-words option, fill in the name of the newsgroup you are looking for, such as *misc.jobs.misc* and click on Search. Check the Usenet list in Chapter 7 for relevant Usenet posting sites.

4. A list of newsgroups matching your keywords will come up. To the left of each newsgroup name is a box and a short description to the right. When you see the name of the group or groups you want to subscribe to, click on

the box and a check mark will appear. When you are finished, click on Subscribe.

5. Repeat this subscription process for as many newsgroups you want. Be careful to type in the correct names of the newsgroups.

6. When you have subscribed to all of the places where you want to post your resume, (or where you want to browse for job openings) click on Close. You'll return to the opening menu.

7. Choose Create an Article. (Or to read only, select Browse.)

8. Fill in subject blank carefully. Use descriptive terms such as *resume of trial attorney* or *resume of UNIX expert.*

9. Click on the Post to Newsgroups.

10. To the right, you will see all of the Usenet groups you've subscribed to in a window with a scroll bar. Click on every group you want to send your resume to. There will be a check mark in a box to the left of the newsgroup after you click on it.

11. You can type in your entire resume here, and then click on Send, but uploading your resume is more efficient. To upload your resume, click on Upload. A blank will appear in which to fill the file name of your ASCII resume. Click on Text (because this is a text, or ASCII, resume) and click on OK. You will see your file appear in the message portion of the screen.

12. Click on Send, and you're done.

Posting to Usenet from Trumpet Newsreader

Another easy way to post to Usenet is via Trumpet, a Usenet newsreader that you can use with a SLIP connection. When you purchase your Internet account, ask about Trumpet. It is a more user-friendly newsreader than the basic Usenet newsreaders like tnn or tin, which you get with a basic Internet account.

The Trumpet newsreading software must, however, be used in conjunction with some other programs, most notably Trumpet Winsock. Some Internet providers are making life much easier for their customers by providing all of this software in a single package. And most Internet providers do not charge extra to get you set up with this software; it usually comes as a part of the package you purchase. This is certainly something you'll want to ask when you are ready to buy an account. And if you have any trouble getting Trumpet installed, please ask your Internet provider for help.

Once you have Trumpet, here's how you post your resume:

1. Log on to your Internet account and access the Trumpet Newsreader option.

2. From the menu bar, choose Group, and then choose Subscribe.

3. Trumpet will automatically check for new newsgroups. While you wait as it does this task, it will display a message that says, "checking for new groups...")

4. When Trumpet is finished checking for new groups, in the Search section, type in the name of any newsgroup you want to post your resume to. Then, when Trumpet finds the group for you, click on Subscribe.

5. Another screen will appear on which will be a list of all of the newsgroups you have subscribed to. To access any of the groups you have subscribed to, double-click on its name.

6. After you double-click on the group name, you will be in the group. This will be apparent because Trumpet will list the messages, or articles, in the group for you.

7. Now you're ready to either read the articles or post. Click on Post. A new screen will open with blanks for you to fill in. Fill in the first blank, Newsgroups, with the name of every newsgroup you want to post your resume to. For example, if you want to post your resume to two newsgroups, type in their names as you find them in the Chapter 7 list, separated by commas, for example, misc.jobs.misc, ba.jobs.misc. This is called cross-posting. Instead of sending one message three different times, you can send one message one time to three different places. It saves space on the network, and it saves time for you.

8. Fill in the subject line with something descriptive of your resume like "resume, C++ expert," or "resume of ESL teacher."

9. Type in an abbreviated version of your resume. *Keep it to two screens or less.* Include your email and other pertinent information, and offer a full length resume on request.

10. Click on Post. That's it.

Posting to Usenet from a Basic Internet Account

If you must access Usenet through a basic Internet account, you will be seeing a black-and-white screen, and you will have a little more cryptic jargon to wade through. But it isn't really difficult, as you'll see:

1. From you Internet account, choose the Usenet option. You should find it as an opening menu option from your account.

2. Look at the top of the screen to see which newsreading program you are using; tnn and tin are two of the most popular UNIX newsreaders, which is what you'll be using.

3. If the program asks you if you want to subscribe to new groups, just push y for yes and n for no. Then press y to "yank" in all newsgroups.

4. Press the slash key (/). A blank will appear asking you what group or pattern you are looking for. Type in the exact name of the group you want to find, for example misc.jobs.misc. Press Enter. The newsreader will find the group for you.

5. Press s to subscribe to the group. Repeat steps 4 and 5 until you have subscribed to all of the jobs groups you want to post your resume to. (Note: if you don't find a group by using "/," try "?". This will tell the newsreader to look backward instead of forward.

6. Once you have subscribed to all of the groups you want, enter a group by pressing the Tab key.

7. Press w, which will allow you to post a message.

8. You will be presented with a blank at the bottom of the screen labeled Post subject: Fill in your subject here,

something that describes your resume. Resumes of librarians and test engineers are good examples. Press Enter.

9. You'll be presented with a new screen. At the top, you'll see the name of the group you're posting to automatically filled in. Press Enter a few times to get into the message area. Or press Tab if Enter doesn't work.

10. Type your resume in the message area. Keep it short! No more than two of your computer screens. (Use your short version of your resume as a guide.) After you're done, press Enter.

11. A prompt will query, "Save modified buffer?" Type in y and press Enter.

12. You will be greeted with another message that gives you three options: Quit, Edit, or Post? Press P for post, and press Enter. Your resume will be posted.

Resist the urge to post more than one resume at a time from this newsreader. Give yourself a little time to browse Usenet and get used to this program first. Be patient, and read the help files (type H while you're in the Usenet reader to access the help files).

Posting to Commercial Online Forums

If you want to upload a file to a commercial service's forum or discussion group, but you don't know how, send an email message to the sysop of that forum. On most forums, the moment you sign on, you will get an automatic response from the sysop of that area. Wait for your automatic message, then email an S.O.S. saying, "How do I..."

If you don't see the automatic greeting, call the toll-free number and ask for customer assistance, or, perform a keyword search on *help* or *customer service.* You will find a customer service area with email addresses to which you can send help messages. Send an email message stating that you want to learn how to upload a file to a group. The customer service department will have the appropriate sysop and email you a response.

Once you've put your resume online, check on it regularly. See if it's still there, and make sure that it looks right on the system you sent it to. You might see lines that are too long or bad spacing. If your sentences don't wrap—that is, go to the next line automatically—insert hard returns in your ASCII resume at the spots you want the sentences to go to the next line. If your spacing is too tight, insert more hard returns to improve the appearance. Then, send an updated ASCII version of your resume.

SAMPLE RUNS

Let's say you're about to complete a course of training as a court reporter, and although you haven't uploaded your resume yet, you have been doing some online cruising, as recommended, and know that there are many jobs in your field listed online—so, you want to try it and see what happens. You have two goals: to have your resume chosen out of a computer search or discovered by an employer who is browsing resumes online, and to use your resume as a networking tool.

With these goals in mind, you go online and look for places to upload your resume. You also look for people to email your resume to. You log on to CompuServe (or wherever your account is) and conduct a keyword search as discussed in Chapter 2, "Online Working Strategies." You begin with the term *court reporter* just to see what comes up, as shown in Figure 3.11.

You find out there's a specific forum or discussion group for your profession. You double-click on the forum to enter it. Looking at the message section, you notice an area for newcomer introductions. You introduce yourself and send along an abbreviated version of your resume as part of your greeting. Figure 3.12 shows the beginning of this process.

You also note that there's a section for classified ads. You enter it, find a job listing well-suited for you, and decide to email your resume to the contact address. You recall from reading this book that you can email your resume to E-Span and to the Online Career Center. Before you log off CompuServe, you look up their addresses in the job list section of this book. You email your resume to these two online areas, and log off, after which you make a note of your submissions in

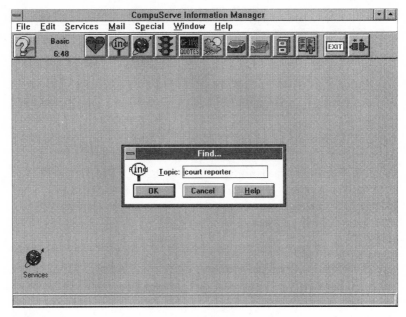

Figure 3.11 Beginning of keyword search in CompuServe for *court reporter*

your job search notebook. Figure 3.13 shows what your email screen might look like as you're sending your resume.

Tomorrow, you plan to browse the Usenet job lists and your local community net to find areas where you can place your

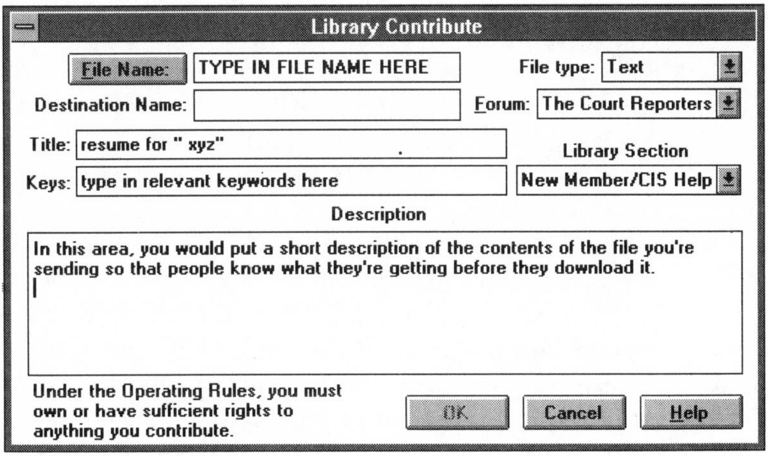

Figure 3.12 The CompuServe screen (Windows version) for sending files to a forum

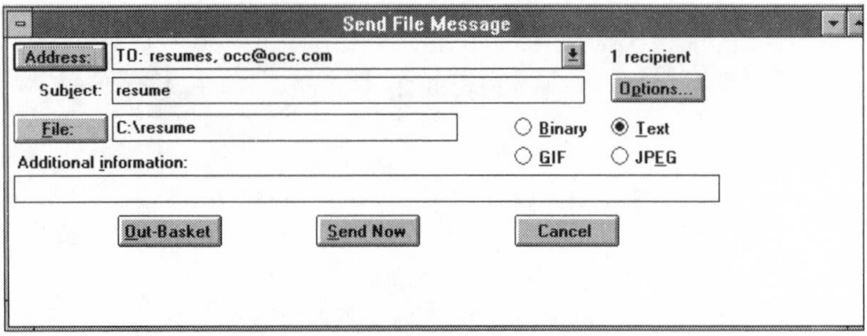

Figure 3.13 Sending a resume to the Online Career Center from CompuServe

resume. You're also going to send a query to your local city government's email address and ask for the appropriate applications.

You're well on your way to finding the job you want. Even though you have many more online areas to investigate, you feel confident that you will be able to accomplish each step of your online job search easily.

In this next scenario, you're a business analyst working for a software consulting firm. You've heard rumors of pending lay-offs, and, not wanting to take any chances, you decide it's time to get going on a job search. You have a connection to America Online, which you plan to use. You know that you can email your resume to the Online Career Center in ASCII, so, you send your correctly formatted resume there first.

After looking at the list of Usenet boards in this book, you choose seven to post your resume to. Going to the Usenet area of America Online (AOL) as shown in Figure 3.14, you post your resume to all seven boards. Still in AOL, you browse the E-Span job listings, see two possible jobs you would be interested in, and you email your resume to the contact email addresses given.

Next you call a large company you've been dreaming of working for, and find out if resumes are accepted via email. If the answer is yes, you jot down the address, and of course, email your resume to the company from your AOL account.

Also on AOL you find several forums that relate to your profession. You upload your resume to the forum libraries and introduce yourself online to the people on the board. (Chapter 4 has details how to do this.)

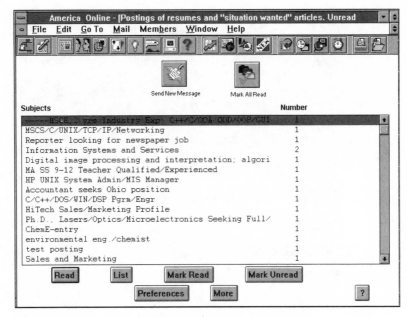

Figure 3.14 Accessing Usenet from America Online

From these two examples, you should have some idea how vitally your resume can affect your online job search. So get your resume online, send it to target companies, and keep it updated.

RESUMES AND THE WORLD WIDE WEB

If you haven't heard much about the Web, you may be wondering how it differs from the Internet. Briefly, know that anything available on the Internet is also accessible by using the Web. But to access the Web, you must have a way to read or browse its documents. Web documents are built in a special way using *hypertext links* and a *graphical user interface*. So, instead of typing in long commands to access a new document or Internet area, all you have to do is to choose a link and press Enter or click with your mouse. This is all explained in Chapter 5, "World Wide Web."

Resumes on the Web differ dramatically from resumes on commercial online services or on the Internet, which are in ASCII format. Web resumes are generally formatted exten-

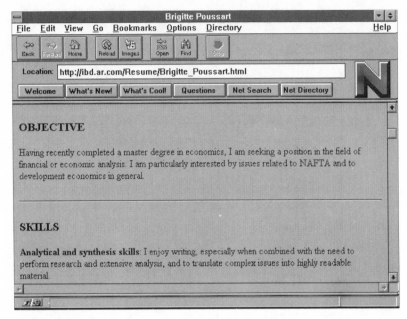

Figure 3.15 The text portion of a WWW resume

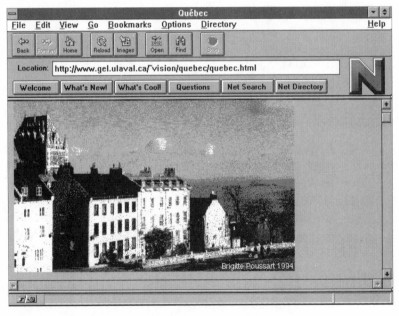

Figure 3.16 The graphic portion of a WWW resume

sively, appear in color, and they may include audio, video, or graphics.

The World Wide Web is growing faster than the Internet, and you'll find that anyone in a computer-centered profession or who just wants to display more information about him- or herself is on the Web. This is not an obscure vehicle that won't catch on for years. Already, large corporations have excellent access to the Web, as does anyone on a college campus.

To whet your appetite for all you can do there, take a look at Figures 3.15 and 3.16; then read on. First we're going to tell you how to network in Chapter 4; then we'll explain how you can spin the Web to suit your purposes, without getting tangled inside it.

NETWORKING ON THE NEW FRONTIER

Networking on the New Frontier

There is no more powerful way to network than to go online. In cyberspace, networking takes on an entirely different dimension, acquires new dynamics, and is dramatically more efficient than traditional networking methods. The online medium gives job seekers access to people otherwise unreachable through traditional means. Geography, time constraints, education, position, and class are irrelevant online. Simply put, electronic networking evens the odds.

THE POWER OF ONLINE NETWORKING

Global Scope

The networking pool in cyberspace is huge. According to estimates, there are some 4 million Usenet users, a breakdown of which showed approximately 58 percent United States sites, 15 percent unknown, 8 percent Germany, 6 percent Canada, 2 to 3 percent each the United Kingdom, Japan, and Australia, and the remainder in various places around Europe. (Usenet, you recall, is a global network of discussion groups called newsgroups, which you can access through the Internet and some commercial online services such as America Online and CompuServe.) Usenet is readable from all continents, even Antarctica. Statistics from commercial online providers reveal that America Online alone, as of February 1995, boasted more than 2 million subscribers. Prodigy, CompuServe, and other online services add an estimated 4 million to the pool.

What this means to you, obviously, is that when you write a message and post it to a Usenet group or commercial online forum such as the Photography forum in GEnie, a lot of people may see what you write. Contrast the online networking scope with that of traditionally made contacts. Clearly, online networking gives you a much greater reach, and much more quickly.

Access to Top Experts

One of the real benefits of participating in Usenet discussion groups and other online networking activities is that they are grouped by topic, and there are innumerable options and topics to choose from. On Usenet alone, there are more than 10,000 discussion groups; on each of the commercial services, there are usually hundreds of discussion groups.

These topical areas attract people of the very highest caliber. They cut across space and time and give you, the job seeker, tremendous advantages. After all, how often now do you get to talk to *the* leading representative of your profession?

Let's suppose that you're one of the daring who's trying to make it in the notoriously cutthroat business of television. How many "players" do you think you'd be able to "take meetings with" in real time? You'll be thrilled to know then that you can go online and talk to someone like J. Michael Straczynski, executive producer of the series "Babylon 5." On the Internet he discusses the ins and outs of Hollywood production with hopefuls. Straczynski saves all of the answers to the questions he's written to a file where people wanting to learn more about television production can download them. If you want to become a television producer, the newsgroup *rec.arts.sf.tv.babylon5*, as shown in Figure 4.1, would be the place to go to get top-level access to a successful series producer. (If you are one of those hopefuls and would like to reach Straczynski, you can post a message on the GEnie Babylon 5 discussion group or on the *rec.arts.sf.tv.babylon5* Usenet group.)

Subject,
author,
date

Original
post

Responses

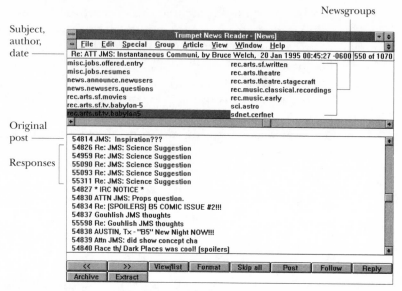

Newsgroups

Figure 4.1 The message headers of *rec.arts.tv.sf.babylon5*. The JMS notices are messages to the series' executive producer, J. Michael Straczynski.

Don't bypass a newsgroup because you think the topic is too far off course or seemingly irrelevant. Be on the lookout for newsgroups that relate obliquely to your profession, such as the example of Babylon 5 and television producers. Don't overlook the obvious, of course, but also take time to browse for the unexpected treasure.

Access to Employers

Right or wrong, the current wisdom among employers is that if you hire someone by networking on the Internet or by using an online job advertisement, you will get a computer literate person and, hence, a better job candidate. John Blakely, director of Software Engineering for Magnet Interactive Studios (which develops computer games and multimedia entertainment packages), regularly scans the Internet to find qualified candidates to hire. He looks for people who have expertise in very specific computer areas on Usenet. "I observe the newsgroups related to my profession all of the time," says Blakely. "I monitor about 12 of them to find people and to make their acquaintance. I believe the people networking online are not only more effective networkers, but they will be better at staying on the leading edge of technology—they've already showed initiative and self-confidence by going online. In my field, these qualities are very important."

And Blakely knows whereof he speaks—he got his dream job designing digital multimedia products (such as computer games and other items) at Magnet Interactive through an on-line job advertised on E-Span. Now *he's* doing the hiring, and finds candidates exclusively through networking on Usenet.

The message is clear: Do your networking, look smart, and be aware that there are many employers out there, watching for good people online. Be subtle, but make your presence felt in a positive way. (See the section "Elements of Online Networking" for details.)

Easy Access to Your Peer Group

Certainly, the volume of people you connect with through networking online is valuable. But more important is the fact that the people you're reaching are your *target audience*—your peers. That's what's exceptional about online networking. You have easy access to the people you must be in contact with to succeed in your field, even if you have an obscure or very narrowly focused specialty, and ordinarily have to travel to conferences to meet those of like profession and mind. There simply is nothing comparable in real time.

Let's say for this example that you're a woman graduating with a Masters degree in microbiology from the University of California, Los Angeles, and you log on to *bionet.women-in-bio*, either from the Internet as shown in Figure 4.2, or from a commercial online service such as Delphi or America Online. Reading the list for the first time, you notice that the newsgroup has top-flight, well-established women biologists discussing weighty issues relevant to their profession, such as "lifestage investing for women," "genetics and ethics," "patriarchal science," and "chromium picolinate."

First you read the group's messages without posting, and identify someone you want to communicate with. At this point, you either respond to one of their posts with a message, (called *replying* or *following up*), or try your hand at a new post or message by way of introduction.

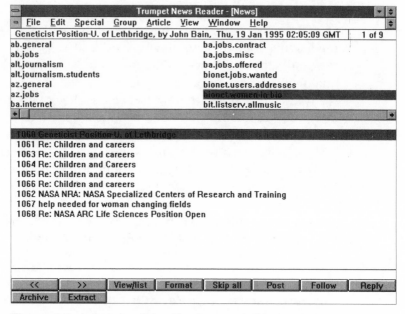

Trumpet News Reader - [News]	
File Edit Special Group Article View Window Help	
Geneticist Position-U. of Lethbridge, by John Bain, Thu, 19 Jan 1995 02:05:09 GMT	1 of 9

ab.general	ba.jobs.contract
ab.jobs	ba.jobs.misc
alt.journalism	ba.jobs.offered
alt.journalism.students	bionet.jobs.wanted
az.general	bionet.users.addresses
az.jobs	bionet.women-in-bio
ba.internet	bit.listserv.allmusic

1060 Geneticist Position U. of Lethbridge
1061 Re: Children and careers
1063 Re: Children and careers
1064 Re: Children and Careers
1065 Re: Children and careers
1066 Re: Children and careers
1062 NASA NRA: NASA Specialized Centers of Research and Training
1067 help needed for woman changing fields
1068 Re: NASA ARC Life Sciences Position Open

<<	>>	View/list	Format	Skip all	Post	Follow	Reply
Archive	Extract						

Figure 4.2 A sample of the *bionet.women-in-bio newsgroup*

Reading the messages on any board for a while without posting gives you a chance to become comfortable with the people who post on the board, and to determine whether they are helpful to others in the group before you decide to post your own message. (This is called starting a thread.)

You create a message. In the header you put "Large vs. Small Schools," and explain in the post that you have just graduated from a large school. You talk about some of your experiences, and ask what it's like going to a small college. You write, "Did you attend a small college? What do you think the benefits and disadvantages were? I'm interested in your experiences." A similar message, shown in Figure 4.3, is an open invitation for conversation, as you haven't addressed anyone in particular.

A header is where you put the subject of a message so that people can see at a glance the topic without having to read through the entire post. Take a look back at Figure 4.1 for a list of headers.

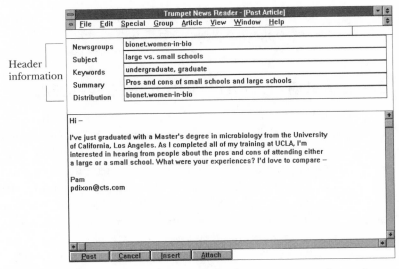

Header information

Figure 4.3 A message ready to post, complete with header and text

This type of post is a benign but interesting way to jump onto a board, and you'll quickly discover that you get all sorts of responses; in fact, we'll assume 15 people respond to your message by the next day. Ten of the responses are posted as follow-ups to your message, and five are emailed to you privately. You notice that a professor from Oxford replied, along with some very well-known researchers in the field.

As a result of this single post, not only do you enjoy a conversation in the group about the pros and cons of large or small schools, you also get your name in front of these important people. Additionally, you are gaining valuable insight as to how people at the top view your academic experience. You are finding out how you need to compensate for your background in an interview situation.

You have also made the first step in developing real online friends. If you stick with it, you could end up with a reference from some of the top people in the world in your profession, or you could be pointed to an opportunity that one of your online contacts hears about.

Within the space of one to two weeks, you can establish meaningful contacts with 15 people from three countries. To do the same in real time, you would have to purchase plane tickets costing several thousand dollars to do the networking in person, and it would have been more difficult to establish quick contact with all of these experts, not to mention a rapport or long-term professional dialog.

YOUR NETWORKING EXPECTATIONS

Online or off, networking is a way to find out where the experts in your field are and to start communicating with them. It is a way to get a sense of what employers, particularly top employers, in your profession are dealing with and what they're looking for in job candidates. Networking is a chance for you to discuss and solve common problems, and to explore areas of mutual interest. Networking gives you the means by which to learn what you need to know and "to be" as an employee.

If you're an excellent networker, you'll discover this kind of information and use it to make yourself a better job candidate. For example, let's assume you're graduating with a degree in journalism, and go online to the Usenet *alt.journalism* group and query politely about how to best go about finding a job in the field. (You can post your query through the Internet or through a commercial service.) Working journalists begin to give you advice you would never have dreamed of getting. One in particular gives you very good information, so you begin a separate email conversation with him, even though he lives on another continent. (A typical conversation is shown in Figure 4.4.) You get many suggestion, such as the one, "Begin with smaller newspapers." You also receive specific resume *do*s and

---

Your post (message) : "Hi -- I've just graduated with a major in journalism from XYZ university. I am looking for a job on a daily newspaper. I'm willing to relocate to get a start. Any suggestions? Thanks -

Response # 1: I recommend that you try at a community paper first. You have the best chance of landing a job quickly, and you'll get the practical experience you need to move on to a larger daily.

Response # 2: You could always apply at a major metropolitan daily paper. Sometimes, editors will pick up highly promising cub reporters -- but it's a longshot. What you really need is experience and a specialty.

Your follow up message to # 1: (Email) Thanks for the advice. Did you start at a community paper?

Your follow up message to # 2: (Email) Thanks for replying to my query. What do you think is the best kind of experience? As far as specialties, I've always been afraid to specialize. I hate the thought of being put into that proverbial box. Is there room for a generalist?

Figure 4.4 A fictional but realistic conversation on Usenet's *alt.journalism*

don'ts for the field, and your email buddy coaches you on potential interview questions and snares.

Although you may not get any actual offers from these types of interaction, you can use the information to help you craft a more focused resume, choose the best places to apply for a job, and shine in an interview. Consequently, even though you're just starting out, you present yourself as on top of your field and as an up and coming talent.

ELEMENTS OF ONLINE NETWORKING

To network online you will need a computer, a modem, and know how to email and post to forums and newsgroups. Most online accounts come with a complete set of instructions on how to accomplish these tasks; here's a quick review. To email, go to your account and log on. On the main menu, choose the Mail or Communications option. Next choose the option that says either Create Mail or Write Mail. Fill in the address your mail is going to in the To: blank; in the From: blank, fill in your email address. Under Subject: insert a one- or two-word description of your message. Press Enter a few times to get to the message area, and begin writing your message. After you're finished, follow the instructions of your system to send the message. Some accounts tell you to press a key series like Control key and X (often written Ctrl+X) to send mail; others direct you to click on a Send button. Most systems post their mailing directions on the bottom of the screen; although, occasionally, you'll see them at the top.

To post a message, go into Usenet. You can get to Usenet through a commercial service by performing a keyword search on *Usenet*. As of this writing, America Online, CompuServe, and Delphi offer Usenet access. (Look for more services to offer Usenet access soon.) From the Internet, access Usenet through your online account. On the main menu, choose the option that says Usenet News, News, Newsgroups, or just Usenet. You will then be in Usenet. How you post a message will vary based on the kind of system you are using. There are, however, some general steps you'll follow and some general help tactics. Once you're in Usenet, if you aren't sure of what to do, take advantage of the Help option. Most are on a clearly marked menu, or via clearly marked instructions at the bottom of the screen. The usual keys to type for help are "?" or "H." Here are the basic steps for posting: Enter a discussion group. Depending on your system, you do this by either clicking on the group or by scrolling through the groups (usually by pressing the Spacebar) and pressing Tab or sometimes Enter to get into a particular group. Once you're in the group, look for either buttons or commands to use.

Another very important—and often overlooked—item you need to network online is familiarity with online culture and environment. If you've never been online before, you may be alternately amused, confounded, and fascinated by the complex etiquette, usually called *netiquette,* that governs online networking. (Netiquette is discussed more fully in an upcoming section.)

Finally, you'll need to have some of the same information at hand that you would use to network in a more traditional manner: a target job, a target company, a real focus as you approach networking, and sincerity and a willingness to help other people. Then, it's a good idea to have some or all of the following goals in mind before you begin to actually network:

- ◆ Goal #1: Seek out experts and people of like mind and interest. When you're online, be focused on finding people who are working in the same profession or the one that you hope to be in. Constantly be on the lookout for discussion groups that fit your specific professional interests. Don't forget to take notes of the contacts you notice on forums and newsgroups, and write down email addresses in a notebook.

- ◆ Goal #2: Exchange ideas. Work hard to find out what the hot topics are in your profession, where the controversial areas are, and what trends are looming on the horizon. For example, if you are an architect, the newsgroup listing in Figure 4.5 offers several jumping-off points for you. Questions to ask yourself from this listing are: What are the new trends relating to stadium design, zero gravity design, and urban planning? How does architecture relate to the Internet? Is this going to be a new career area? Submit, after thorough research of course, some ideas of your own to add to discussions. Add buzzwords and recurring themes or ideas to your notebook.

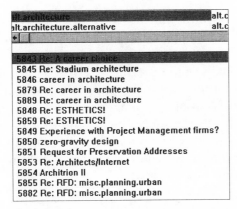

Figure 4.5 An architecture newsgroup, whose topics are leads to areas of research for job hunters.

- ♦ Goal #3: Find out, specifically, what you need to be or to do to be competitive in your job market. Have you been busy studying for a degree the last couple of years? Have you been worked to the bone at a company that just downsized you out of a job? In either case, you're probably out of touch with the general marketplace. You need to know who and what employers are looking for, so this is one of the major areas you must focus on as you network online.

- ♦ Goal #4: Determine the specific requirements for jobs in your profession. To be competitive, obviously, you need certain broad qualities—depending on your profession, perhaps a degree, a general expertise, or a certain viewpoint. But you also need to know what specific skill sets are necessary. Exactly what are employers asking employees to have as a knowledge or experience base? Get as many specifics as you can.

- ♦ Goal #5: Uncover and discuss common problems and areas of concern. Are you a systems engineer who's looking for a new job? Find out what employers' pet peeves are. You can usually figure this out simply by reading what they write. Chances are, these will show up in the form of questions in interviews, so you'd better be prepared. And remember, discussing possible solutions to problems reveals your expertise while it helps you see how other people in the field look at the problem.

- Goal #6: Keep your name in front of the right people. No one can get to know you and help you unless they know you're there. Tune into people who have the authority to hire you. Usually, signature files are the big giveaway to such people. If you don't see a revealing signature file, watch the posts closely. People who are online frequently reveal a lot about themselves—what they do for a living and so on. Over time, and with continual, intelligent exposure, you'll earn a good reputation. And who knows where that will someday lead.

- Goal #7: Try to make contact with people who work in your target company or job. This is sometimes a difficult goal to accomplish. Nevertheless, it should be on your list. You should be looking for people who can give you inside information about the job you want or the company you want to work for. It's just a matter of getting yourself online and into a lot of discussions.

 One of the biggest mistakes you can make in the online world is to develop one-sided relationships, where you're always at the receiving end of others' help. Never forget to find ways of reciprocating that help. You, too, are expected to provide useful information when you can, give referrals if you have them, and generally have a generous, helpful attitude. Don't go online, find top experts, use them to help you get a job, and then just log off without giving anything back. "Thank you" should definitely be a part of your words and deeds.

Online Jargon Recap

Before you go online to network, it's not a bad idea to review some of the terms we've been using and that you'll frequently see online:

Posting—sending a message to Usenet or another discussion group. Refer back to Figure 4.3 to see a sample posting.

Threads—strings of discussions. In Figure 4.6, you can see an example of a thread.

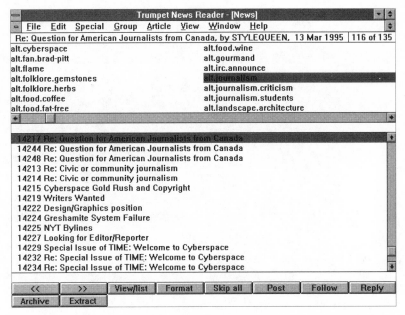

Figure 4.6 This is the newsgroup *alt.journalism*. Messages #14244 and 14248, Re: Question for American Journalists from Canada, are two in a thread. Messages 14213 and 14214 are part of the thread, or discussion of, Civic or community journalism. Message #14229, Special issue of TIME...., is an original post, while the two messages following are responses to it, which make up a thread.

Follow-up—sometimes called a reply, this is simply a response to someone else's post. Your reply to a post adds one more message to a thread.

Flame—Unpleasant comments and/or responses, sometimes erupting in online *flame wars*, tantamount to arguments. Look at Figure 4.7 to see a flame, but note that this is not a common occurrence. Most people are polite, but just like in "real life," there are always a few who must cause trouble. The best advice to flaming is to stay out of it. No one

---

Query: I'm a chef (I specialize in providing desserts for resorts and hotels) and I'm trying to relocate from Chicago to Los Angles. Are there any West-coast based chefs with any suggestions? I don't want to attempt the move unless there is a good market.

Flame response: Well, for one, why don't you get a clue about how to spell? It's Los ANGELES not Los "Angles."

Figure 4.7 A fictional flame

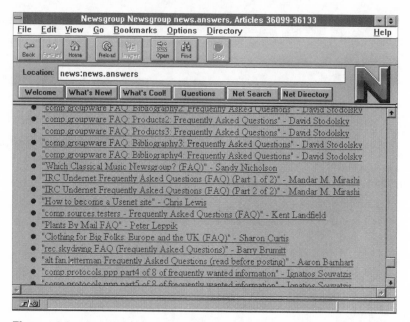

Figure 4.8 The Usenet group *news.answers* contains many FAQs that answer common—and repeatedly asked—questions. Some FAQs can be very long documents.

looking for a job can afford to develop a reputation for being ill-tempered.

FAQs—*frequently asked questions.* A FAQ is usually posted as a permanent message on a discussion group so the participants aren't bothered by having to answer the same questions 100 times. In Figure 4.8, you'll notice a list of FAQs for people to read. FAQs are musts for new participants to read before they join in.

Emoticons—the so-called smiley faces that people add to their electronic communications to show humor, sarcasm, irony, or other emotions (hence the name emoticons) that are lost in online communication. Here are some examples (hint: turn the book sideways):

;)   This winking smiley face is often used when telling a joke or using a pun.

:o   Denotes surprise

:(Expresses unhappiness; for example, "I'm dieting! :("

HOW TO NETWORK ONLINE

Practice Good Netiquette

Every online area has its own rules of conduct, and if you go online without familiarizing yourself with these rules, you do so at your professional peril. Think how carefully you prepare for "real life, real-time" meetings. You dress, speak, and generally behave in the manner appropriate to the situation. It's no different online. Here are some basic netiquette guidelines that will help to keep you out of trouble.

- *Be polite.* Don't rebuff people for their ideas, spelling errors, or foibles. Don't act like you know everything about the topic you're discussing. Be tolerant of other viewpoints.

- *Post only to appropriate groups.* If you are trying to find a job as a high school teacher, don't begin posting to every educational board available. Find two, three, or four boards that really suit you and spend time nurturing your contacts there. After a few months of networking, look around and branch out. But give yourself time to become more skilled at online networking before you do this.

- *Read a group's FAQs and a week's worth of messages before you post.* Otherwise, you may miss the "feel" of a group or forum. Some discussion groups are very businesslike and serious; others are more light-hearted. Don't make the classic mistake of jumping in before you read.

- *Don't waste other people's time or money.* Don't post unnecessarily long messages, headers, or subject lines that aren't specific; quizzes, surveys, advertisements on the wrong boards, and too-general "can you help me" messages. (Find a more subtle, professional way to approach this. This is discussed further in the upcoming section, "Make Your Debut.")

- *Don't post multiple messages to different places; instead, post copies.* This means that if you are going to send either a message or your resume to more than one board, simply send the message once and *copy* or forward the message to all the places you want it to go. To do this, in the Newsgroups blank, type the names of all the newsgroups you want the message to go to, separated by commas. (Exhibit some self-restraint here, though, since it's considered bad form to post your resume to every resume board at once because your messages take up valuable bandwidth.)

♦ *Don't advertise yourself.* You're networking with very specific goals in mind, and "Hire me!" tactics are inappropriate. On commercial services, your advertisement will probably be removed by the sysop. On Usenet, your advertisement will earn you contempt and will damage your networking efforts dramatically.

Set Your Career Goals

Before you send any messages or even decide where to network, decide what you want to do, and who or what company you want to work for. What are your salary goals? These are basic career planning questions you'll need to have answers for as part of your networking effort.

Research Online Discussion Groups

Your next step is to get online and uncover the best areas for you to network. Is Usenet the place for you? How about a presence on the World Wide Web? Remember that it is quality of your target audience that you are seeking, not quantity. If you find three discussion groups that are focused on your profession, you are doing very well, indeed.

If you have a commercial online account, you can log on to the account and compile your list. Here's how to do this:

1. Perform a keyword search, as described in Chapter 2, for your career area. For example, if you are in marketing, type in *marketing*.

2. Quickly scan the groups you discover to see if they interest you or will be worthwhile to participate in. But scan—don't read in-depth at this point. On commercial online services, newsgroups usually cost extra. Once you have chosen a few groups, use navigation software, as discussed in Chapter 2, to save time and money. Naviga-

Artists	Physicians, medical
comp.graphics	sci.med
rec.arts.fine	sci.med.pharmacy
rec.arts.misc	
	Publishing
Attorneys	rec.arts.books
misc.legal	
	Scientists
Computer Specialists	sci.bio
comp.admin	sci.research
comp.answers	
comp.misc	**Teachers**
	misc.education
Financial	
misc.taxes	**Writers**
Managers	misc.writers

Figure 4.9 A sampler of Usenet newsgroups

tion software allows you to retrieve and post messages much more quickly, thus saving you time and money.

3. Check the "Resources" appendix for a list of Usenet groups that might be relevant to your job search. Go to the Usenet portion of your service and browse groups you think may be helpful in your job search. Remember to open a capture file and to do your serious reading offline. Some possible groups for an architect are shown in Figure 4.9.

Choose Your Contacts

After you've determined the discussion groups you want to join, choose one or two, and read the messages for at least a week, noting the people who are participating. Observe the interactions among the participants, and analyze which kinds of discussions are of most interest to the people on the board. Do you see people getting philosophical? Or do you see a lot of good-natured joking? What are the hot issues on the board? Who appears to be the most outgoing, easy-to-get-along with person on the board? These are all impressions that will help you plan whom you will contact first and by what means. These impressions will also help you decide on the content and tone of your messages.

Again, remember to keep your networking goals in mind. Write them down and tack them near your computer. It will help you keep focused as you go about your online networking.

To Email or Post, That Is the Question

When you post a message to a group, everyone browsing or reading in that discussion group sees it. When you email, only the individual to whom it is addressed will read your message. The online rule of thumb is to email first. For instance, if you were browsing, *misc.writing*, and someone wrote, "Did you see the article in *XYZ Journal?* I was intrigued by the ....," it would be a waste of time and network space for you to write, "I saw that article too. It was really interesting" and post it to the group (this is referred to as a *copycat* reply). If you really want to extend the conversation with the initiator of the message, refine the message by adding why the article was interesting you, mention perhaps a paper or article you've published or discovered on the subject, and send it to the individual who posted the original message. But only post to the group if there's a compelling reason to do so, such as a lively group discussion.

In general, it is better to build individual relationships through emailing replies, and to reserve posting for those situations for which you want general exposure. The best strategy is to use both, but wisely. Here's are some guidelines:

Email if:

♦ The message is personal or directed to only one other individual.

♦ You want to develop a relationship with an individual. If, for example, you notice a particularly articulate peer, send him or her an email following up on one of the group posts. Your reply could be more personalized and longer, so that you come to this person's attention and develop a professional online friendship.

♦ The message would be boring to an international audience. Remember, most newsgroups and forums have a global reach, so your posts must be relevant to the entire group. Even if you are posting to a chemistry discussion group, and you've just found out about a regional conference the coming weekend, it's still better to send email to the appropriate people on the list; that is, the people who could ostensibly attend the conference. International readers wouldn't be able to attend, so spare them reading your message.

Post a message if:

♦ You have an insight or information that will benefit the group as a whole.

♦ You are trying to gain international exposure. For instance, suppose that you have a research paper that has just been published in a scholarly journal. You can make a polite announcement of the topic of the paper that was published, noting the publication it was in and the date.

♦ You want to reply to a thread with a relevant, meaningful comment.

Plan What You're Going to Say

One of the most wonderful things about online networking is that it allows you to moderate your communications, an opportunity you don't have in real-time situations. So take advantage and consider carefully what you want to say and how you want to say it. Write out your messages before you log on, and think about these elements as you compose:

♦ Does my message move me closer to my networking goals, or am I just speaking for the sake of saying something?

♦ Am I writing in the accepted style for the group? (See the following section for more on this.)

♦ What do I want the other people reading this message to do or to say?

♦ Does my message encourage a reply?

♦ Would my message be more effective as an emailed reply to an individual or as a post to the group?

Write for the Electronic Medium

Never forget the enormity of what you're dealing with when you go online: Approximately 3 million people participate in

Hello --

I'm a public relations professional with 7 years
of work experience. For the past 5 years I've been
the director of public relations at a large engineering
company. Now, I'm interested in finding a position
as a public relations director for a non-profit organization.

Can anyone offer me any advice on making this career
move?

Thanks

Figure 4.10 A message in electronic style

Usenet, and as many as 5 or 6 million people use the online
commercial services such as CompuServe. English is not necessarily everyone's first language, and many people are paying to
read the messages, and many, especially Usenet users, are very
picky about message style because Usenet developed in the era
when the Internet was populated primarily by academics and
researchers. Any advertisements or messages that are not on
the topic are frowned upon by this core group. Even though
Usenet has become more commercial in the past few years, its
distinctive "personality" persists.

As a result of the sheer numbers and diversity of people
online, a certain "electronic style" of writing has developed to
keep things moving smoothly and quickly. The hallmarks of
this style are simple language, short and to-the-point statements, and clear concise references (see Figure 4.10 for a
sample). Don't be the one who inadvertently irritates or of-
fends any of the people who can potentially help you in your
job search.

Be Clear

Read and reread your message. Ask yourself: Can anything you
have written be interpreted a second or third way, or be misin-
terpreted entirely? Is there anything that could be misunderstood by someone not fluent in English? (This is especially
important if your profession crosses international boundaries
or you are trying to find a job in another country.) Keep in

mind that subtleties, witticisms, slang, and abbreviations don't travel well online—stick with a very direct, clear approach.

For example, look at the following message posted to a group discussion on fractals:

"I read your post about a job opening in NE. I am expert in COBOL and Visual Basic. Here's my email address."

There are a lot of things wrong with this message. First, it shouldn't be posted to a group, but emailed to the individual, since the message is off the group focus. Also, is it safe to assume that international group of participants are going to know the terms COBOL and Visual Basic? And what does "NE" stand for? Nebraska? The northeast? Niger? (NE is that country's international mailing symbol.)

Think globally, and spell out all acronyms and abbreviations, no matter how simple and straightforward they may seem to you. You never know when someone from another country will have a splendid insight for you or an inside tip. Make sure your language can be understood by everyone.

Don't Forget the Basics

Use correct grammar and spelling, and use upper- and lower-case letters, as usual. Don't type all in uppercase or all in lowercase letters either from laziness or as an attempt to stand out. All uppercase letters come across as shouting online, and all lowercase letters make it difficult to see the beginnings and ends of sentences. And don't forget to check your spelling! Look at these two messages to understand how you can reduce your chances simply by not following basic writing rules.

"HI, I AM TYRING TO FIND OUT INFORMATION ABOUT ...."

"hi i'm trying to find out infomation about a company in boston. this company ..."

Both messages are difficult to read, and both make the person who wrote them look less than professional, complete with typos. Don't make the mistake of overlooking the obvious.

Be Aware of Time Differences

Messages can be delivered at different times in various portions of the Net, and people don't pick up their email every day. So when you write a follow-up message, whether by email or by posting to Usenet, always refer to the original message in your reply. In your newsreading software, when you begin to type a reply to a message, you will have the option of including the original message. The original message will appear with chevrons in front of each line of text, as shown in Figure 4.11. Your reply will appear without the chevrons.

If you don't refer to a specific message of a specific date, your reply may be rendered meaningless when it's received two weeks later. For example, if you are thinking about switching careers from dentistry to dental instrument manufacture and design, you may be haunting several manufacturing newsgroups to get a feel for the profession before you leap into it. Let's say you spotted a message that mentioned something about designing tools for physicians.

To follow up, you email the person in question, referring to his or her post. You express your interest in what he or she was doing, and invite the person to talk with you. But if your message refers vaguely to "your post yesterday," and the recipient doesn't pick up his or her messages for two weeks, your reply might get tossed because the recipient can't figure out when "yesterday" was and to which post you were referring.

From: xyz@e.mail
Subject: Re: listing of all newgroups
Date: Fri, 19 Jan 1995 10:10:18

In article < xxx@e.mail> writes:
>I'm trying to figure out how to get a listing of all newsgroups.
>Does anyone have any suggestions?

Here, following in this text, are a couple of previous posts on the subject. The information will cover much of what you're looking for. For more help, email me directly.

Figure 4.11 A note with the original message included. Note the " >" before each line of original text.

Keep It Short

The longer your message, the less likely it is that people will read it or respond favorably to it. Before you send two pages of brilliant theory over the wires, think again. Edit that prose down to a half page at the very most.

Remember, some people pay a premium price for access to online areas, and they don't want to waste their time and money wading through long messages. They want to go online, capture text, and then get off line as soon as possible. Wordy, glib messages tend to get passed over, since most experienced users know better than to leave long messages.

Use Accurate Headers

When you prepare to write a message, be specific and exact in the *header*—the subject portion—of you message. Be aware that most system operators set up sites either on Usenet or on commercial services to display the subject lines of articles first. People can then browse a list of subject headings to decide which articles they want to read. So, if you have a subject heading that is too broad, many people will just ignore the article and go on to the next one.

For example, on the Usenet group *rec.music.early* (recreational, early music discussion group), it is standard for performing groups to post their schedules. It's a simple way of letting the world know about their upcoming concerts. The most effective headers give specific information, as shown in message #16579 in Figure 4.12a. The least effective headers say something vague like, "Performing schedule."

And when you post your resume, headers are your first calling card, as you can see in Figure 4.12b. So, be as specific as you possibly can. Before you mail your message, ask yourself, does my header accurately describe the contents? Have I been as specific as possible?

Keep your headers to 40 characters or less because some systems will cut off the headers at 40 characters. Character count is determined simply by counting all the letters and the spaces in the header.

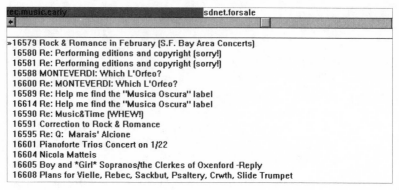

Figure 4.12a Headers for *rec.music.early*. Note message #16579 giving location, title, and date of performances.

Format Simply

People view Usenet messages on hundreds of different type of monitors and computer systems. To ensure that your message can be read from any system, keep the text free from extra characters like tabs or formatting attributes such as boldfacing and italics or fancy typefaces. Set the line length to no more

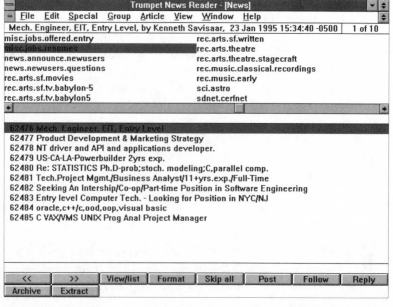

Figure 4.12b Resumes posted in *misc.jobs.resumes*. Which resume would you look at, based on the subject headers?

than 80 characters per line (from the left side of the monitor to the right side of the monitor, count no more than 80 letters and spaces).

MAKE YOUR DEBUT

It's time: You've decided on a group, figured out what to say, who to say it to, and how to say it. Our advice for your initial forays online is to stay low-key, and realize that after the first post, things get easier. If you're still hesitant, here are a couple of opening lines for you to work with and adapt to suit your personality and your professional needs.

The "jump from the post" opener:

> Hi Dave, I read your post about marketing with interest. I, too, majored in communications and ended up in a marketing job. I find that my degree has actually been more of a help than a hindrance. Is this what you've discovered?

To ask for advice:

> Hi. I just graduated from Columbia College, a small private school in South Carolina. I'm currently applying for a number of jobs where I'm competing with graduates from the other Columbia, as in Columbia University. I'm wondering how I can compete for a job with a less prestigious degree?

Or:

> Hi. I'm just starting to look for a new job in arts administration. I haven't job hunted in a long time, so my search skills are a little rusty. Are there any new trends I should know about regarding resumes? Does anyone know what types of interview questions employers are currently asking in this field? Any advice on starting points?

General conversation starter:

> I recently had lunch with a colleague, and he made quite an argument for using resume tracking software to help manage resumes. I disagreed with him then, but now I'm wondering what other people working in human resources think about this issue.

Follow Up

Once you've posted to a group, you'll begin getting replies. At this point, assess carefully what you've received and decide whether to answer via post to a group or through one-to-one email (review the previous discussion in this chapter if necessary to help you decide which type of post is appropriate. But whatever you do, take the time to answer within a day or two. As with all other types of communications—phone calls, memos, letters—people don't like to be ignored, put off, or forgotten.

Maintenance

Once you have made your initial contact, you'll be faced with the task of maintaining your professional online relationships. Keep your networking goals in mind, and evaluate how your online contacts fit into your goals. If you started networking while still employed or well in advance of graduating, you will have time to plan a long-term strategy and let your online relationships develop slowly and naturally.

If, however, you're one of the unfortunate who lost your job unexpectedly and you need another job immediately, a word to the wise: No matter how anxious you are and desperate you may feel, don't push friendships or relationships online any more than you would offline. You will only impact negatively on your attempts to obtain worthwhile help and job leads.

Keep the long view in mind. Find out more about your contacts' professional experiences, particularly any published works they may have so that you can show you have a real interest in them, in their work, and in what they have to offer. You'll have to do some research to ferret out this kind of information, but that will only make you look better to the profession, too. And if this sounds like work, it is. As we said in Chapter 1, looking for a job is a job in itself.

Don't be a pest. When you're preoccupied looking for work, you'll have a tendency to forget how busy other people are. Your own needs, like the impending rent or mortgage payment, may cloud you ability to consider the lives of others. Just remember, to maintain a professional online relationship, you have to think long-term. Keep your networking goals always in the front of your mind.

As we admonished earlier in this chapter, never forget that online relationships are reciprocal. So while you're busy trying to make contacts for yourself, also be on the lookout for cross-referrals you can make between those you've met online. Can you help out someone who has given you advice? Did you see a job offer that wasn't right for you but might be for someone you chatted with in a group discussion? Pass it on! What goes around, comes around, and your good deed will not go unnoticed.

Also keep your eyes open for *virtual cafe* notices. A virtual cafe is when several people from an online group get together. Usually, these meetings are announced online and held in large cities. If you don't see such a message, and you notice there are a lot of people within driving distance of each other who are active in the discussion group, then suggest one yourself. Of course, you'll want to be well-established in the discussion group before you do suggest an in-person meeting like this.

And speaking of meeting in person, another good way to maintain and extend your online relationships is to find out if any of you regularly attend the same conferences. If so, plan a brief meeting over coffee. Or, if you happen to be traveling to the place where your contact lives, do the same thing. To repeat though, don't push this initially any more than you would in *real time*. You'll know when the time is right to take a relationship to another level. Just don't let your concern over finding a job mislead your ordinarily trustworthy instincts.

WHERE TO NETWORK

We've discussed all these places earlier in the book, but it's relevant to repeat them here to refresh your memory. The general guideline is that you can network in any online areas where there are opportunities to form discussion groups or to exchange information. *Your* best networking spot will depend on your profession and on your goals. Here's a recap of the major online networking hotspots. (Another reminder: Before you jump online, be tuned into the different and distinct environments of each area you enter.)

Usenet

Usenet, or network news, is a very large network of computers that communicate with each other. Over this network, millions of people send jokes, read notes, hold long discussions, and—in short—talk about anything and everything. For job hunters, the real value of the Usenet discussion groups is that they offer places to post your resumes and unparalleled access to key people in virtually all professions.

As we've mentioned before, Usenet is an independent computer network that you can reach through the Internet or through online commercial services. Usenet is an excellent place for job seekers to look for discussion groups that relate to their professions. Usenet is a little more difficult to use than the commercial online service discussion groups, but you also have more opportunities to find a group that suits you simply because there are more groups. Refer back to Chapter 2 "Online Working Strategies" for complete details on Usenet's structure.

Commercial Online Services

America Online, GEnie, CompuServe, and almost all of the other commercial online services offer places where people can discuss topics near and dear to them. The discussion groups on these services differ significantly from Usenet in that there are fewer people and the discussion groups usually have moderators, people who monitor the discussions to keep them on track.

If you are looking for a professional discussion group, CompuServe is arguably your number one choice. It offers many business discussion groups such as the PR & Marketing Forum you saw in Chapter 2. Call CompuServe's toll-free number and ask a customer service representative about specific groups in your profession. America Online and GEnie also have professional discussion groups, but there are fewer choices, and the groups don't always have the same level of seriousness as on CompuServe. Again, you'll need to call the toll-free numbers and ask the customer service reps which groups are available for you.

Most services offer a one-month trial period. Take advantage of these offers—go online for a month with as many commercial online services as you can, and then make a final choice after you've investigated them. Ultimately, only you can decide which service has the groups that offer you the most networking opportunities and best fit your needs.

The World Wide Web

Currently, Web's main purpose for job hunters if for circulating their resumes and *home pages*, topics that are covered in depth in Chapter 5.

Bulletin Boards, Community Nets, and Freenets

Dial-up employment boards and local bulletin boards offer job seekers the opportunity to network at a community level. This is very useful if you are determined to find a job in a particular geographic area. Also, some of these boards are good places to try out your online skills before you log on to Usenet, an

Figure 4.13 The California Job Bulletin Board. All of the jobs listed are available only in California, thus the name.

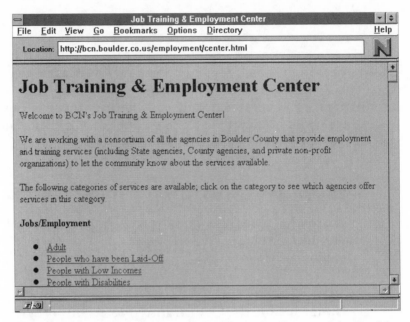

Figure 4.14 The Job Training & Employment Center of the Boulder
Community Network

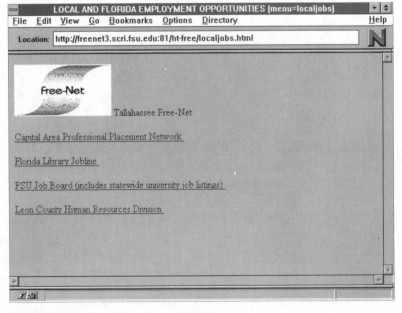

Figure 4.15 The Tallahassee Free-Net

international forum. It's sort of the online equivalent of off-Broadway tryouts before heading to the Great White Way. As valuable as they are, however, remember that they are not usually national, and therefore cannot possibly expose you to the best discussions or the most knowledgeable people in your field. Figures 4.13, 4.14, and 4.15 show a sample of each of these.

TROUBLESHOOTING

We'd like to be able to tell you that networking is always a breeze, and everyone you meet online will be helpful, kind, and polite. Well, it's not the case, and just like in-person interactions, you're bound to run into some difficult situations or people online, so it's best to be prepared. The following discusses some of the more typical difficulties you might face and how to sort your way out of them.

No One Responds to Me!

If you are getting ignored, probably you have done one of the following:

♦ Targeted the wrong group.

♦ Been too broad in your statements.

♦ Communicated inappropriately in some way.

Here are some suggestions for diagnosing the problem:

♦ Privately email someone in the group you've been posting to. Choose the most reasonable and kind person. Ask him or her for some feedback on how your presence is regarded by others in the group.

♦ Start over with a new group. You may just have encountered a "cliquish" newsgroup. If you still aren't getting responses, you may either be too passive in your responses or too aggressive. Reread the guidelines for networking and follow them. Listen before you speak; be courteous and respectful.

♦ Download a series of messages in a board you are interested in, and study them. Try to figure out what makes them work—or not. When you see someone getting flamed or ignored, try to analyze why.

♦ Go back to your target board and start over. If you have been rude, apologize through email. If you have been too quiet, gather the courage to step into the public eye more often.

I Got Flamed!

It happens to everybody. You post a message, you've followed all of the rules and, one day, you find a truly nasty little note waiting for you in your electronic mailbox. Flames usually follow two formats. You get flamed because you've inadvertently done something that violates netiquette, like inappropriate multiple posting (when you should have emailed an individual). The flame in response to your error will usually be along the lines of, "How dare you clutter up the Net? Are you a newbie (a new kid on the block) or what?"

The second kind of flame usually comes from a know-it-all, who clearly thinks you, your information, and your opinions are worthless. This type of flame usually reads something like, "I saw your post on Monday. According to my sources, your theory is completely off base. Let me give you the real facts!"

The best way to put out most flames is to ignore them, unless you believe it is absolutely essential to defend yourself; and if you do, be polite. You never know when an anonymous person from the Net will materialize in your daily life. Above all, resist the temptation to whip out an equally obnoxious email. You'll only end up looking as bad as the person who offended you. No matter how angry you are, wait 24 hours, and give people the benefit of the doubt. Keep in mind, too, that misunderstandings can occur more easily online because you don't have the benefits of body language and voice tone to determine if someone is joking, being ironic, and so on.

Online Discretion

I Lost My Temper

It cannot be emphasized enough that electronic networking is a powerful way to reach many people. The down side of this power, though, is that if you misuse it—say by losing your temper or behaving inappropriately—you can discredit yourself just as dramatically.

If you do have a particularly bad day and lose your temper on the Net, it can be difficult to repair the damage. A potential 4 million people may have witnessed your tantrum. The best advice is to own up quickly, apologize to the people involved, and then vow that you will not send any more flames or rude communications.

More on Privacy and Copyright

Janet Attard, a sysop for GEnie's workplace round table and other forums says, "People don't realize that any statement they make on a bulletin board is a public statement. It's especially important that job seekers *don't make comments about their present employers.*" Further, any libelous or slanderous statement you make can get you in some real legal trouble. So if you hate your boss, refrain from broadcasting the fact through cyberspace. Don't say anything you wouldn't be proud of at any time in any discussion group.

Posting copyright. Newsgroups are regarded as a form of publishing. So, if you are putting something online that you want to make sure stays yours, you must include a copyright symbol on your work to indicate that. You can also request that the information not be used for any purpose other than educational or for nonprofit. Remember, anything you send to a newsgroup, no matter which one, is considered to be in the public domain.

In addition to protecting yourself, you have an obligation to regard the rights of others. Therefore, don't forward other people's email to anyone else unless you have received the author's permission. Forwarding email without permission is considered to be a serious breach of netiquette, to say the least.

WORLD WIDE WEB:
THE JOB SEEKER'S GOLD MINE

World Wide Web: The Job Seeker's Gold Mine

Do you remember the first time you watched "The Wizard of Oz," and marveled when Dorothy left her black-and-white Kansas world for the technicolor magic of Oz? That's what the World Wide Web (the Web, WWW) has done for the information superhighway. It's turned a formidable, daunting phenomenon into a world that is accessible and inviting to everyone. And because of this, the Web is attracting businesses and organizations of all sizes, government agencies, and first-class research institutions, which are all advertising their job openings on their Web home pages in career centers such as Career Mosaic, The Monster Board, and the Interactive Employment Network.

The Web's success lies in its use of graphical user interfaces (GUIs). In the same way that these so-called user-friendly interfaces swept the computer industry a few years ago, the World Wide Web has become the darling of the Internet by acknowledging that people prefer clicking on icons, navigating with a mouse, and selecting actions from pull-down menus to typing commands. What this means to you, the online job hunter, is that, instead of typing in commands to retrieve text documents that reveal all the secrets of online jobs, you can point with your mouse, click on an icon, and retrieve a document. You do

140

not—as in the early days on the Internet—have to learn the forbidding Unix language, with its cryptic commands that kept many of us less-than-technically-fluent people away in droves.

SPINNING THE WEB

The Web has become such an important place for job seekers to understand that this entire chapter is devoted to explaining all about the Web, what it is, how it works, how to search it, and how to use it in your job search. First, a little background: The World Wide Web was developed as a hypertext project primarily at the European Laboratory for Particle Physics (CERN) just outside of Geneva, Switzerland. Hypertext itself was a phenomenon of the not too distant past, when Apple Computer released its HyperCard program, an authoring language bundled with the Macintosh that facilitated storing and interactively retrieving on-screen cards containing text, bitmapped graphics, sound, and animation.

The World Wide Web is aptly named. Like a spider's web, with thousands of strands that intersect at key points but seem no have to "top" or "bottom," Web links between documents are completely interactive. There are many points that can function as a starting point, and on the World Wide Web, it is up to you as to where you want to start looking or browsing.

The Web makes use of *hypertext*, which, briefly, is text that has predefined or user-created links (called *hyperlinks*) that permit the reader to pursue associative trails as desired. Look at Figure 5.1 to see what how hypertext and hyperlinks work. A hypertext link is represented here by underlined words. For example, the first underlined word in the list is Agencies. When you click on Agencies with your mouse—whoosh!—you're off to a new, and related, location. The numbers in parentheses—in this example, 261—represent the number of Web sites that will be listed if you follow this link. When you click on and activate a hypertext link, the link then tells your Web browser to establish a new connection and display whatever is on the other end of that link.

A link can also be graphically represented, like the pictures in Figure 5.2. Note the five icons above the underlined text. You can click on the picture and go to a new location. This is an

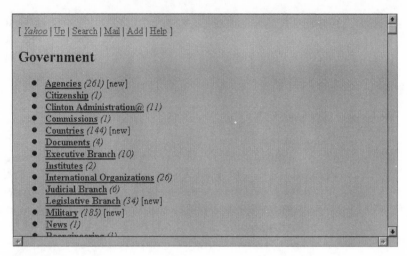

Figure 5.1 All of the underlined text in this figure represents hypertext links.

example of a link that is hidden, or *embedded* in a graphic. For example, if you clicked on the picture of the computer (second from the left), you would go to a database maintained by Job Search. You can even access audio links if you have the proper

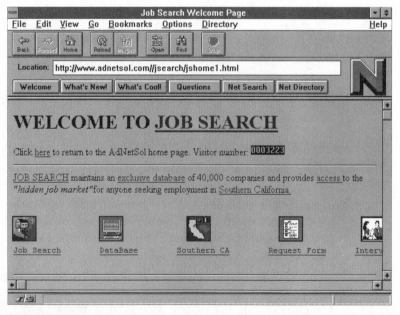

Figure 5.2 Graphic hypertext links in Job Search

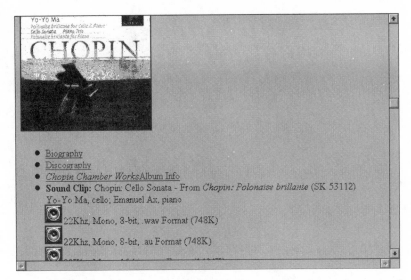

Figure 5.3 Hypertext hiding behind the speaker icons in one of Sony's home pages. Click on the speakers and hear the heavenly sounds of Emanuel Ax.

software. (To hear audio, you will need a sound card in your computer. You'll also need what's called a *helper application* from Netscape. More on this later.) Look at Figure 5.3 to see how audio hyperlinks are represented.

A hyperlink can lead to whatever the author of the Web document feels would help the reader to understand something better. A hyperlink can also lead to a mail session, allowing visitors to immediately send mail to the author of that page. In Figure 5.4, note that Martin Marietta Energy Systems, Inc. has added an email link that lets visitors to their home page send immediate feedback by clicking on the email address.

Later in the chapter we'll explain how to write hypertext commands, in the section entitled "Designing Your Own Home Page." For now, all you have to know in order to navigate the Web is that you choose a hypertext link and click or press Enter.

Uniform Resource Locators (URLs)

Probably the only things that might get you trapped in the Web are the lengthy and seemingly unintelligible addresses known as *uniform resource locators*, or URLs for short. Believe it or not, a

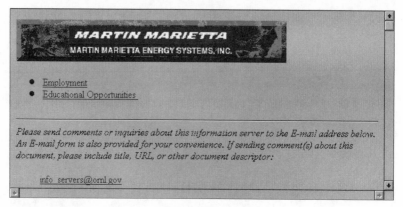

Figure 5.4 Martin Marietta's instant email link for feedback. You can see the email link at the very bottom of the figure. Also note the links to employment just under the company logo.

URL is actually a logical way of writing a Web address, and we're going to break one down for you so that you can understand the setup of these all-important elements. Here's a typical URL for you to look at:

http://dragon.yukon.ca/~gilford/HTML_Editor/Documentation.html

The basic setup follows this order: the *protocol*, the *machine name*, the *directory/file name*. Here's the breakdown of our sample address:

♦ **http:** These initials stand for *hypertext transfer protocol.* A *protocol* is the set of rules that govern how data will be exchanged between different programs. The Web rules say its documents must be retrieved via hypertext, which is why its addresses begin with http, hypertext transfer protocol.

♦ **//:** The two backslashes precede the first part of the address. The slashes separate the *protocol* (how to retrieve the information) from the actual *address* (the physical location of the information).

♦ **dragon.yukon.ca:** dragon in this URL is the *machine name,* which is an arbitrary moniker given to a machine. Some people create names based on a physical location; others just use numbers or letters for their machine names; yukon is the facility name. The last segment of this section, ca, tells us that this address is in Canada. (All international addresses contain a two-letter country code at this portion of the URL. These codes—more than 250 of them—are set by the International Standards Organization. The Resources appendix contains a list of these codes.) In U.S.-based URLs, a three-digit code replaces the country code, in this case, ca. The three-digit United States code tells you whether the address is commercial (com), educational(edu), government (gov), organizational (org), or military (mil). (These are like the extensions for email addresses.) So, in this Internet address,

http://sealevel.xyz.com/

sealevel is the machine name, XYZ is the facility name, (arbitrarily chosen) and com denotes a commercial site in the United States.

♦ **/~gilford/HTML_Editor/Documentation.html:** The rest of our sample address or URL is comprised of directories and file names, and your destination would be reached in this order: first, the home directory of gilford; next, the subdirectory called HTML_Editor, where you would get a document named Documentation.html. The *directories* are separated by slashes, with the actual *file name* always last in the URL.

Hopefully, now you can see that although URLs are cumbersome, there is a "rhyme and reason" to everything in them. Just remember the order: protocol, location, directories/file name.

▤▤▤ WHAT'S ON THE WEB

Anytime you want information about your profession, look on the Web. You will unearth people, organizations, and research projects having to do with your areas of professional interest. You can then translate these contacts and this knowledge into networking savvy, interviewing expertise, and skill-building blocks. You can look for experts, find information about cities, governments, and traveling, all on the Web.

Use live Web focus groups to keep yourself on top of just about every subject you can name. The *interactive* groups are becoming popular on the Web, and according to many Web experts such as Mike Rowe at the Interactive Employment

> **B. Media Roundtable** - The first Chiat/Day Communications interactive media
> roundtable on the Internet will focus on the future of the news delivery process.
> How will journalists' jobs change? How will instant access to news impact
> consumers? How will corporations, government and other entities interact with
> journalists? Who will act as news gatekeepers? Which mediums will survive?
> Tuesday, March 7, 1995
> 10 AM PST
> Maximum 20 journalists and 20 other guests
>
> **C. Kids' Market** - Kids still eat the same basic things, grow at the same basic
> rate, and especially, still need all the emotional support that little people have
> always required. So, as 1995 debuts, what is the list of "must-haves" for
> youngsters? What products and services are the backbone of today's kids'
> market? Will Cheerios still launch their days, does Oscar Mayer still have a way
> with B-O-L-O-G-N-A, and will an hour of Sega a day keep the doctor away?
> Thursday, March 9, 1995
> 10 PM EST
> Maximum 20 guests

Figure 5.5 Live online focus groups from Chiat/Day Communications

Network, "Interactivity is blossoming on the Web because it
takes a medium that is machine-dependent (online technology) and really adds the human element." In Figure 5.5, you
can see a partial list of Chiat/Day Communications (a public
relations/marketing company) focus group topics. Notice that
each topic has a set number of *chairs,* or available spots for
attendees. Joining one of these groups is a simple matter of
filling out an online application form, as shown in Figure 5.6.
You click on the letter of the focus group you want to join, give
your name and other information, and then click on the Submit Sign-up button on the bottom of the screen. If there is a
chair left, you're sent a password. Further on down in the form
(not visible in this figure) is a button you can click on that says
Join Focus Group, which enables you to join the online talk
when you are ready. Talk about great networking!

You can also access Usenet newsgroups through the Web,
and although access is slower through the Web, presentation is
better because Web browsers, like Netscape, display the messages in a nice font.

Chapter 6 contains many URLs that allow you to connect to
vast, constantly updated online libraries of information. You'll

find a selection of specific URLs and the addresses of some *meta-lists* (lists with links to many other documents, such as the Yahoo list you saw in Figure 5.1). These lists are usually organized by subject area.

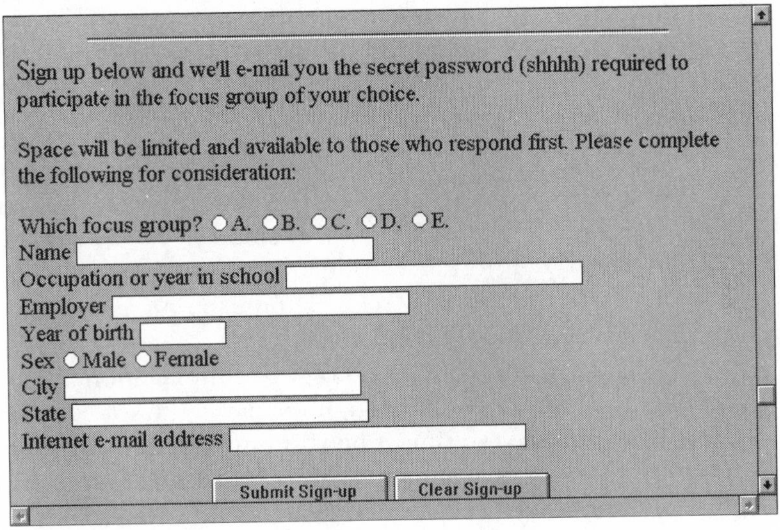
Sign up below and we'll e-mail you the secret password (shhhh) required to participate in the focus group of your choice.

Space will be limited and available to those who respond first. Please complete the following for consideration:

Which focus group? ○A. ○B. ○C. ○D. ○E.
Name
Occupation or year in school
Employer
Year of birth
Sex ○Male ○Female
City
State
Internet e-mail address

Submit Sign-up | Clear Sign-up

Figure 5.6 A typical online application form for getting a seat in an online focus group.

FINDING AND USING WEB BROWSERS

Once you're on the Web, all of the off-putting elements—commands, long addresses, and the like—become transparent. Even the most complicated searches are invisible to the user. To access the world's most current information, you don't have to be a technical wizard; all you need to know is how to use a Web browser.

Most Macintosh users prefer Netscape, and most PC owners use either Netscape or Lynx. Netscape is so popular because it's a smooth graphical interface that will allow you to access the whole Internet and the Web with just a click, which is why it's called a *multiprotocol browser.* It browses many protocols, such as http, gopher, telnet, and more. If you have a fast modem (14,400 bps or higher, which means that the modem transfers data at the rate of 14,400 bits per second) and run

Windows from a PC, then you can run a graphical Web browser like Netscape. Be aware, though that you will need a SLIP or PPP account from your Internet provider. Netscape and other graphical browsers are also available for Macintosh computers.

If you have an old computer and a slow modem, Lynx may be the browser for you as it will operate with older (and newer) PCs, including DOS-based computers. (That means you don't have to have Windows to use Lynx.) Lynx also works with Macintoshes. We'll show you how you can access Lynx in this chapter. All you need is a PC computer, a modem, and a basic Internet connection. You won't get to see the graphics, but you will have access to all of the textual information available via the Web. If you're a Delphi member, you can access Lynx by typing "go Internet Gopher" at the main menu. Then press Enter. At the next screen, choose menu item number 18 – WWW and you'll be in Lynx.

You can also contact Prodigy for information about how you can get on the Web through its services, but to access the Web from Prodigy, you must be running Windows or some kind of windowing environment from a PC-based computer. As of this writing, Web service for Macs was not available, though it is planned for release in a few months. As of this writing, no other commercial online services offer a full graphical interface to the Web, but the race is on! Expect all of the major online services to be offering full graphical interfaces to the Web by the end of 1995 or 1996.

Remember, for Web and Internet account information and contact phone numbers, refer to Appendix A, "Getting Yourself Online."

Netscape

Netscape is arguably the most popular of the Web browsers, because it is by far the smoothest and fastest currently available, and there are versions available for both PCs running Windows and for Macintoshes.

We're going to get you up and running with Netscape here, but for the complete, and definitive guide to this browser, access Netscape's online handbook at this address:

http://mosaic.mcom.com/home/online-manual.html

This is a complete manual that covers all Netscape features in detail. To get your own copy of Netscape, contact this address for instructions on where to find copies of Netscape online. You'll also find instructions for downloading it, and information about Netscape helper applications that allow you to access video and audio files with your computer.

http://home.netscape.com/info/how-to-get-it.html

You can also call Netscape Communications to order, at (415) 528-2555. For now, though, here is a quick course in Netscape that will get you spinning in no time.

Following Links

To follow a link in Netscape, point your mouse at an icon or underlined text, and click. Netscape does all the work for you. Within a few seconds, depending on network traffic, you will be at a new location. That's all there is to it. Figure 5.7 shows Netscape's opening menu. This is the first screen you see when you log onto your SLIP or PPP account with Netscape. To scroll the page, position your mouse pointer over the arrows at the

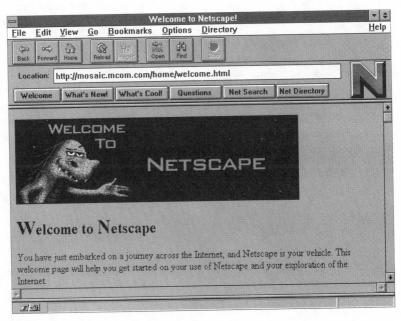

Figure 5.7 Netscape's opening menu

right and bottom of the page and click. The Location field above the row of buttons shows the address of what you are looking at. The large N is blue when viewed on a color screen, and when Netscape is accessing a document, it waves slightly to let you know it is active.

To begin our Netscape browse, we clicked on the Net Search button, which resulted in the screen shown in Figure 5.8. This screen has the beginning of information about *search engines,* which are tools that allow you to ferret out all kinds of information in a variety of methods (more on these valuable tools later in the chapter). Scrolling down the page, you will see more information. Figure 5.9 has the start of valuable information on the Lycos search engine which lets you search for document titles and content. In the six-month period from June to November 1994, this database contained 862,858 documents. This should give you some idea of the tidal wave of information awaiting you on the Web. Figure 5.10 shows the second engine mentioned in Figure 5.9, the Web Crawler.

What is so interesting about following links is that you can float around and create your own pathway on the Net. It is doubtful that any two people have chosen all of the same links

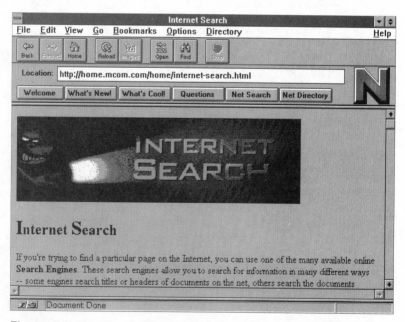

Figure 5.8 Netscape begins to explain how to use search engines.

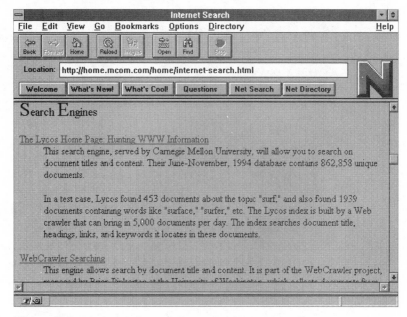

Figure 5.9 Two search engines available via Netscape

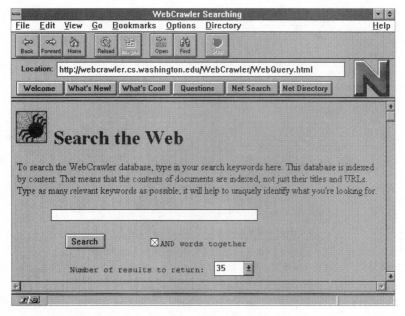

Figure 5.10 It couldn't be easier to use Web Crawler Searching. Just follow the on-screen instructions.

Figure 5.11 Netscape's toolbar, menus, Location field, and buttons

in any two sessions on the Web. Grabbing information in this way is so wonderfully human and eccentric. A jaunt online can be as serendipitous or as logical as you wish it to be. You can even go backward if you like, say to revisit that great URL you whizzed by earlier. Just click on the Back button in the toolbar at the top of the screen isolated in Figure 5.11 (the left-pointing arrow). One click takes you back one step, two clicks take you back two steps, and so forth. To proceed forward again, all you have to do is click the Forward (right-pointing arrow) button in the same way.

Navigating Netscape

Here's a quick survey of the other Netscape buttons:

Top Row Buttons

♦ The Home button will bring Netscape's home page (Figure 5.7) back to your screen. This may be useful for finding Netscape information or for grabbing a copy of its online manual.

♦ Pushing the Reload button brings a fresh copy of the current Web page to your screen. This is useful for when you have gotten a page with marred text due to a bad transfer.

♦ The Images button loads the graphics onto the screen. (Netscape will do all of the graphics for you—you don't need any additional graphics programs to make it work.) You can choose (via the Options menu) to turn on or off Auto Load Images. When it is on and you push the Images button, the graphics for the current page will load. Note that people often have Auto Load Images turned off because browsing the Web is much faster this way—graphics take much longer to compile than just text.

♦ The Open button lets you open a new URL. After you click on the button, you will be given a blank to fill in. Type in the URL you want to access and click on Open.

♦ The Find button lets you perform a keyword search of the Web page currently on your screen. For example, if you are looking at a copy of the latest White House press releases, you may type in a keyword specific to your profession. Netscape will find any occurrences of the word. This allows you to search for profession-specific information much more quickly.

♦ The Stop button halts any transfer of information. You may want to use the Stop button if a Web page is taking too long to load or if you decide to go off online in the middle of a transfer.

Bottom Row Buttons

♦ The Welcome button takes you to the page you see in Figure 5.7. It is an introductory page designed to help you use Netscape and find your way around. Check out the "getting started" online tutorial accessible from this page.

♦ The What's New button links you to updates to the Yanoff meta-list.

♦ The What's Cool button takes you to a list of interesting sites. You may find some business items here, but, you may also find yourself distracted! The day we accessed this button, it listed links to the Virtual Vineyard, (where you can select and purchase wine online), Federal Express (where you can track your Federal Express packages online), and Virtual Flights (for a virtual flight in a Russian Mig 29 fighter jet).

♦ Clicking on the Questions button will take you to a FAQ (*frequently asked questions* list). The FAQ will answer questions about how to use Netscape and Netscape software.

♦ Choosing the Net Search button will take you to the screen you see in Figure 5.8. It lists some of the most popular Web search engines such as Lycos and the Web Crawler.

♦ The Net Directory button takes you to a Yanoff meta-list link.

Netscape Menus

We are not going to cover Netscape's menus comprehensively, but we will cover the menu items that are critical to use for job hunting purposes.

Bookmarks

You say you're still put off by those lengthy URLs, and imagine that you'll wind up who-knows-where because you typed one letter wrong? Then the Bookmarks feature is for you. When you find a spot on the Web that is valuable to you, Netscape gives you the ability to insert a bookmark in the file, thereby saving the document's URL. You can call up the file and access the saved document at any time. Needless to say, using a book-mark list beats typing in those long URLs every time you want to see something. With bookmarks, you only need to type a URL *once*. To add the current document URL to your book-mark list, follow these steps:

1. Click on the Bookmarks menu.
2. When the menu drops down, click on Add Bookmark.

You're all done! Your item will have been added to your hotlist. When you want to see your hotlist, click on Bookmarks again. Then, click on View Bookmarks to see the items you have added to your hotlist. In Figure 5.12, you can see what a hotlist looks like.

As always, use the scroll bars to the right to view all the items. To go to a location, just click on the URL of your choice; then click on the Go To button in the upper right-hand corner of the bookmark list. The Find button will help match keywords, and the Edit button will open a submenu that allows you to delete items from your hotlist.

Opening URLs

If you decide that browsing through links is too casual an approach and too time-consuming, and you don't have a book-

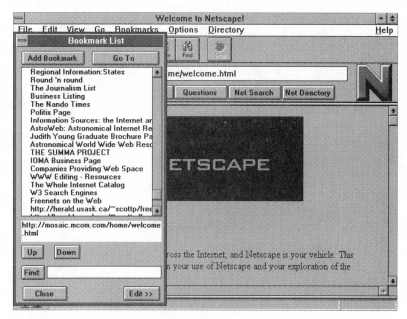

Figure 5.12 A portion of a bookmark list in Netscape

mark list yet, you will need to make use of specific URLs. There are many prize ones listed in Chapters 6 and 7 for you to begin with. Let's take an example from Chapter 6, for our purposes here, the Interactive Employment Network; its address is http://www.espan.com. Here are the steps you'll take to access this excellent career resource.

1. From the Netscape menu, click on either the Open button or the File. (If you click on Open, skip to step 3.)

2. Click on Open Location.

3. A dialog box will open on your screen (see Figure 5.13). Fill in the blank with the complete URL, taking care not to make typos; it must appear exactly as given or your access attempt will fail. If your attempt fails, Netscape will send you a message that says, "Unable to locate host" or "Badly formed address." To type, click the mouse pointer on the blank once, and begin typing. The address may run off the screen, but Netscape will still record it correctly (see Figure 5.14).

4. Press Enter, and in a few moments, Netscape will open the Interactive Employment Network for you.

Figure 5.13 The blank in which to type the URL you want to reach

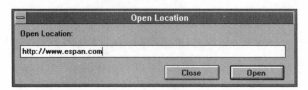

Figure 5.14 The correct address of the Interactive Employment Network. To go to the location, click on Open

Saving the Information You Find

Often, you'll want to save the information you find in a Web document; this is both time- and cost-effective, two objectives you should always keep in mind when job hunting. You have three options available to you: print, save to a file, or send to an email address.

To print information from Netscape, follow these steps:

1. Click on the File option.

2. Click on Print

3. A submenu, shown in Figure 5.15, is where you confirm that the correct printer driver is installed, set the number of pages, and so on.

4. If you need to change any of the print options in this screen, say the wrong printer is identified, click on the Setup button, and you will see a screen similar to Figure 5.16.

5. Here you can change the printer designation, paper size, and orientation. The Options button on this screen, if chosen, will lead to the screen shown in Figure 5.17, where you select whether to print in color (only if you have a color printer), the print speed, and the type of paper.

6. Press OK two times to return to the first screen.

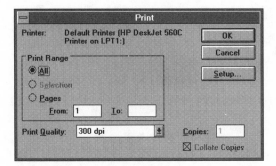

Figure 5.15 The first print submenu of Netscape

Be aware that printing from the Web can take a while when traffic is heavy, so be prepared to wait a few moments for your document.

To send documents to your email address, follow these steps:

1. Choose the File menu option.

2. Click on Mail document.

3. A blank will pop onto your screen. Fill the blank in with your email address, click on Include Document Text, and press Enter. That's it. The Web document will be mailed to whatever email address you give. (Note: no graphics will be mailed.)

If you want to save a document to a file, here are the steps you take:

1. Go to the File menu.

2. Click on Save As.

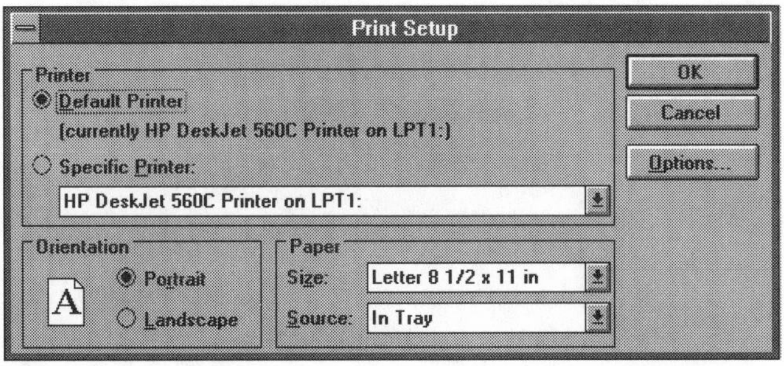

Figure 5.16 The second print submenu of Netscape

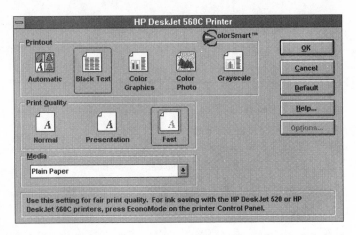

Figure 5.17 The third and last print submenu of Netscape

3. Fill in a file name to save the document to or simply use the default file name that you find already in the blank. You can save the document to your hard drive or to a diskette. We recommend that you always view Web documents before saving to a file to be sure there are no problems that could corrupt your file. To view the Web document from your word processor, go to your file selection option and type in the file name. Press Enter, and see if your word processing program can convert it.

4. Press Enter. Netscape will save your document in a matter of seconds.

Netscape is truly an easy Web browser to use, and we assure you that after you've used it a couple of times, you won't need to refer to this section again.

Directory

Much of what you find in the Directory menu repeats what is available on the toolbar buttons (the buttons provide quicker access). But an option only available via this menu is the Go To Newsgroups option. This is how you access the Usenet newsgroups from Netscape.

To get to Usenet, just go to the Directory menu, choose the Go To Newsgroups option, and click. You'll be presented with a screen that lists three newsgroups for you automatically: **news.announce.newusers**, **new.newusers.questions**, and **news.answers**. To subscribe to a newsgroup, fill in the blank provided. (See Chapter 7 for a list of job-related Usenet groups and their addresses.) Press Enter. Netscape will then print the name of the newsgroup in your list as a link. To access any of your subscribed newsgroups from Netscape, just click on the name of the group.

Once you're in Usenet, you'll see immediately that to post, you click on post, and so on for all actions. Usenet is very intuitive and easy to use from Netscape. Usenet from Netscape, however, is very slow. The information takes more time transferring because of the graphical interface.

Options

On the options menu are several useful items. The first item you will discover is the Preferences item. This option lets you direct Netscape as to how you want it to accomplish certain tasks, like using Telnet. Note: *When you first begin using Netscape, you will not need to set any of Netscape's preferences.* We recommend that you familiarize yourself with the Web for a few months before using this menu option. The technical wizards at Netscape suggest that you read their online manual thoroughly. All information about preference-setting is included.

Other menu options you will find in the Options menu are Show Toolbar, Show Location, Show Directory Buttons, Show Security Colorbar, Auto Load Images, and Show FTP File Information. As a new navigator, we recommend that you keep everything "on." To turn these options off and on, just click on the option with your mouse. If you see a check mark beside the option, the option is on; if there is no check mark, the option is turned off.

The toolbar is the top set of buttons you see in Figure 5.11. The location is the long blank in which the URL of the document you are currently viewing is shown. It's just below the toolbar. The directory buttons are the small ones below the toolbar. The Show FTP File Information lets you see the transfer process as it's occurring. When you navigate, you'll see this information at the bottom of the screen, in the left-hand corner.

Look ahead to Figure 5.28. There, we've turned off all of the options in order to get more text onto the screen. You can see that the only thing showing is the menu bar and the title of the home page just above it. As you can see, the button bars really make navigating a lot easier. To turn everything back on in this screen, we went into the Options menu and clicked on the options again.

The only option we recommend that you turn off with any frequency is the Auto Load Images option, because it makes navigation faster. Loading images takes longer than loading text. But with the images off, you won't see the graphics.

LYNX

If you are accessing the Web via a basic Internet account, then you will probably be using Lynx as your browser. Lynx is a very simple text-based Web browser, and, if you don't have Windows, it is your way out of a major computer upgrade.

Most of you will find Lynx already installed by your sysop. This means that when you purchase an Internet account, the sysop will have put Lynx on the menu as an option. (The Lynx program is actually running on the Internet provider's machine—you won't have to pay extra to use it, and you won't need to download it to your machine.) Look at your opening menu. Does it say "World Wide Web" anywhere? If so, then that menu option will likely use Lynx to get you on the Web. If you are a Delphi user, you can find Lynx by typing "go Internet Gopher" from the main menu. You will find Lynx at menu option number 18.

Telnet is an Internet and Web tool that allows you to connect to remote computers. You will find Telnet on the network itself; there's no need to purchase it. The benefit of Telnetting is that you can access machines all over the world through your local Internet connection.

The process of Telnetting is very simple. The first thing you need is the machine name you're going to telnet to. Machine names are like the first part of URL addresses. They can appear as **122.323.1.444** *or* **adams.poly.edu** *(relevant Telnet addresses are listed in this book when you need them). Once you know the address, find a Telnet prompt. For* *most of you, this will mean logging on to your Internet account and looking at the main menu. You should see a Telnet option. If you don't, call your Internet provider and ask where the Telnet option of your account is located. When you locate your Telnet option, choose it, and you will be at a Telnet prompt. This looks like:*

Telnet>

Your cursor will be blinking to the immediate right of the prompt. Type in the address you want to reach and press Return, for example:

Telnet> adams.poly.edu

If you do not see a new screen, type the word Open in front of your Telnet address, as:

Telnet> open adams.poly.edu

Press Return. One of these methods will work for you. Once you arrive at the remote host, you will often be prompted for a login. If a login is required, you will be told by the person listing the address for you. (We always list the logins when they are required.) Many times, the login is actually printed in an information screen for you so that you may log in without any help from a book or listing.

Once you're in the remote system, you will be given instructions on how to get back to your original menu listed for you on the screen. Usually, the logoff command is **logoff**, **Quit**, *or something very similar. You can always press the question mark for a list of commands while you're using Telnet.*

If you don't find a Web or a Lynx option from your menu, then you can Telnet to a public Web site. Recall that Telnet is another Internet tool that allows you to log on to remote computers and, using a set of simple commands, retrieve data.: Here's how to use Telnet to a public Web site:

1. Log on to your Internet account and choose the Telnet option.

2. At the Telnet prompt, type:

   ukanix.cc.ukans.edu

3. Press Enter, and wait until a new screen comes up.

4. When you are prompted for a login, type WWW and press Enter. In a few moments, the Lynx opening screen will appear.

Once you are on Lynx, you can access the complete Lynx user's guide by opening the following URL:

http://www.cc.ukans.edu/lynx_help/Lynx_users_guide.html

You will find this guide, written by the authors of the Lynx program, to be extremely thorough and helpful. If your basic Internet account doesn't have Lynx, you can even give your sysop this address and request that he or she puts Lynx on the system for you. All the information they will need is in this document.

This is a list of Telnet addresses you can use to access the WWW, where you can find Lynx or a variation thereof.

Academy of Science, Slovakia
sun.uakom.cz
login: WWW

CERN; Geneva, Switzerland
info.cern.ch
login: WWW
Note that this site is often overloaded with connections; so always try other Telnet sites first.

Center for Computing, University of Arizona, Tucson, Arizona
lanka.ccit.arizona.edu
login: WWW

Computer Network Center, Hungary
fserve.kfki.hu
login: WWW

Finnish University Research Network
info.funet.fi
login:WWW

Hebrew University of Jerusalem
vms.huji.ac.il
login: WWW

Legal Information Institute,
Cornell Law School
fatty.law.cornell.edu
login: WWW

New Jersey Institute of Technology
www.njit.edu
login: WWW

University of Kansas
ukanaix.cc.ukans.edu
login: WWW

Lynx Navigation

Lynx, as mentioned, is a very simple browser. Most of its commands are self-explanatory, but the following list identifies those you'll need immediately. For the lowdown on all Lynx commands, refer to the Lynx user guide at the URL just given.

?   Help
q   Quit
a   Add the current link to bookmark file
g   Open a new URL
m   Return to the main screen (home)
p   Print or mail a file
v   View your bookmark file
=   Show file and link information

To navigate in Lynx, use the up and down arrow keys. To move from one highlighted bar (link), as in Figure 5.18, press the down arrow to move forward one link; press the up arrow to move to the previous link. When you land on a link you want to see, press Enter. Lynx will then move you to the new location. Lynx screens are in black and white, so the highlight bar will look like a moving rectangle as you navigate. Note in Figure 5.18 the convenient navigation help at the bottom of the screen.

Opening URLs and Creating Bookmarks with Lynx

Like Netscape, Lynx makes it possible to directly access a URL and maintain a bookmark list for greater efficiency as you

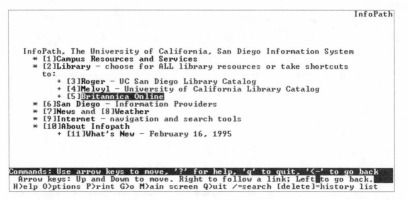

Figure 5.18 The highlighted area is what Lynx uses to follow links. To activate the bar, press Enter.

spend more time on the Web. Here's how to do both with Lynx.

To open a URL:

1. From any screen in Lynx, press g, for go.

2. Fill in the blank that appears near the bottom of your screen. Be sure to type in the complete URL, again, taking care not to make mistakes. Notice at the bottom of Figure 5.19, we've again typed in the URL for the Interactive Employment Network.

3. Press Enter. After a few moments, Lynx will take you to your destination.

To create a Lynx bookmark list:

1. When you have something on-screen that you want to *bookmark*, press a. The link will automatically be added to your file without any other effort from you.

2. To later access your bookmarked files, simply press v, and using your up and down arrows, choose a file. When the highlighted bar is on a link you want to see, press Enter.

Printing and Mailing Lynx Files

To save or print a Lynx document, press p, and a screen (shown in Figure 5.20) will appear that asks you what you want to do: save the material to a local file, mail the file to yourself, or print to the screen. At the bottom of the screen , Lynx asks

```
                                                              InfoPath

 InfoPath, The University of California, San Diego Information System
    * [1]Campus Resources and Services
    * [2]Library - choose for ALL library resources or take shortcuts
      to:
        + [3]Roger - UC San Diego Library Catalog
        + [4]Melvyl - University of California Library Catalog
        + [5]Britannica Online
    * [6]San Diego - Information Providers
    * [7]News and [8]Weather
    * [9]Internet - navigation and search tools
    * [10]About Infopath
        + [11]What's New - February 16, 1995



URL to open: http://www.espan.com
  Arrow keys:
 H)elp O)ptions P)rint G)o M)ain screen Q)uit /=search [delete]=history list
```

Figure 5.19 The URL for the Interactive Employment Network being accessed via Lynx

you to enter a valid Internet mail address. To do this, simply begin typing. The cursor is automatically positioned in the right place for you to begin typing in your email address.

We like the Mail the file to yourself option, because after filling in the blank with the address you want the document sent to and pressing Enter, Lynx sends the document immediately. It takes less than 30 seconds.

Printing to the screen is a little more complicated. If you choose the Print to the Screen option, the Lynx program will type the document to your screen rapidly. And, if you have a capture file open, it will save the text Lynx typed to your screen. Then, you can print it out later. If you want to do this, you will need to open a capture file on your modem software. Every

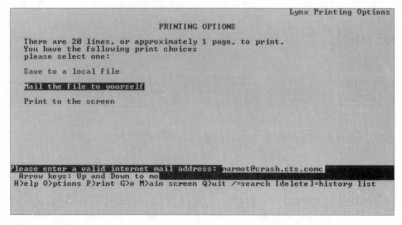

Figure 5.20 The Lynx Printing Options screen.

communications software program is different, but usually, you open a capture file by finding the File option, then the Capture Text option. (Be sure to read your software documentation software before you do this, in case it differs in any significant manner.) Then you name the file and press Enter. Lynx will print the text to your screen quickly. Later, you can go offline and read the captured file.

The final option on this screen, Save to a local file, should be used only after you have checked with your local sysop. It is almost always better to mail the file to yourself or print to your screen than to use this option, as this choice takes up valuable disk space on your Internet account—for which you are usually charged.

If you have no other means of accessing the Web, Lynx is a great tool. Even if you do have access to the Web via a SLIP account using Netscape, consider using Lynx if you are in a hurry to find text-only information. Because you can't see graphics with Lynx, it is much faster than a graphical browser.

OTHER GRAPHICAL BROWSERS

Mosaic and Cello

If Andy Warhol was right, that fame for most people lasts a scant 15 minutes, popularity on the information superhighway must be measured in milliseconds. Mosaic, a very capable and (briefly) popular graphical browser, was superseded by Netscape within *one month* of the latter's release, thanks to its faster, simpler and more efficient interface.

Nevertheless, Mosaic is still a good graphical browser that comes in versions for Macintosh, Microsoft Windows, and X-Windows. If you want to try Mosaic or if you just want complete information about how to use Mosaic, open the following location:

http://www.usc.edu/NCSAMosaicHome.html

Cello, another graphical browser that you may hear about, never caught on like Mosaic, and certainly never achieved the acceptance of Netscape, but it does still provide a decent graphical interface.

For more information on Cello, use the following URL, which contains complete information on where to get Cello and how to use it:

http://www.law.cornell.edu:80/cello/cellocfg.html

For more information about other Web browsers not covered here, access this location:

http://www.w3.org/hypertext/WWW/Clients.html

WEB SEARCH ENGINES

A search engine is software designed specifically to help you search the Internet more effectively and efficiently. Instead of following link after link with a Web browser, Web search engines let you type in a keyword or sets of keywords, and they find the relevant information for you.

Two years ago, these wonders were not available—at least not in the quantity and quality of today's. This is another area of tremendous growth on the Web, so always be on the lookout for others to add to the list of our favorites given here. And the good news is, this software is downloadable from the Internet—no expensive packages to buy.

The URLs of four Web search engines we particularly like are:

Web Crawler

http://www.biotech.washington.edu/WebCraw ler/WebQuery.html

Lycos

http://fuzine.mt.cs.cmu.edu/mlm/lycos-home.html

Galaxy

http://galaxy.einet.net/www/www.html

World Wide Web Worm

http://www.cs.colorado.edu/home/mchryan/wwww.html

And here is the address of a search engine meta-list, shown in Figure 5.21, which is not just one search engine but a site listing almost every search engine available.

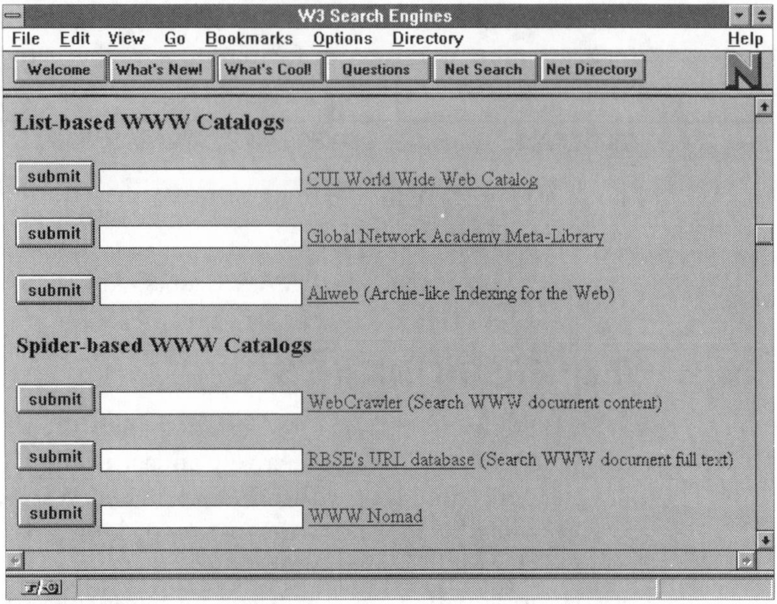

Figure 5.21 Web search engines, as seen from a meta-list containing many Web searchers

Search Engine Meta-List

http://ageninfo.tamu.edu/meta-index.html

How Search Engines Work

Looking at Figure 5.21 you will notice the screen divided into two sections: Spider-based WWW Catalogs and List-based WWW Catalogs. These terms refer to how a Web search engine looks for material. List-based search engines look through a previously determined list of materials for your keyword, such as a particular catalog. Spider-based Web search engines literally crawl through the entire network looking for your keywords. They don't limit their search to one catalog or list.

Other search engines search in-depth at one Web server, move on to the next, and repeat the process until they have searched through a huge number of Web servers. Others search the Web in a breadth-first manner, accessing just a few files from each site before moving on to the next one. These engines also look for documents in different ways. Some search by URL, others by document content.

Fortunately, all of this variance is invisible to you, the end user. The only thing you see when the search engines are busy hunting through the network is a blissfully blank screen.

To operate a Web search engine , follow this procedure:

1. Log onto your Internet account and access the World Wide Web. Once you are on the Web, go through the appropriate steps to open a new URL. (From Netscape, go to Open Location, type in the URL, and press Enter. From Lynx, press g, type in the URL, and press Enter.)

2. Type your keywords in the blank. Every Web search engine uses a simple fill-in-the-blank method. See Figure 5.21.

3. Press Enter or click on Submit.

That's it. The search engine does all of the research for you. In a few moments, the engine will return a list of results based on your keyword(s). Then, all you have to do to complete your search is to browse the documents the engine found for you.

Always use more than one search engine to look for material. We like to use Web Crawler and Galaxy, because we always get a good mix of information with these two. You may, after experimentation, find that you prefer using a different combination of search engines. As an experiment, try the same search in more than one search engine. You will see as you look over the results that some documents have been found by all of the search engines, but that other sources were found by only one search engine. This is a reflection of the different methods used by these engines and the reason you should always use at least two different search engines. For detailed information about how each search engine works, access the information from the search engine's URL.

During peak business hours, most search engines are very busy. You may need to try the most popular engines, like Lycos, during nonbusiness hours (early morning or later in the evening).

A Sample Search

Let's see how these engines work by performing a sample search. We'll start with the Web Crawler and use the keyword *conservation*. Then we'll use Galaxy to do the same thing so that you can compare the results from each. (Note: In Chapter 6, we'll use the same keyword to practice using gopher, and you can then compare those results with these to get a real idea of how all these tools operate.)

1. Type in the URL for Web Crawler:

   http://www.biotech.washington.edu/WebCrawler/
   WebQuery.html

2. Fill in the Web Crawler search blank with our keyword (see Figure 5.22). Because we want to limit the results for our purposes here, we chose 35 in the "Number of results to return" box at the bottom of the screen. (We could have clicked on 10, 100, or 1,000.)

3. Click on Search and wait.

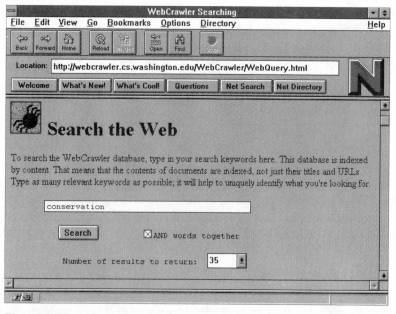

Figure 5.22 Here we have typed in our keyword *conservation*. We will click on Search to start the search engine.

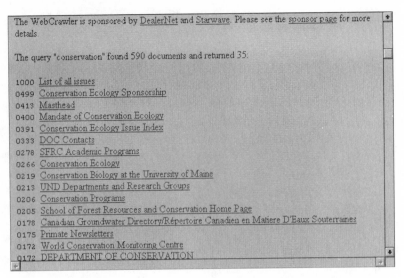

The WebCrawler is sponsored by DealerNet and Starwave. Please see the sponsor page for more details.

The query "conservation" found 590 documents and returned 35:

1000 List of all issues
0499 Conservation Ecology Sponsorship
0413 Masthead
0400 Mandate of Conservation Ecology
0391 Conservation Ecology Issue Index
0333 DOC Contacts
0278 SFRC Academic Programs
0266 Conservation Ecology
0219 Conservation Biology at the University of Maine
0213 UND Departments and Research Groups
0206 Conservation Programs
0205 School of Forest Resources and Conservation Home Page
0178 Canadian Groundwater Directory/Répertoire Canadien en Matiere D'Eaux Souterraines
0175 Primate Newsletters
0172 World Conservation Monitoring Centre
0172 DEPARTMENT OF CONSERVATION

Figure 5.23 Results from Web Crawler search on *conservation*

4. The top 35 results shown in Figure 5.23 (scroll down for the rest of the list), can be printed, saved, or accessed immediately by clicking on those we want to view.

We clicked on DOC Contacts, #6 in the list, which looked like a good place for digging up names and phone numbers. In Figure 5.24, you can see what we found when we followed that link.

Now, let's see how Galaxy performs.

1. Type in the Galaxy URL,

   http://galaxy.einet.net/WWW/WWW.html

2. Fill in the Galaxy search blank with the keyword, as in Figure 5.25.

3. Press Enter. (Whenever you don't see a Submit button on a Web searcher, just press Enter to start the search.)

4. Figure 5.26 shows a portion of the 73 results from the Galaxy Web search on the keyword *conservation*. You can print the list out or begin to browse it.

Following the first link we see, The World Wide Web Virtual Library Forestry, which has a score of 1,000, we arrive at the veritable gold mine of information you can see in Figure 5.27.

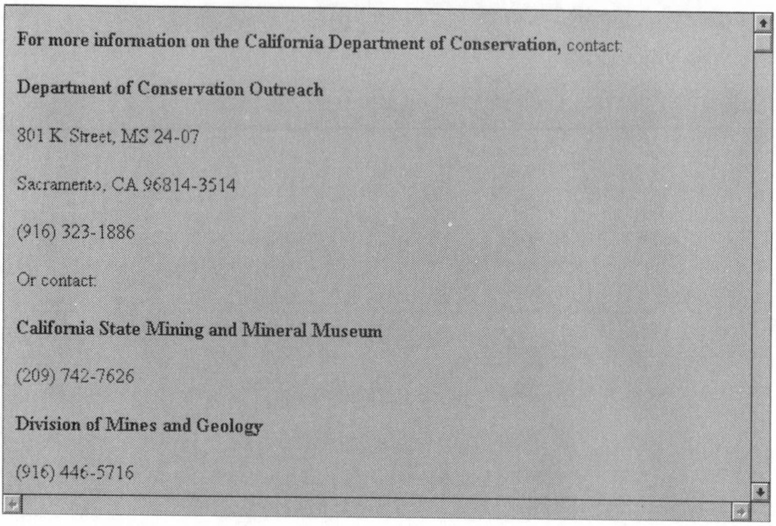

For more information on the California Department of Conservation, contact:

Department of Conservation Outreach

301 K Street, MS 24-07

Sacramento, CA 96814-3514

(916) 323-1886

Or contact:

California State Mining and Mineral Museum

(209) 742-7626

Division of Mines and Geology

(916) 446-5716

Figure 5.24 Following the DOC Contacts link

The score in a Galaxy search, which you can see to the right of each entry in Figure 5.26, refers to the "fit" of the document to your keyword. The higher the score (the maximum is 1,000) the better the chances that the document will give you what you're looking for. We must admit, though, we have found some excellent documents with a low score. So be sure to browse any document that interests you, despite its score.

Other search engines, such as Lycos and the World Wide Web Worm, are every bit as easy to use as Web Crawler and Galaxy. Just follow the same process we used in the steps for Web Crawler and Galaxy.

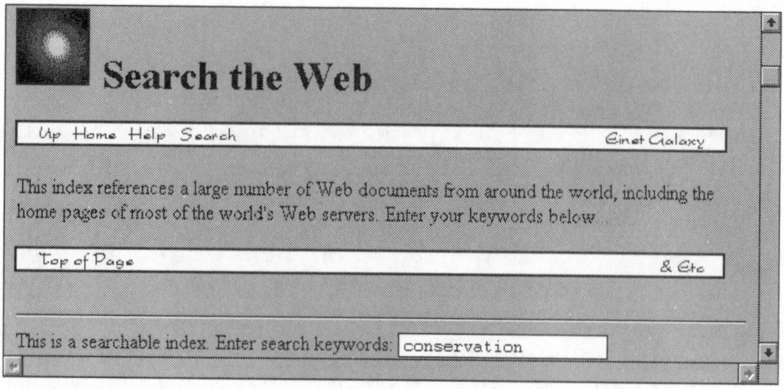

Search the Web

Up Home Help Search   Einet Galaxy

This index references a large number of Web documents from around the world, including the home pages of most of the world's Web servers. Enter your keywords below.

Top of Page   & Etc

This is a searchable index. Enter search keywords: conservation

Figure 5.25 Searching the Web using the Galaxy search engine

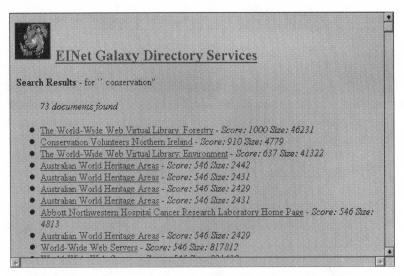

Figure 5.26 Results of the Galaxy Web search on the keyword *conservation*

And keep on trying new search engines. All it will take is a few moments of your time. Even if you decide you don't like a particular search engine, at least explore it once in a while just so you won't miss the unexpected treasure.

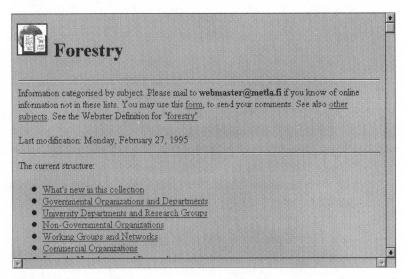

Figure 5.27 The links here appear invaluable to anyone interested in forestry.

HOME PAGES AND MULTIMEDIA RESUMES

A picture is worth a thousand words, or so they say, and this is the idea behind home pages. Instead of just writing about yourself or your company or organization, you can add photos, graphics, sound clips, and video to embroider your words and give them more punch. And, of course, when you're looking for a job, the more you've got going for you, the better. Your home page should be a place where people can go to get more information about you. For example, if you have sent your ASCII resume to an employer, you will want to have your URL listed on the resume for the employer to contact for more information. If the employer is interested in you, he or she will type in your URL and take a look at your home page. Keep in mind that adding your URL address to your ASCII or paper resume is a major trend right now.

A *home page*, simply defined, is an electronic presence, where individuals, corporations, small businesses, government agencies, organizations, even cities stake their claim on the Web. Currently, there are many thousands of home pages on the Web, and a flood of new ones go up every day. With all of this activity, you may be wondering how your home page will ever get noticed. That's what this section is all about: how to develop an effective home page that will help you achieve the online goals you've set for yourself, whether it's finding a job, consulting with experts, or networking for future reference.

A home page may contain whatever the designer of the page wants, including audio, graphics, text, and video in any combination. Hypertext links on a Web page lead to other documents: samples of articles you've written, graphics, your email address, and so on. Remember Joseph Evans' resume from Chapter 3, which included his photograph? Figure 5.28 shows another portion of his home page. And, as you can see by the underlined segments, clicking on any one of these leads to other aspects of Evans' background, skills, and interests. Figure 5.29 shows the start of a research project listed under the third link, titled My Research Interests.

If you want to add images, video, or audio to your home page, this is not something that will just magically happen. You must have the graphics files, digitized video clips, and digitized audio files to add. You can find and purchase these kinds of

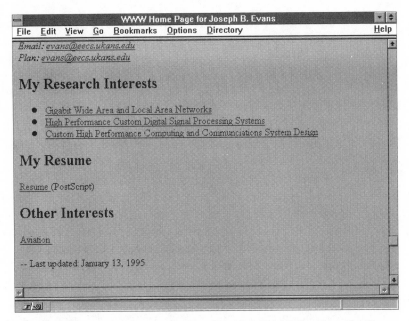

Figure 5.28 Professional links available from the Joseph Evans home page

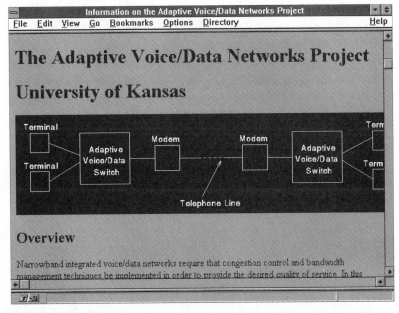

Figure 5.29 The result of following the third link on Joseph Evans' home page

files in computer stores. If you have the right equipment, you can also create these files at home. (For example, if you have a scanner, you can scan your picture into your computer. You will be able to use this as a graphic file for your home page. If you have a video translator and editor, you can work with video files.)

Getting the right equipment involves a lot of shopping around and expensive computer upgrading. We do not recommend that, as a beginner, you add audio or video to your home page. We do, however, recommend beginning with graphics. You'll find boxes of electronic "clip art" in almost every computer store. Each piece of clip art will have a file name; if you find something you want to add to your home page, you'll be all set. Be sure to get a booklet that shows what each piece of clip art looks like in the package, in case you're not able to view the graphics in your computer program. Many new word processors allow you to import and view clip art; others don't. Clip art packages can cost anywhere from $10 to $50, and usually include hundreds of images.

When you purchase your clip art, you may also want to ask about an inexpensive graphics viewer. This is software that will let you view the graphics files on your computer. These programs usually cost about $35 to $100.

If you want to go all out, you can purchase a computer graphics program that lets you draw, paint, and create your own graphic files. These programs currently cost from about $100 to $350. Ask for a full computer graphics program at the store.

Recently, the first Web-only resume database was created. This database, the Internet Business Directory, is a place where people in all professions from all over the world can put their Web or multimedia resumes—for free! (The Internet Business Directory is sponsored by Internet Business Services. It is a place where high-tech businesses can, for a fee, list their home pages.) Figure 5.30 is an example of one found on the database, belonging to Brigitte Poussart. (Note the prominence of the career objective section of this resume. Recall from Chapter 3 how important this element is to your presentation.) Earlier in this book, you saw one of her photographs of Quebec. Here is another portion of her home page, her resume written in hypertext. Look for more of these Web home page

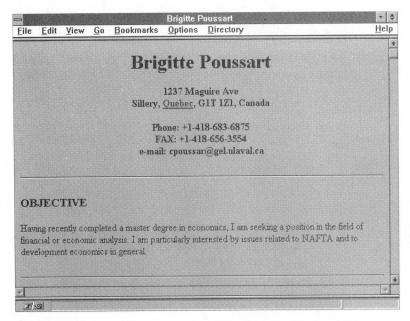

Figure 5.30 A sample resume from the Internet Business Directory, a free Web-only resume database

"corrals" in the near future as people find ways to organize themselves on the Web.

To access the Internet Business Directory resume section, use this address:

http://ibd.ar.com/Resume

You'll be happy to know that many businesses, too, put their home pages in this directory, making it a doubly valuable place for you to visit.

DESIGNING YOUR OWN HOME PAGE

General Page Tips

The trouble with something so full of possibilities for creativity, like designing a home page, is that people often have a tendency to go overboard. We caution you against overkill in your design. Like someone who is overdressed, the focus turns to the costume and away from the person underneath. Your goal is to be noticed, of course, but for your skills and experience, not because you have the most elaborate or exotic home page. In general, remember Proust: Less is more. We suggest that before you even begin your own, you "shop" other home pages; make notes as to what you like and what put you off. Which ones were the easiest to read? Which ones were so graphics-heavy and took so long to upload that you canceled them before ever seeing the completed page? Here are a few guidelines to consider:

◆ The average length of a home page is from one to two screens of online text and/or graphics.

◆ Break up your home page by subject as frequently as you wish, and make sure to provide round-trip links; for example, if you write a home page that links to your resume, don't forget to include a link back to your home page from your resume.

◆ Don't go wild with graphics. Anything too graphics-heavy will encourage home users to abort the download. Never forget that many people look at the Web without images or with their online images turned off to speed things up, so you may be wasting your time anyway, (unless, of course, your profession requires that you display your ability to use graphics effectively). When you do include graphics, make sure they "mean" something in regard to your resume; and aim for clean designs that don't scream at the viewer. To that end, be aware that yellows and oranges don't work well in large quantities in online graphics. Cool, clear colors seem to translate best online. Reserve yellows and other brilliant warm colors for accents.

◆ The same admonition applies to audio and video files. These files, too, take *forever* to download. Use these files as you see fit, yes, but don't make your document depend on them.

If you decide, for whatever reason, that you don't want to create your own home page, you can hire someone to write one for you. Skip to the section, "Hiring Someone to Spin Your Web Page." This is not to say that you should relinquish responsibility for its design. We recommend that you have ideas of what you want and don't want, and be explicit

in your instructions to your ghost home page writer, in the same way you would be with someone helping you to write a paper resume

Home Page Anatomy

Before we get to the nuts and bolts, we're going to add a couple of more terms and concepts to your expanding online vocabulary. First is something called HTML, which stands for *hypertext markup language*. This is nothing more than the formatting language used to create hypertext links. HTML, much like your word processor, inserts codes that set the attributes, such as boldfacing and italics, for the text in your document. The codes are visible only as you write in HTML, but when the Web document is displayed, you see the page formatted and designed as you intended. HTML also lets you set the links to other URLS online. This is what separates HTML from regular word-processing programs, and it's what makes the Web so special.

Home pages are made up of a body and a head in one to an infinite number of files. The body and the head are created using HTML *tags*, which are markers identified by the "open" (<) and "close" (>) brackets. These tags operate like doors to the information enclosed between them. (You'll see this clearly in a moment.)

The Head

In a home page, there are two levels, one of which is not visible to the online viewer. This invisible level, usually of instructions, is called the *head*. The head contains information about the document that is not displayed in the online document, including the document title, the document's URL, and links to other documents. The title of your document should never be more than five or six words describing the contents of the document; for example, the title of your Web resume could be "Mary O' Leary, electrical engineer" or "Resume of Joe Smith," or even just your name.

The Body

The *body* contains the part of the document or page that is displayed to the online viewer. The tags used in the body define headings, line breaks, lists, menus, paragraphs, and graphics; and they specify font attributes such as boldface and italics. Your goal should be to make the body organized and readable, and to identify links to other documents.

Step by Step to Your Own Home Page

A Beginner's Template

The following is a basic template that will get you started. If you follow these instructions carefully, you will end up with a basic Web page. After learning how to do this simple home page, you'll be able to get creative and make your own snazzier version.

The template you'll be copying is shown in Figure 5.31 To reproduce it, open your word processing program, such as WordPerfect or Word, and simply begin typing a new document as if you were writing a regular letter. Type everything exactly as shown, including the open and close brackets that indicate tags (< >). Look at Figure 5.32 to see how this template looks when viewed with a Web browser.

Be aware that some tags (see Title, HTML, Body, and Address in the template) require a slash mark following the open bracket in the second, or closing, tag. For a complete list of tags, access an html primer. A good one to look at is available at:

http://www.ncsa.uiuc.edu/General/Internet/WWW/HTMLPrimer.html

Now let's examine the template line by line. As you see, the entire document is bounded by the <HTML> tag; it opens and closes the document. The next element is the head tag; it indicates that this portion of the document will remain unseen when displayed online.

Next is the title tag. What you write between the title tags will show in the text bar at the top of your Web Browser. Refer back to Figure 5.9, for example, where the title shows up as "Internet Search" which you can see at the very top of the figure.

Next in the template, the head portion of the page is closed with </HEAD>. This is followed by the body tag. <BODY> indicates that you are in the "guts" of the document, and that

```
<HTML>
<HEAD>
<TITLE>My HTML TEMPLATE</TITLE>
</HEAD>
<BODY>
<H1>My Resume</H1>
<HR>
<H2>My Qualifications</H2>
Paragraph 1.
<P>
Paragraph 2.
<P>
<HR>
<ADDRESS>me@hostname.com</ADDRESS>
</BODY>
</HTML>
```

Figure 5.31 A basic HTML resume template

what you write now will be displayed on screen. (Of course, the tags themselves aren't displayed, but everything between them is.) Remember, once you are in the body portion of a Web page, the HTML tags that you add format the page and make it look good. In our second sample template, you will see body tags that also create hypertext links. There are a variety of tags you can choose from.

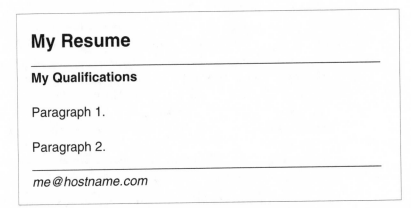

Figure 5.32 The template viewed with a Web browser

To create the large heading that starts our document, we used the <H> tag, which controls headings. The <H> tag comes in six levels. <H1> is the largest size typeface, and they decrease in size to level 6. You can use any combination of <H> tags in your document.

Next notice the <HR> tag. This tag inserts a horizontal line across your page, as you can see in Figure 5.32. We like to use this tag to separate important sections of text. (Note that this tag does not require a slash to close with.)

Since HTML uses tags to format text, you must tell it when a new paragraph begins. The <P> or paragraph tag is used to indicate a new paragraph. (This tag does not require a slash to close it.)

In the template, the lines Paragraph 1 and Paragraph 2 are where you will write the actual contents of your resume. Finally, the <ADDRESS> tag at the end of the page is very important. If you don't include your email address, people will not be able to find you.

Make It Your Own

At this point, take the time to fill in your own data between the title tags, the header tags, and the address tags. Again, in place of the paragraph lines, fill in the details of your resume. You may use as many paragraphs as you need, but be sure to precede and close each with the <P> tag. Once this is done, save the document to ASCII. (Save it to a diskette as well as to your computer's hard drive.) Then all you have to do is mail the diskette to your system operator. He or she will place your home page on the Web server or system for you. If you don't know who the sysop is, call your Internet provider. Ask what the charge is for *housing* Web pages (more on this in a moment) and ask who you can send your completed home page to. (Tell them you'll be mailing a diskette.) Your Internet provider will be able to give you the appropriate contact name.

Here's a brief review of the steps to create a basic home page:

1. Open a blank document on your word processing program.

2. Type in the HTML template exactly as you see it in our example.

3. Personalize the template with your own information.

4. Save the file in ASCII to a diskette.

5. Give the diskette to your system operator.

That's it, a very basic Web page. Of course, you'll no doubt want to learn how to add some more creative elements to your home page—after all, that's one of the benefits of these hi-tech resumes, so read on.

A Bells and Whistles Template

Once you have created your basic resume in HTML based on the basic template, you can expand your knowledge to create a snazzier Web document. Following, you will see a fictitious resume we created using HTML. We've included many elements that you may want to add to your Web resume or home page, including graphics and links to other documents. The finished Web page is shown first, in Figure 5.33; the codes used to achieve it are shown in Figure 5.34. Then we explain what everything means.

Look at the first part of the Abigail Basset home page. You'll notice that the tag <HTML> opens the document, as with our basic template. Next, you'll see the <HEAD> tag, which indicates that what you're about to type will not be displayed in the completed document.

Following the <HEAD> tag is our pair of <TITLE> tags. Obviously, in place of Abigail D. Basset-Vocalist you would type the name you want for your document. Remember to add the backslash to the second and closing <TITLE> tag. For your title tag, add a short but descriptive set of words that suits you. This completes the head portion of the Web page, so we close it with </HEAD>.

Next, we open the body of the Web page by typing the <BODY> tag. From this point on, everything will be displayed online. The heading tag comes next. This is the tag that determines the font size of everything displayed online. We chose <H3> tag for Abigail's name. To display your name in a larger font, choose <H1> or <H2>; for a smaller font, choose <H4> to <H6>.

Because we did not want the rest of the address to be large, we simply typed in the address with no tags. Type in your address here, adding your phone and fax numbers if you wish.

Abigail D. Basset
P.O. Box 849
Cardiff by the Sea, CA
92007

 Vocalist

• Member of the Metropolitan Opera Chorus since 2001.

• Concertized in extensive tours of Europe, Asia and the United States from 1999-present.

• Extensive chamber experience in **French art song**.

To see my complete **resume** and **discography**, click **here**.

To see a **photo** of me in performance, click **here**.

Other links to vocal-related documents:

The **Vocalist Page** is an excellent jumping-off point for information about opera, opera festivals, and other vocal information. The **Yahoo** list has many musical links for you to follow.

If you would like to send me feedback regarding this page, or if you have any helpful information, send it to *marmot@crash.cts.com*

Thanks for visiting my home page!

Figure 5.33 Making use of attributes to highlight a Web home page

The next tag you see is the <HR> tag. Remember from the basic template that this tag will create a horizontal line across the page. Now you will find a new tag, <PRE>. It records hard returns and spacing information. This is how we created a double space in Abigail Basset's Web page. If you want three spaces in your Web page, type the <PRE> tag and push the Return key three times and add the closing tag, </PRE>.

```
<HTML>
<HEAD>
<TITLE>Abigail D. Basset - Vocalist</TITLE>
</HEAD>
<BODY>
<H3>Abigail D. Basset</H3>
P.O. Box 849
Cardiff by the Sea, CA
92007
<HR>
<PRE>

</PRE>
<IMG SRC="notes.gif" ALT="Music Notes"> <H2>Vocalist</H2>
<PRE>

</PRE>
<UL>
<LI>Member of the Metropolitan Opera Chorus since 2001.
<LI>Concertized in extensive tours of Europe, Asia, and the United States from
1999-present.
<LI>Extensive chamber experience in <B>French art song.</B>
</UL>
To see my complete <B>resume</B> and <B>discography</B>, click
<A HREF="resume.html">here</A>
To see a <B>photos</B> of me in performance, click <A
HREF="photo.gif">here</A>
<PRE>

</PRE>
Other links to vocal-related documents:
<P>
The <A HREF="http://caruso.met.edu/usr5/vocal/vocal.homepage.html">
Vocalist Page</A> is an excellent jumping-off point for information about opera,
opera festivals and other vocal information. The
<A HREF="http://harvard.edu/yahoo/vocal/music.html">Yahoo</A>
list has many musical links for you to follow.
<P>
If you would like to send me feedback regarding this page, or if you have any
helpful information, send it to <ADDRESS>marmot@crash.cts.com</ADDRESS>
<P>
Thanks for visiting my home page!
```

Figure 5.34 The codes used to create the home page in the previous figure

Now you'll find another new tag, the graphics tag. Adding an image is just as easy as any other format tag. The basic form is: <IMG src= "my-note.gif">. This tells HTML to insert the gif file, or graphical file, my-note.gif. Note: If you want a photograph in your Web page, you must scan it in. If you don't have access to a scanner, you can use standard clip art files to add graphics to your resume. Netscape users will actually see the graphic image, whereas Lynx users only see text.

Next you see a <PRE> tag again, simply because we wanted to double space here. Again, you can adjust the number of spaces you want by hitting Enter for as many spaces as you desire.

The next tag, <UL>, creates a bulleted list. Following the <UL>tag are the <LI> tags, each of which includes text following each bullet. Note that after we finished the list, we closed the list with the </UL> tag. (Note the backslash.)

Now notice that surrounding the words "French art song," "resume," "discography," and "photos" is the <B> tag, which directs the computer to boldface the text between the open and close brackets text.

The anchor —<A>—tag is next, and it's an important one, as it creates the highlighted/underlined text in the document that, when clicked, transports you to a new location or document; this is the tag that creates those all-important hyperlinks. By creating an anchor tag, you are automatically creating a highlighted and underlined link. In the Abigail Basset Web page, the tag: <A HREF="resume. html">here</A> HREF= "resume.html" is the part of the anchor that tells HTML where to find the new document. This will be the document's file name; in this case, the new document is located at "resume.html". Of course, fill in the actual file name of your documents here. After you've listed the file name of the document you want to link to, then the anchor is closed with the >. Next comes the text "here" as it will be seen highlighted and underlined in the document. And, finally, the entire anchor is closed with an </A>. If you want different text highlighted, simply type a different word or phrase in the last portion of the tag.

The next anchor is of a photo. You handle photo anchors exactly the same way you handle the resume anchor. The only difference is the file name for the photo. In this case, the anchor is: <A HREF="photo.gif">here</A>. Again, you will add the correct file name for your document. And as a review, "here" is what will be highlighted.

Following our paragraph tag are two more anchor tags, which lead to two other Web sites. If you don't want to link to other sites, of course, you will leave this information out of your Web page. If you do want to link to other sites, you will add the relevant URLs. The format is the same as for the photo and resume anchors in this resume, but instead of typing a file name between the double quotations, you will type a URL.

In Abigail Basset's page, we are linking to two fictitious pages. Here are the anchors. As seen on the Web page:

The Vocalist Home Page is an excellent jumping off point ...

As seen in the HTML page:

The <A HREF="http://caruso.met.edu/usr5/vocal/vocal.html"> Vocalist Page</> is an excellent jumping off point ...

The next anchor, the Yahoo meta-list, is handled in exactly the same way, except that between the double quotes we typed the correct Yahoo URL.

To end, we just added a paragraph tag to indent our "feedback" paragraph. Next, we added an <ADDRESS> tag that encloses Abigail Basset's email address. We finish our Web page by closing the </BODY> and <HTML>tags. This completes our Web document.

Here's a review, and also some additional pointers:

1. To make the home page snazzier, open a blank document on your word processing program.

2. If you want to link to other Web pages, have the correct URLs ready to type into the anchor tags.

3. If you want to include graphics, you must have the graphic files to link to. To get your photo in an anchor, scan it in and save it in a .tif or .gif format. Name the file and add that file name between the double quotes in your anchor tag. If you don't have a scanner, you can use clip art files. The name of the file goes between the double quotes in the anchor tag.

4. If you link to graphics files in your anchors, copy the files in .tif or .gif to a diskette. Name the files on the diskette *exactly* what you named them in your anchor.

5. After you have finished writing your home page, save it in ASCII to the same diskette that has the graphic files. Keep it simple, something like"Homepage.html."

6. Give the diskette to the system operator to put up on a Web site. If you want to try and put the material up yourself, you'll need to ask the sysop, as he or she will have special rules for you to follow.

Review of Commonly Used HTML Tags

<B>**This text will be bold.**</B>

<I>*This text will be italics*</I>

<P>This tag opens a paragraph. No closing tag needed.

<HEAD>This tag tells HTML not to display what you write.</HEAD>

<HTML>This tag opens and closes your entire Web page.</HTML>

<BODY>This tag tells HTML to show what you're writing.</BODY>

<PRE>This tag will display text and formatting exactly as you typed it between the tags.</PRE>

In our sample home pages, we did not use all the HTML tags that are available to you as you format your home page, but we covered the most popular and important ones. To obtain a complete rundown, refer to the excellent HTML primer for beginners located at:

http://www.ncsa.uiuc.edu/General/Internet/WWW/
HTMLPrimer.html

There are a number of products available online to help you write your home page. These software products are called HTML editors or converters and are available for both the Macintosh and IBM platforms. If you want to explore these products, use one of these addresses:

http://mosaic.mcom.com/mcom/tricks_docs/tools_docs/index.html

http://www.w3.org/hypertext/www/Tools/Overview.html#he1

Both Microsoft and WordPerfect are including HTML converters in their latest releases. This is fabulous news for all of us—it means that we can write our Web pages without having to see the codes.

___

Hiring Someone to Spin Your Web Page

If you decide that you don't want to design your own home page, there are people who will do it for you—for a fee, of course. But be very careful if this is what you decide to do, because this is a new area for HTML-literate entrepreneurs, and some are less trustworthy than others.

In addition, you'll find great variance in the fees that these experts charge, so at the very least, shop around. In general, we recommend thinking twice if the fee goes above the $35 to $50 per-page range. If you have a Prodigy account, look there for these Web writing services, as this commercial service is promising reasonably priced rates to its members.

You will also hear about Internet Presence Developers in this regard, and there are some excellent consultants available to help as well; to find them go through trustworthy channels, such as your local computer society, the computer department at a local college or university, and national computer societies such as The Internet Society, which can be reached by email (isoc@isoc.org) or by voice (703-648-9888). Further contact numbers can be found in the "Resources" appendix.

If you are attending college, check with your career placement office; it may offer to design home pages free of charge. You can also contact your local Internet provider. You can bet you'll find Web page writing services.

≡ DEVELOPING YOUR WEB PRESENCE

When you put your page up on the Web, it is called "developing a Web presence" or "getting a Web presence." Before you have your page put up on a Web server, shop around. Go for the lowest price. Keep in mind that your home page doesn't have to be on a Web server near your particular geographical area. And again, we refer you to Prodigy, which will be offering a site to put up a home page for just the cost of membership—that's about $10.00 a month. That's an unbeatable deal.

Currently, Prodigy is the only commercial online service that plans to offer Web page services to its subscribers. Do check with your commercial online service provider to see if by the time you read this, it has plans to offer this type of service.

If you don't go with Prodigy, try to find a provider that will charge you by the number of accesses your page has instead of a flat fee. Charging by the number of accesses is by far a more fair system for you, the user.

Check Appendix A, "Getting Yourself Online," for contact numbers. As a general rule, $50 a month (flat fee) for a Web page is at the absolute top limit. A standard per-access rate of $.01 is acceptable.

Once you have your Web page online, you're ready for the next step: getting people to look at your page. If you have created a Web resume, by all means add it to the Internet Business Pages (IBD), and send along a thank you to the system administrator. To add your resume to the IBD, you'll need to access the IBD and read its Resume FAQ, which will give you instructions for getting a resume to its sysop. If you have a problem with any of the directions, email a query to the sysop. You will find his or her address listed on the bottom of the IBD home page.

Next send messages to the Lycos and Web Crawler search engine sites notifying them that you would like your URL included in their database. (That way, your URL can be found in keyword searches.) To send messages to the Lycos and Web Crawler search engine sites, open the URLs for each location. Read the opening instructions for the search engines. You will find directions and email addresses for sending your home page.

Finally, list your page with the "Complete Home Page Directory of Internet Personalities." Open the URL listed below under Complete Home Page Directory and follow the instructions for inclusion you will find there. Usually, it's just a matter of sending email. And by the time you read this, there will be many more sites on which to place your Web resumes and other home pages. To check on this type of information, look at the World Wide Web Virtual Library at the CERN pages. Check under the subject "people" or "finding people." (The wording may change, but the idea will remain the same!).

Here are the addresses we've discussed so far:

Complete Home Page Directory

http://web.city.ac.uk/~cb157/pages.html

World Wide Web Virtual Library

http://info.cern.ch/hypertext/DataSources/bySubject/
Overview.html

Search Engine addresses

Refer back to the URLs listed under the heading "Web Search Engines" earlier in this chapter.

For more information about getting a home page on the Web, browse the following addresses:

Home Page Development Tools

http://mosaic.mcom.com/home/manual_docs/graphics.html
#RTFToC3

Style Guide for Hypertext

http://www.w3.org/hypertext/www/Provider/Style/Overview.htm

Using Your Home Page to Network

Now that you have a home page, use it to augment your networking in the job market.

Home pages can be used as a corollary to your other networking practices. Most people add their URLs to their paper business cards, give it out to contacts over the phone, and add it to their email signature files; and in your online conversations, you can suggest that people browse your home page if it contains something you think is of interest. A home page is a simple, nonpushy way for other people to find out detailed information about you at their convenience.

Another way to get your home page noticed is to link it to other pages. (A link to another page is created by putting in an anchor tag, as you'll recall from our discussion of the bells and whistles template.) A current networking phenomenon is that if your home page is interesting or valuable to other people in some way, you'll be asked, "May I link to your home page?" Consider this a compliment, and realize that the more people you link to, the more networking exposure you will have.

Attorney Robin Diane Goldstein is an excellent example of how home page linking works as a Web networking tool in the professional world. Goldstein has her home page, which is a shining example of a professional home page, by the way, filled with information about her law practice, directions to her office, and information about one of her projects, "Web Legal." (If you want to see her home page, you can find it at **http://www.zoom.com:80/Robins_sandbox/**.) Goldstein also links to other attorneys and to places such as the U.S. Patent and Trademark Office, the U.S. Copyright Office Gopher, Patent Law Documents, the Villanova Center for Information Law, and much more. Her links have created a one-stop network of information about intellectual property, (which is her specialty) as well as a network of selected other attorneys on the Web.

Once you have your home page, you can begin looking around for people you want to link to. Contact relevant professional organizations online and ask if you could link to each other. If your page provides enough great information, you could also contact meta-list keepers such as Yanoff and Yahoo and tell them about your specialized resources. Getting a link from a meta-list is great exposure for your home page.

It is in this way that you spread the good news about your Web page. At every opportunity, mention your home page. Keep your eyes open for links, and meanwhile add your URL to your paper and ASCII resumes. And watch the Web closely for new places to post your Web resume.

Look before you link! If there is anything questionable on another person's home page, think carefully before you link to it. Web "law" is still being formulated, and no one knows where the responsibility for linked information is going to fall. In any case, you don't want to be held responsible for someone else's inaccurate or misleading information, so trust your instincts, and when in doubt, don't link.

══ CONCLUSION

When it comes to resumes, Web pages are a long way from Kansas, as it were. The World Wide Web, with all of its capacity for color, sound, and graphics, represents the direction the online world is taking. If you haven't hopped on the Web yet, now's the time. The Web is a great place to see and to be seen. It's the most upscale place you could possibly look for a job. Expect to rub elbows with the world's top executives as well as with sharp-minded small business owners. You never know what good things will happen when you put your home page up on the Web.

Information at Your Fingertips

Remember the old Yellow Pages jingle, "Let your fingers do the walking..."? Today, your fingers can travel a lot more extensively—in fact, they can get you just about anywhere in the virtual world via your computer keyboard. It's impossible to exaggerate the scope of the information you can access from your desktop: Pay a visit to the Louvre in Paris, (see Figure 6.1), stop by an Irish pub, review the schedules of all the opera houses in the world, watch a video of a dance recital, view a snapshot of a city you want to move to—it's all online, waiting for you.

The downside of this "reach" is that it may exceed your grasp, simply because there is too much available, and you might not know where to begin. That's what this chapter is for, to give you some places to start. We've collected a group of starting-point resources from all over the Internet which will enable you to concentrate on your job search instead of on aimless searching.

This chapter is divided into two sections. First we discuss how to access the electronic addresses you'll find in this chapter. Then under the heading "Alternative Search Tactics" we discuss more Internet search tools and explain how you can use

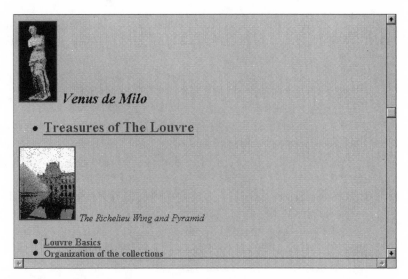

Venus de Milo

• Treasures of The Louvre

The Richelieu Wing and Pyramid

• Louvre Basics
• Organization of the collections

Figure 6.1 The Louvre online

them to find career and professional information. The difference between the Internet search tools in this chapter and the Web search tools we discussed in Chapter 5 is that Web search tools are designed to work with the hypertext documents unique to the Web. The Internet search tools presented in this chapter work with nonhypertext documents—in short, anything *not* on the Web.

We've stressed the information available on the Web throughout this book, but the Internet documents accessible (through gophers, for example) are also valuable, and we want to make sure you can search these gold mines as well. And a reminder: If you have a SLIP/PPP connection and are using a graphical Web browser, you can still use these Internet tools designed for nonhypertext documents. That's the great thing about the Web—you can search both the Web and the Internet. And if you don't have a SLIP/PPP connection, you're still in luck, because as long as you have a connection to the Internet, you can use all of the Internet search tools we mention. You don't need anything extra to use them.

In the second section, "Starting Points," we give you a list of career resources that will serve as jumping off spots for your Internet information exploits. Specifically, in the "Career Resources" section you will find listings that will tell you how to conduct interactive interviews, provide resume tips and general career advice. In the companies listing that follows, you will find addresses that will take you to databases loaded with in-depth profiles of companies you may want to work for or find out more about, as well as databases that will give you detailed financial information such as 10K reports.

We know that, usually, you will tap Usenet for contacting experts and peers, but we've uncovered additional areas and ways for you to locate the top people in your field, and they're given here, too. You'll find online phone books and online associations, so if you need to talk to someone in the know, you'll be able to do so.

Use these listings to find out the most current information about your area of interest or chosen career. You can find articles, dissertations, research studies, statistics, discussions, and bibliographies all having to do with how you make your living or how you want to make your living in the near future. And finally, you can use the listings as a way out—of your current geographical area, that is. You'll find online addresses for the best geographic information currently available. If you want to make a major move, this information will help you get prepared. You can even find a real estate agent online!

The majority of listings in this chapter are World Wide Web resources. If we didn't succeed in encouraging you earlier in this book to obtain access to the Web, we recommend that you reconsider. And it's never been easier. Prodigy, a popular online commercial service, now offers graphical Web access (call toll free, 800-776-3449 to set up an account). Delphi, another commercial provider (800-695-4005), offers Lynx access to the Web (Lynx, as you'll recall from Chapter 5, is a nongraphical Web browser). Call your commercial online service provider for updated information about Web access. Most major online services plan to offer it within the year. Also, many private Internet providers offer graphical or Lynx access to the Web. Appendix A, "Getting Yourself Online," has a list of Internet providers. And if you already have Internet access through a basic account. (which gives you gopher and Telnet, but not Web, capabilities) review Chapter 5 for ways to gain full access to the Web without spending a fortune upgrading your computer or account.

ACCESSING THE LISTS

There are four types of "addresses" cited in the resources in this chapter:

- voice telephone number for commercial online services
- Web addresses
- telnet addresses
- gopher addresses

A year ago, you would have seen primarily gopher and telnet addresses, with some others tossed in, but the phenomenal growth of the Web has relegated all of the other Internet services to the secondary role as references for archived information, and not as sources of up-to-the-minute information.

We have emphasized the Web because it is, to put in colloquially, "where it's at." In the past six months alone, the process of getting on the Web has become a much more user-friendly experience. Many service providers hand you the Web in a package. And, as we mentioned earlier, Prodigy now offers Web access, as does Delphi, which offers text-based Web access through Lynx. For you this means all you have to do is point and click your way through the information. If you are currently using a graphical Web browser to access the Internet, read about how you can open URLs (the electronic addresses for the Web) to reach the addresses listed in this chapter. If you're using anything else, read the Lynx and Gopher sections so you can find out how to access the addresses we list.

In the upcoming sections, we also cover using gopher, Veronica, and Jughead as a means of accessing all the resources listed in the chapter and throughout the book. It's your choice. You'll want to use these tools to mine information that is on the Internet but that is not hypertext based. Again, this means that the documents or files are available on the Internet, and are accessible through Web browsers, but the documents themselves contain no hypertext links and are thus indexed differently and searched with different search engines.

Getting the Goods Via the Web

Using Graphical Browsers

Navigating with a Web browser is an intuitive experience. We explained in detail in Chapter 5 how to use some of the most popular of these tools, and the following steps provide a quick review:

To access the addresses on the Web from a graphical browser like Netscape, do the following:

1. Log on to your PPP, SLIP, or high-speed Internet account.

2. The opening menu will come up, and will—no matter which browser you use—have an option available that says something like Open or Go to. On Netscape, choose Open Location, as shown in Figure 6.2.

3. Fill in the blank that appears with the address you find in the listing, as you can see in Figure 6.3.

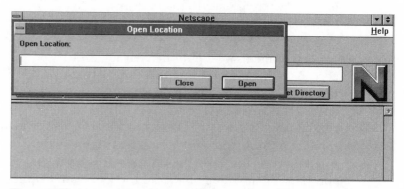

Figure 6.2 Netscape's menu to open a new location

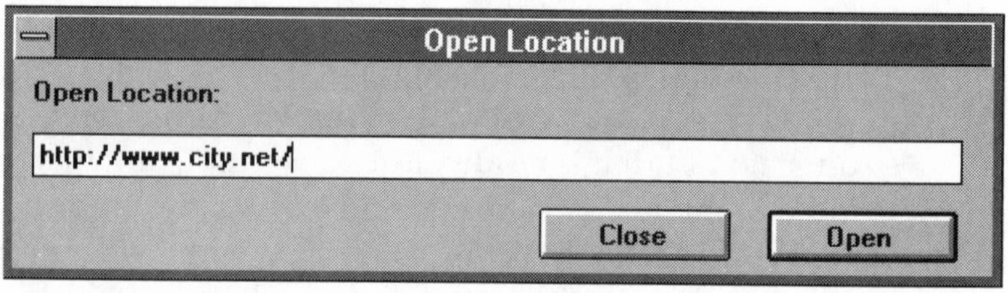

Figure 6.3 Netscape filled in with City Pages' address

4. Press Enter. In a few moments, the address will be contacted and will appear on your screen.

5. Once you are at the address, to navigate, use a mouse to point at an underlined (or, on a color monitor, a blue or purple) link and click. It's that simple. (That's why everyone loves the Web.)

6. If you get the message "Can't connect," the port may be busy or the address may have changed. If it's busy, try later at a slower time. If the address has changed, conduct a keyword search to find the new address.

To access an address from a text-based browser like Lynx, follow these steps:

1. Log on to your Internet account.

2. Select World Wide Web from the menu options. (It is not likely, but if you don't have a Web option, you may need to telnet to a Web site. See Chapter 5 for full details. After you telnet, the rest of the steps are the same.)

3. Select the URL option and type in the address you want to reach, as shown in Figure 6.4a.

4. Once in the Web, you can press G, for go, at any time to open a new URL blank, as shown in Figure 6.4b. Your

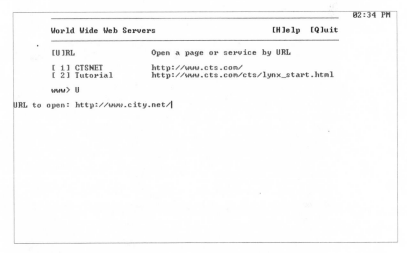

```
                                                                02:34 PM

    World Wide Web Servers                        [H]elp  [Q]uit


    [U]RL                     Open a page or service by URL

    [ 1] CTSNET               http://www.cts.com/
    [ 2] Tutorial             http://www.cts.com/cts/lynx_start.html

    www> U
URL to open: http://www.city.net/
```

Figure 6.4a URL option for a text-based Web browser

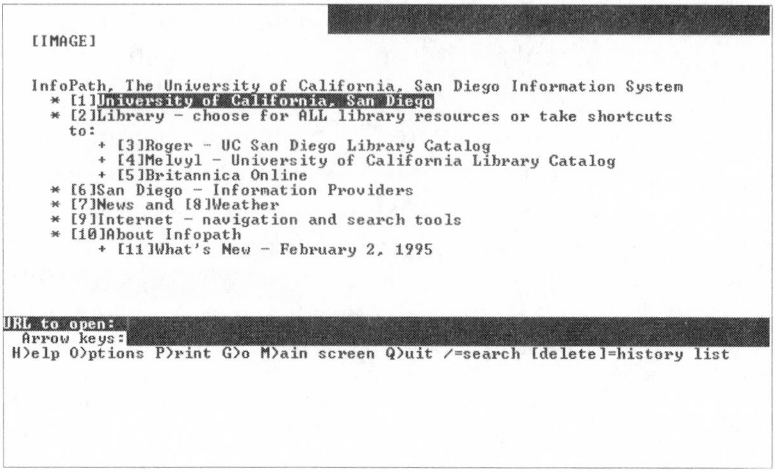

```
[IMAGE]


InfoPath, The University of California, San Diego Information System
 * [1]University of California, San Diego
 * [2]Library - choose for ALL library resources or take shortcuts
   to:
       + [3]Roger - UC San Diego Library Catalog
       + [4]Melvyl - University of California Library Catalog
       + [5]Britannica Online
 * [6]San Diego - Information Providers
 * [7]News and [8]Weather
 * [9]Internet - navigation and search tools
 * [10]About Infopath
       + [11]What's New - February 2, 1995


URL to open:
  Arrow keys:
H)elp O)ptions P)rint G)o M)ain screen Q)uit /=search [delete]=history list
```

Figure 6.4b The command to open a URL in Lynx, a text-based Web browser. Note the blank to be fill in at the bottom of the screen.

system may be slightly different, in which case, use the help function for your system's commands.

5. Type in the new URL. In the example in Figure 6.5, we typed in the address for the City Pages. Note the address format.

6. Press Enter and wait for the computer to contact the address. Once there, you can follow the links either by choosing a number or moving the highlighted bar over

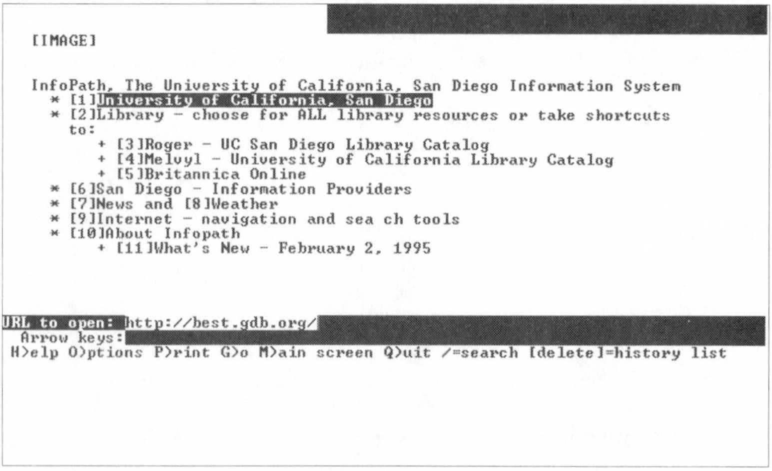

```
[IMAGE]


InfoPath, The University of California, San Diego Information System
 * [1]University of California, San Diego
 * [2]Library - choose for ALL library resources or take shortcuts
   to:
       + [3]Roger - UC San Diego Library Catalog
       + [4]Melvyl - University of California Library Catalog
       + [5]Britannica Online
 * [6]San Diego - Information Providers
 * [7]News and [8]Weather
 * [9]Internet - navigation and sea ch tools
 * [10]About Infopath
       + [11]What's New - February 2, 1995


URL to open: http://best.gdb.org/
  Arrow keys:
H)elp O)ptions P)rint G)o M)ain screen Q)uit /=search [delete]=history list
```

Figure 6.5 Typing in a URL from Lynx

the links and pressing Enter on the links you want to follow. See Figure 6.6 for an example of what the highlighted bar over a link looks like.

Text-based browsers are not as pretty as their graphical cousins, but you get the ease of movement and, most important, access to the information you need.

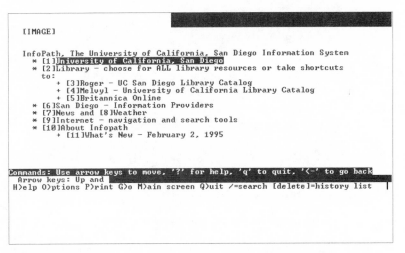

```
[IMAGE]

InfoPath, The University of California, San Diego Information System
    * [1]University of California, San Diego
    * [2]Library - choose for ALL library resources or take shortcuts
       to:
       + [3]Roger - UC San Diego Library Catalog
       + [4]Melvyl - University of California Library Catalog
       + [5]Britannica Online
    * [6]San Diego - Information Providers
    * [7]News and [8]Weather
    * [9]Internet - navigation and search tools
    * [10]About Infopath
       + [11]What's New - February 2, 1995



Commands: Use arrow keys to move. '?' for help. 'q' to quit. '<-' to go back
  Arrow keys: Up and
  H)elp O)ptions P)rint G)o M)ain screen Q)uit /=search [delete]=history list
```

Figure 6.6 Navigating with Lynx. Note the highlighted bar over University of California at the top of the page. To follow this link, press Enter.

Getting the Goods Via Gopher

Gopher is one of the simplest Internet tools around. To use it, follow these steps:

1. Log on to your Internet account. Look at the menu. You should see an option for gopher. (It is *very rare* that an Internet account provider or college campus system won't carry a gopher option. If, however, this is the case for you, you'll need to telnet to a public gopher site. Read the telnet sidebar for instructions.)

2. Choose the Gopher menu option and press Enter.

3. Once in gopher, either browse by choosing menu options, or press O to type in a specific address as shown in Figure 6.7. After you type in the address, press Enter. Note the format used in this figure.

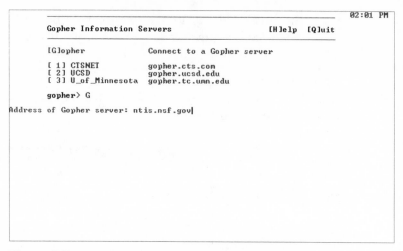

Figure 6.7 A gopher address being typed in at the prompt

4. Follow the menus you're interested in by pressing the number of the menu item you wish to see, and then Enter.

Some additional notes on gopher:

◆ When you get into one gopher system, you have access to all gopher systems.

◆ To contact a specific gopher address, either perform a veronica search (see the next section) and press the item

```
Gopher Help File (1k)                                                  86% |
lqqqqqqqqqqqqqqqqqqqqqqqqqqqqqqqqqqqqqqqqqqqqqqqqqqqqqqqqqqqqqqqqqqqqqqqqqqqqqqqk
Bookmarks
---------------------
a : Add current item to the bookmark list.
A : Add current directory/search to bookmark list.
v : View bookmark list.
d : Delate a bookmark/directory entry.
---------------------
Other commands
---------------------
s : Save current item to a file.              ove around
D : Download a file.
q : Quit with prompt.
Q : Quit unconditionally.
= : Display Technical information about current item.
o : Open a new gopher server           item/Go up a level.
O : Change Options
/ : Search for an item in the menu.
n : Find next search item.
!, $ : Shell Escape (Unix) or Spawn subprocess (VMS)
0-9 .................:   Go to a specific line.
m .................:   Go back to the main menu.
mqqqqqqqqqqqqqqqqqqqqqqqqqqqqqqqqqqqqqqqqqqqqqqqqqqqqqqqqqqqqqqqqqqqqqqqqqqqqqqqj

[PageDown: <SPACE>] [Help: ?] [Return to Menu: u]
```

Figure 6.8 A portion of the gopher command menu

number you want to see from the list that your search reveals, or, as already mentioned, use the gopher command O to move to another site. Again, this command results in a fill-in blank for the gopher address.

◆ Figure 6.8 has a partial list of other gopher commands. For a full list, type the question mark (?) in any gopher system.

ALTERNATIVE SEARCH TACTICS

Although having lists of pertinent addresses is a great way to access online information, the reality of the information superhighway is that change is constant: addresses might be different than what you see here; lists will have been updated, added, or eliminated. This means that you must also be able to use other search tactics so that you are not left out in the online cold.

Chapter 2 explained how to perform keyword searches on commercial online services. You already know that you can log on to any of these services, go to the "find" or "search" areas, type in your keywords, hit Enter, and wait for the service to find what you want. In Chapter 5, we discussed how to search using the Web.

But what about searching the Internet from a basic account or searching for non-hypertext documents? (A basic Internet account is also called a *shell* account. With this kind of account, you do not have a SLIP or PPP connection to the Internet, thus you will be using gopher, telnet, and Lynx to do a lot of your Internet browsing.) Even if you do have Netscape or another graphical Web browser, you will find that you cannot search gophers using a search engine designed for Web documents, such as the Web Crawler. You'll need to use a search engine designed to search gophers. Never fear. As on the Web, there are search engines available on the Internet. The search engine we are about to discuss is called veronica, an engine that will tame gopherspace for you.

Veronica

Veronica, an Internet search engine that searches about 15 million documents hiding out in gopher holes, is first and

Telnetting to Gopher

Most of you will never have to telnet to a public gopher site, because gopher is readily available from most Internet accounts and college campus systems. But, just in case, here are the instructions:

1. Go to a telnet prompt by choosing the Telnet option from your menu. Once at the prompt, enter the telnet command followed by one of the addresses listed below.

2. When prompted for a login, type gopher. If, for example, you want to telnet to the Michigan State University's campus system (which has a good gopher) you would type: telnet gopher. msu.edu.

This list represents only a portion of the gophers available through Telnet. We have chosen connections that are stable and that aren't constantly busy. Once you connect to any of these gophers, you will have access to all gophers. (You can hop from menu to menu to navigate, or you can use the gopher command O to open a specific gopher. See the heading "Burrowing into the Web Through a Gopher Connection" in this chapter for an example of how to do this.)

U.S. gophers (login: gopher)

consultant.micro.umn.edu	University of Minnesota
ecosys.drdr.virginia.edu	University of Virginia
gopher.msu.edu	Michigan State University
gopher.ohiolink.edu	Ohio Library and Information Network
gopher.unc.edu	University of North Carolina, Chapel Hill

International gophers (login: gopher)

gopher.denet.dk	Danish Research and Academic Network (DENet)
gopher.th-darmstadt.de	Technische Hochschule Darmstadt, Germany
gopher.ncc.go.jp	National Cancer Center, Tokyo
info.sunet.se	Swedish Network

Note: These are not comprehensive lists, just some places to get you started. Keep in mind that it's always best to telnet to a gopher in your geographical area.

foremost a gopher tool. Like so much of the terminology in cyberspace, veronica is another of the ubiquitous acronyms. Its letters stand for "very easy rodent-oriented netwide index to computerized archives." You can access veronica both from the Web and the Internet, and it always works the same way.

Veronica searches specified keywords in the titles of more than 5,000 gopher servers; it amounts to indexes of some 15 million items. And all you have to do is to type in your keywords of choice.

On some systems there are Veronica help files available for you to read. If you see this Help option, it's a good idea to take the time to read the files before you perform a search.

By way of example, let's say you are a conservationist currently working for the federal government. You have an interview next week with a paper manufacturer in an area of the country where you've always wanted to live—Seattle, Washington. You want this job not just because of the contributions you can make, but also because you want to move to this area. So, you're looking for the most current information about conservation and about Seattle. Here's how you use Veronica to help:

1. Log on to your Internet account.

2. Go to gophers, remembering that once in a gopher, you have access to all gophers.

3. Choose the Veronica option by moving the cursor down to it; then, press Enter. (The actual option number will change, depending on which gopher system you are accessing.) Figure 6.9 shows what the gopher menu looks like. The Veronica option has been highlighted, ready for the Enter command. (To create this example, we accessed gopher through a multiprotocol Web browser.)

A multiprotocol Web browser is a software program like Netscape or Mosaic that allows users to browse the World Wide Web and Internet items such as gopher, too. It's the electronic way of "one-stop shopping."

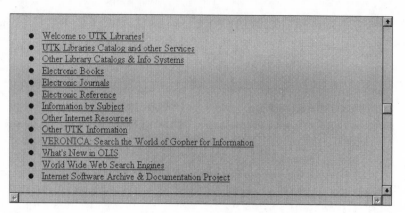

Figure 6.9 A gopher menu with veronica highlighted

4. A screen like the one in Figure 6.10 will appear. Choose one, and press Enter.

5. Fill in the blank with keywords appropriate to your search. Note that at the bottom of the screen in Figure 6.11, the blank has been filled in with the keyword *conservation*.

6. Press Return, and wait for a list of resources to appear on your screen. The list from our veronica search appears in Figure 6.12.

7. Now, simply choose an item to browse. You may find it instructive at this point to compare the results of our *conservation* searches on the Web in Chapter 5 with the results of our veronica search.

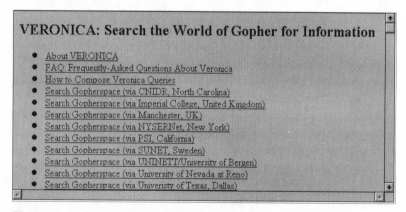

Figure 6.10 A list of Veronicas that you can choose from to perform a search

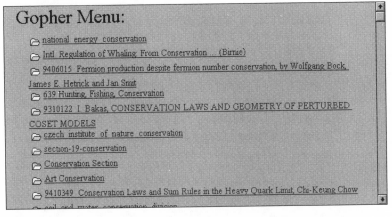

Searchable Gopher Index

gopher://gopher.umanitoba.ca:2347/7-t1%20%20

Please enter words to search for.

Search Index: conservation

Figure 6.11 Getting ready to search. Note that your screen may look different, based on the type of account you use, but veronica always works the same way.

Gopher Menu:

📁 national energy conservation
📁 Intl. Regulation of Whaling: From Conservation ... (Birnie)
📁 9406015 Fermion production despite fermion number conservation, by Wolfgang Bock, James E. Hetrick and Jan Smit
📁 639 Hunting, Fishing, Conservation
📁 9310122 I. Bakas, CONSERVATION LAWS AND GEOMETRY OF PERTURBED COSET MODELS
📁 czech institute of nature conservation
📁 section-19-conservation
📁 Conservation Section
📁 Art Conservation
📁 9410349 Conservation Laws and Sum Rules in the Heavy Quark Limit, Chi-Keung Chow
📁 soil and water conservation division

Figure 6.12 The results of a veronica search on *conservation*

When you are searching Veronica, you can use the connector words AND, NOT, OR, and wildcards to narrow your search.

♦ AND instructs veronica to find gophers containing all the words connected. For example, you can search for *conservation and forestry*.

♦ OR directs veronica to find one search term *or* another. A search criterion with *conservation or forestry* will result in hits of either of the words, whether they appear together or not. These searches typically bring up more documents than AND searches.

♦ NOT eliminates obvious but unwanted hits from your search. *Conservation not forestry* instructs veronica to find conservation information only—no forestry information will be picked up.

♦ Wildcards are characters such as asterisks and question marks that stand for any other character that may appear in the same place. A search of *conservation** tells veronica to find *conservation, conservationists, conservationism*, etc.

You can also direct veronica as to the number of results you want. You may choose 200, 1,000, or unlimited search results. If you want 200 hits from your search, just write the keyword; for example, *conservation*. If you want 1,000 hits from your search, write the keyword and add -m1000; for example, *conservation-m1000*. If you want all possible hits, add -m-all; for example, *conservation-m-all*.

Jughead

Jughead is another Internet search engine available through gopher. Thankfully, it is not another cutesy acronym. It is, however, an alternative to using Veronica. When you perform a Veronica search, millions of items are examined, and sometimes this may be more than you want or need. If you aren't interested in such a comprehensive gopher search, consider Jughead.

To use Jughead, you follow the same steps you follow for a Veronica search. The basic pattern is that you log onto your Internet account, access gopher, and look for "Internet tools" or "Internet search," or something very similar on your menu. This is where you will find Veronica and Jughead options.

1. Once in gopher, type O. Enter the following address in the Hostname field that appears: **liberty.uc.wlu.edu**

2. Press Enter (you won't need to type in any additional information) and wait for the opening screen to come up. You will be connecting to the Washington and Lee University gopher system.

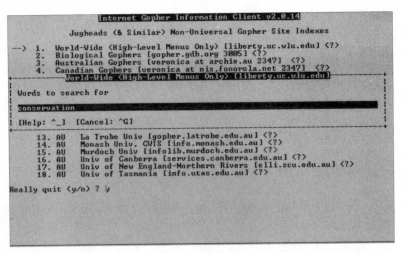

Figure 6.13 Searching Jughead for conservation information at Washington and Lee University

3. At the opening screen, press option #5, "Finding Gopher Resources."

4. At the next screen, choose #3, "Jugheads and Similar non-Universal Gopher site Indexes."

5. Choose a logical place to search and press Enter. You will be prompted for a keyword. Take a look at Figure 6.13. You will see that the cursor (which looks like an arrow) is positioned at option number 1, World Wide (High-Level Menus Only). We simply pressed Enter at option number 1, and the fill-in-the-blank opened onto our screen. For comparison purposes, we typed in our favorite keyword, *conservation.* Of course, you will type in your profession-specific keywords here.

6. After you type in your keyword, press Enter.

7. You will see screens full of results come up. Now, you can browse for information. Look at Figure 6.14 and 6.15. They are the first two (of six) pages of results. (The backslash at the end of each entry indicates that it is a directory.) For example, in Figure 6.15, item number 30 says CONSBIO – Conservation Biology List .../. This tells you that if you press Enter at this menu item, you will be taken not to a single document, but to a whole new gopher menu, called a directory. You will see not one

document, but many menu choices filled with multiple documents.

The difference between these two search engines is that Veronica would have given us the contents of the directory. Jughead gives us the directory. It's your choice. When you search with Jughead, you are limiting where you look for information.

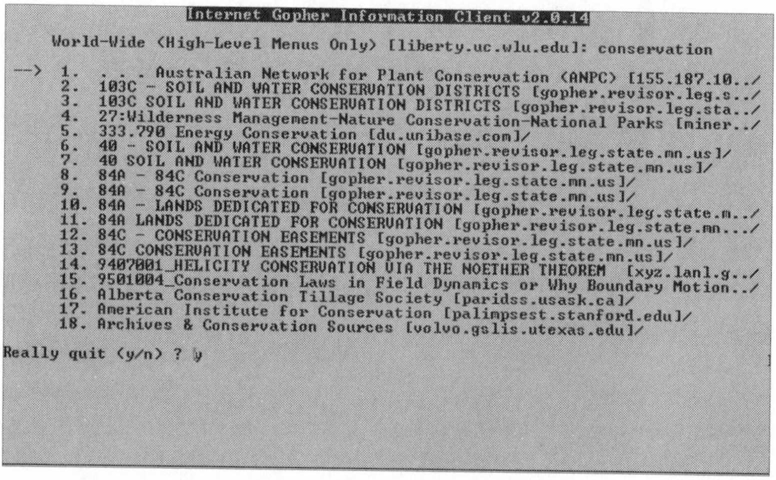

```
Internet Gopher Information Client v2.0.14

    World-Wide (High-Level Menus Only) [liberty.uc.wlu.edu]: conservation

-->  1.  . . . Australian Network for Plant Conservation (ANPC) [155.187.10../
     2.  103C - SOIL AND WATER CONSERVATION DISTRICTS [gopher.revisor.leg.s../
     3.  103C SOIL AND WATER CONSERVATION DISTRICTS [gopher.revisor.leg.sta../
     4.  27:Wilderness Management-Nature Conservation-National Parks [miner../
     5.  333.790 Energy Conservation [du.unibase.com]/
     6.  40 - SOIL AND WATER CONSERVATION [gopher.revisor.leg.state.mn.us]/
     7.  40 SOIL AND WATER CONSERVATION [gopher.revisor.leg.state.mn.us]/
     8.  84A - 84C Conservation [gopher.revisor.leg.state.mn.us]/
     9.  84A - 84C Conservation [gopher.revisor.leg.state.mn.us]/
     10. 84A - LANDS DEDICATED FOR CONSERVATION [gopher.revisor.leg.state.m../
     11. 84A LANDS DEDICATED FOR CONSERVATION [gopher.revisor.leg.state.mn.../
     12. 84C - CONSERVATION EASEMENTS [gopher.revisor.leg.state.mn.us]/
     13. 84C CONSERVATION EASEMENTS [gopher.revisor.leg.state.mn.us]/
     14. 9407001_HELICITY CONSERVATION VIA THE NOETHER THEOREM  [xyz.lanl.g../
     15. 9501004_Conservation Laws in Field Dynamics or Why Boundary Motion../
     16. Alberta Conservation Tillage Society [paridss.usask.ca]/
     17. American Institute for Conservation [palimpsest.stanford.edu]/
     18. Archives & Conservation Sources [volvo.gslis.utexas.edu]/

Really quit (y/n) ? y
```

Figure 6.14 Page 1 of our Jughead search results of *conservation*

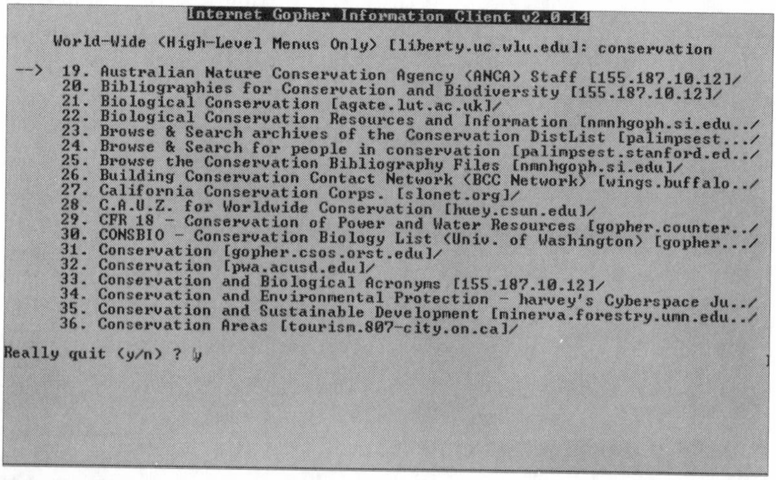

```
Internet Gopher Information Client v2.0.14

    World-Wide (High-Level Menus Only) [liberty.uc.wlu.edu]: conservation

-->  19. Australian Nature Conservation Agency (ANCA) Staff [155.187.10.12]/
     20. Bibliographies for Conservation and Biodiversity [155.187.10.12]/
     21. Biological Conservation [agate.lut.ac.uk]/
     22. Biological Conservation Resources and Information [nmnhgoph.si.edu../
     23. Browse & Search archives of the Conservation DistList [palimpsest.../
     24. Browse & Search for people in conservation [palimpsest.stanford.ed../
     25. Browse the Conservation Bibliography Files [nmnhgoph.si.edu]/
     26. Building Conservation Contact Network (BCC Network) [wings.buffalo../
     27. California Conservation Corps. [slonet.org]/
     28. C.A.U.Z. for Worldwide Conservation [huey.csun.edu]/
     29. CFR 18 - Conservation of Power and Water Resources [gopher.counter../
     30. CONSBIO - Conservation Biology List (Univ. of Washington) [gopher.../
     31. Conservation [gopher.csos.orst.edu]/
     32. Conservation [pwa.acusd.edu]/
     33. Conservation and Biological Acronyms [155.187.10.12]/
     34. Conservation and Environmental Protection - harvey's Cyberspace Ju../
     35. Conservation and Sustainable Development [minerva.forestry.umn.edu../
     36. Conservation Areas [tourism.807-city.on.ca]/

Really quit (y/n) ? y
```

Figure 6.15 Page 2 of our Jughead search results for *conservation*

WAIS

WAIS is a jewel of an Internet keyword-search engine. Its letters stand for Wide Area Information Searching. This is a tool that everyone on the Internet should take time to investigate. There are several ways of performing a WAIS search, and we're going to take you along the simplest route—via gopher.

The reason to include WAIS in your Internet toolkit is for the same reason we used two different Web search engines in Chapter 5. Even though WAIS and Veronica function very much the same way, you will find the results may be different. And, since searching WAIS through gopher is so simple, it would be foolish not to use this excellent resource. Here's how:

1. Log onto your Internet account.

2. Access gopher.

3. Open the Washington and Lee gopher system by typing O and entering this address: **liberty.uc.wlu.edu**

4. Choose menu option number 4, Explore Internet Resources and press Enter.

5. Choose option number 1, Netlink Server, WAIS, Gopher, Telnet, WWW, sites.

6. Now you can access WAIS. Go for broke, and choose the option that says List of all WAIS Sources. You will be presented with a list of over 500 members, and every site is a massive database repository that you can now keyword search. (In Appendix C, "Resources," we list these sites for you so you can read through them off-line to get an idea of what site will help you the most.)

7. Choose a WAIS database to search by menu number and press Enter.

8. You will be presented with a keyword blank just like the one you see in Figure 6.16, which resulted from our choice, #1. AAS_jobs.src. (The src extension always indicates that it is a WAIS resource.) Fill in this blank with your profession-specific keywords and press Enter. (Your cursor will automatically be positioned correctly.) Notice that the name of the WAIS database appears in a little box atop the keyword pop-up menu.

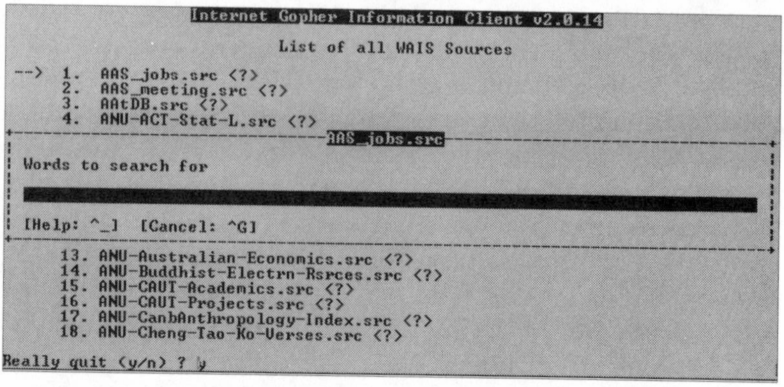

Figure 6.16 Getting ready to search WAIS through gopher.

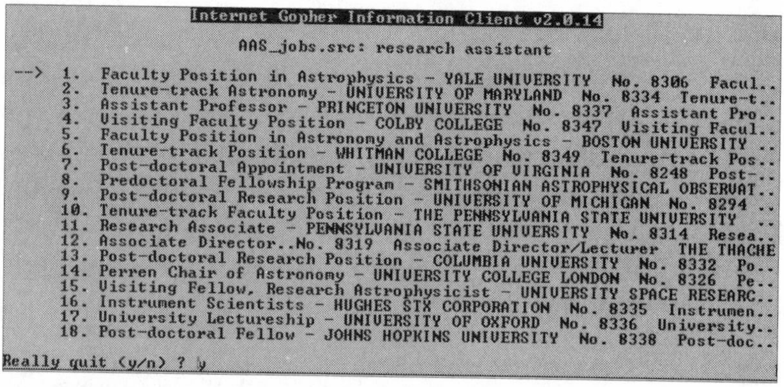

Figure 6.17 Results of our WAIS search in the AAS (American Astronomical Society) database

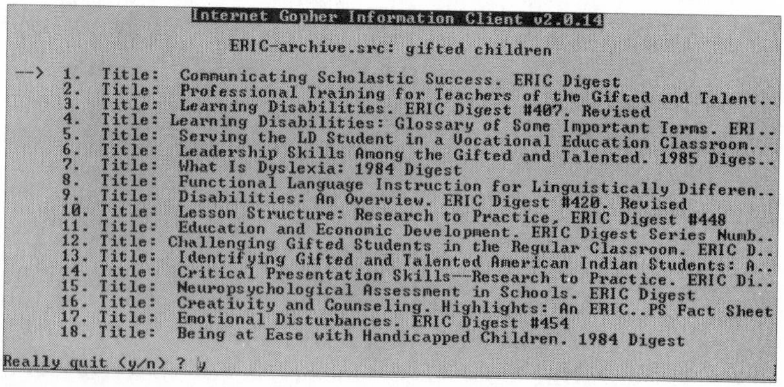

Figure 6.18 A gold mine of information via a WAIS search of ERIC, an educational resource database

9. Wait for the results. For our sample search, we chose to enter the words *research assistant.* In Figure 6.17, you can see that our search was not in vain. The WAIS search found 25 positions that match the keywords. (The rest of the positions are on the next screen.) Figure 6.18 shows another example, this from ERIC, an educational resource database that we searched for information on gifted children.

SAVING GOPHER INFORMATION

We know that you'll find information via Veronica, Jughead, and WAIS searches that you'll want to save. There are several ways of doing this.

♦ Create a bookmark so you can return to the information easily. (See the upcoming section, "Bookmark Regularly" for instructions.)

♦ Mail files to yourself. This is our favorite option for saving gopher material. From any gopher document, press m. A blank will open on your screen, prompting you for a correct email address to send the file to. Fill in your email address and press Enter. That's it. You'll find the entire document waiting for you in your email box.

♦ Capture text with your communications software. To open a capture file, go to the File menu in your communications software, look for a Capture Text or Capture Screen option, and select it. If you wish, you can open a capture file on your communications software and capture text while you're online. The downfall of this method is that the commands and prompts are captured right along with document text.

♦ Save to a file. When you save to a file on gopher, you are actually storing the file on a remote computer. Every system operator has a slightly different method for doing this, so you'll need to give them a call and ask what the procedure is. If you are a beginner, we recommend that you stick with mailing files to yourself or using capture files.

When you conduct any Veronica or WAIS search, go through the results of the search rapidly, reading just the first paragraph of each item. If an item looks good, bookmark it, then mail it to yourself. You can move very rapidly through search results this way, saving hours of connection time. At the end of your session, go to your mailbox and print out your mail, save it to a file, or capture the text.

BURROWING INTO THE WEB THROUGH A GOPHER CONNECTION

If you have access to a gopher, you can get yourself on the World Wide Web through some fancy burrowing. This will give those of you with a simple computer setup the option of accessing all of the best resources on the Web. Of course, if you have a SLIP connection and you're running Netscape, you won't need to bother with this. But if you have an older computer on your desktop, this trick will save you a computer upgrade. You can do that after you land your new job! Here's what you do:

1. Log onto your Internet account.

2. Access a gopher.

3. Type O to open a gopher location. Fill in this address: **liberty.uc.wlu.edu**.

4. Press Enter.

5. Choose option #4; then press Enter. Choose option #1, and press Enter.

6. Choose WWW sites. Press Enter.

7. You will be presented with a list of WWW sites you can telnet and gopher to. Choose the menu number you're interested in and press Enter. Gopher will do all the telnetting for you, and will take you directly to the site. If you need a login, the gopher will give you a message about what you should type (usually WWW).

This will give those of you with a simple computer setup the option of accessing all of the best resources on the Web.

IF ALL ELSE FAILS (BACKDOOR SEARCH METHODS)

It's only fair to warn you that, because of the astonishing growth in the number of travelers on the information super-highway, you will run into online "traffic jams," particularly when using Veronica. In the same way you learned the value of an alternative route to avoid ending up in bumper-to-bumper car traffic, it's a good idea to know some tricks to help you avoid online pileups.

Bookmark Regularly

You learned the value of bookmarking when using the Web in Chapter 5. You can make use of this same method of electronic placemarking in gopher, too. Here's how to add a bookmark on gopher:

1. Find a gopher you like. We chose an Entomology gopher from the Smithsonian.

2. From the gopher menu, type the letter a. This will add an item to your bookmark list, as in Figure 6.19. (The screen you see in the figure just pops up after you type the letter.)

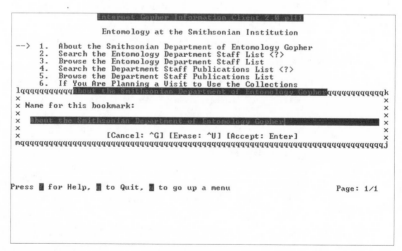

Figure 6.19 Gopher bookmark menu

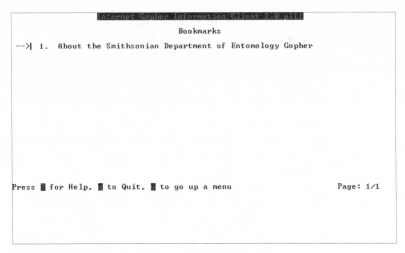

Figure 6.20 Our new entomology bookmark

3. Note that the gopher software fills in the blanks for you. All you do is press Enter. Here, we've pressed the lower-case a, so we've just bookmarked one item on a gopher. (Looking at Figure 6.20, you can see that we bookmarked just menu item number 1, "About the Smithsonian Department of Entomology Gopher.") If you press the uppercase A instead, you will bookmark an entire directory.

4. To view a bookmark, press v. Figure 6.20 shows what you'll see after you've added bookmarks. You can view your bookmarks from anyplace in any gopher—just get into a gopher, press v and your bookmarks will pop up.

5. To see your bookmarks at any time, press v as in step 4. Then all you do to access the bookmark is to move the cursor to the gopher you want and press Enter.

Head for the Hills

Another good way to avoid a dreaded online traffic tie-up (see Figure 6.21), is to "get of the beaten path"; in other words, take the road less traveled. Online, that usually means you'll have to try accessing through more remote sites. There are also some nongopher hotspots that can really help you out of an information crunch.

Gopher Menu:

0*** Too many connections - Try again soon. ***

Figure 6.21 A Typical "too busy" message

CARL

CARL is a snazzy bibliographic database that you can search by keyword, name, title, or author. Some 44,000 entries are added to the CARL database every day. For a job seeker, this database is best used to find articles that will help you prepare for interviews, further develop your expertise, or to find names of experts. For example, one physician we know uses this database to keep abreast of what his competition is publishing. He searches for articles related to his area of expertise, rhinoplasty, every month. He finds out, instantly, what other surgeons in this specialty have been up to. What would have taken him hours in a medical library to locate, he can accomplish in less than 15 minutes from his home. To access it, use this address:

telnet pac.carl.org or through gopher menus.

Access to CARL is free. You'll get the bibliographic information about your topic that you need: where, by whom, and when an article was published. You can set up an account and have CARL fax you an article or articles within 1 to 24 hours. A word of warning: Once you're in CARL, it can become expensive—faxing an article usually costs about $11.00.

Marvel

Marvel is the Library of Congress gopher. Its great virtue is that it's organized by subject, so you can jump from menu to menu by topic to get the information you want.

STARTING POINTS

The lists that follow should set you on the right path as you begin your Internet explorations. You'll find, for example, where you can go to evaluate a company's financial status *before* you accept a job and move your family across the country. You'll also find online phone books where you can locate that long-lost employer who will write you a glowing reference. And if you want the latest tips on preparing a resume, you'll find the address for E-Span's terrific resume articles and career tip sections.

You will want to search for additional resources, of course, so that you can expand on what's here, and you'll discover that some of the addresses have changed—the bane of online technology. To locate new resources, or update addresses, all you have to do is perform a search using either a Web or an Internet search engine (depending on the resource). Use the name of the resource as the search term, and you'll find the address you want. For example, if the Bureau of Labor Statistics, the first address we list, has moved, then just go to the Web Crawler and type in *Bureau of Labor Statistics.* You will usually find the title or something very similar listed in the search results. Voilà, your new address. If you don't find it, try another search engine. If that doesn't work, (it probably will, though) try going to the Yahoo list and browsing around topically. For the Bureau of Labor Statistics, you would probably try *Government* listings first.

CAREER RESOURCES

Nobody likes looking for a job. It brings out everyone's insecurities and doubts. But online technology can help to assuage your concerns as you go through this difficult process. Many resources are available that contain current information on preparing an effective resume, tips on successful interviewing, and a host of other job search-related topics.

In this section, we list only career resources available on the Internet, not on commercial sites; they are included in Chapter 7, which features actual online job listings and resume database sites.

Internet Sites

Bureau of Labor Statistics

Access: **http://stats.bls.gov/blshome.html**

Content: More numbers and statistics about employment than you can digest in one sitting. If you are looking for very specific statistical information about your profession or field of interest, check here.

Career Choices Page, Catapult

Access: **http://arthur.physics.wm.edu:80/~charette/ choice.html**

Content: This is a listing of links to information that will help you make career choices about various professions. Not comprehensive but worth a look to see if your profession is covered.

Career Mosaic

Access: **http://www.service.com:80/cm/**

Content: In addition to its renowned company listings and job openings, Career Mosaic offers a fine career resource called the *Employment Directory Guide to North American Markets.* This directory lists the employment lowdown on the top 50 U.S. markets and the top 10 Canadian markets. Demographic information and employment analysis is great for job seekers and marketing professionals.

Directory of Executive Recruiters

Access: **http://www.careermag.com/careermag/**

Content: This is a service provided by *Career Magazine,* and it's a great one. Many executive recruiters are listed, with more adding their names each month. If you're interested in finding a recruiter, especially in another location, don't miss this site.

Employment Opportunities and Job Resources on the Internet

Access: **http://www.wpi.edu/~mfriley/jobguide.html**

Content: This is Margaret Riley's (an academic librarian at Worcester Polytechnic Institute) list of links to other employment sites. It is an in-depth list in which every entry is explained in detail. A good way to begin is to read it first, then visit the areas that apply to you. If you're in a hurry to browse, this is a good place to start. You'll find links to many of the resources mentioned in this section of our list.

Interactive Employment Network

Access: **http://www.espan.com**

Content: There are many excellent career resources at this site. Figure 6.22 shows the first menu. Notice *The Occupational Outlook Handbook,* a fabulous way to research any career area; it is shown in part in Figure 6.23. Figure 6.24 shows a portion of practice exercises available to help you as you prepare your job search. Check out the interactive interview! A version of the Interactive Employment Network (called E-Span) is also available via America Online, CompuServe, Prodigy, and eWorld.

Labor Trends

Access: **gopher gopher.enews.com**

Content: General labor trends. Good resource for statistical employment information.

National Center for the Workplace

Access: **gopher uclink.berkeley.edu**

Content: Many menus on workers' rights and recent employment legislation.

The Career Manager has all you'll need for a successful career search:

- Career Fair Calendars
- Salary Guides
- Resume Writing Tips
- Networking Advice
- Spotlight Pages featuring top companies
- The Occupational Outlook Handbook for 94-95
- ...and much more!

Figure 6.22 A general menu of the career resources available in the Interactive Employment Network career resources area

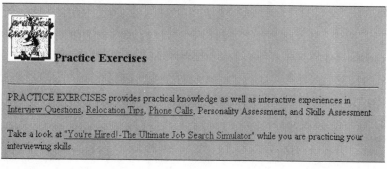

> **Tomorrow's Jobs**
>
> Every 2 years, the Bureau of Labor Statistics develops projections of the labor force, economic growth, industry output and employment, and occupational employment under three sets of alternative assumptions-low, moderate, and high. These projections cover a 10- to 15-year period and provide a framework for the discussion of job outlook in each occupational statement in the *Handbook.* All of the approximately 250 statements in this edition of the *Handbook* identify the principal factors affecting job prospects, then discuss how these factors are expected to affect the occupation. This chapter uses the moderate alternative of each projection to provide a framework for the individual job outlook discussions.

Figure 6.23 A portion of the *Occupational Outlook Handbook,* available in many areas of the Net, here, accessed via E-Span's Web site

> **Practice Exercises**
>
> PRACTICE EXERCISES provides practical knowledge as well as interactive experiences in Interview Questions, Relocation Tips, Phone Calls, Personality Assessment, and Skills Assessment.
>
> Take a look at "You're Hired!-The Ultimate Job Search Simulator" while you are practicing your interviewing skills.

Figure 6.24 Practice exercises at Interactive Employment Network

Online Career Center

Access: **http://www.iquest.net/occ/**

Content: Many good career links. Figure 6.25 shows OCC's opening menu of resources. After clicking on Career Assistance, Figure 6.26 shows you what other resources you'll find at OCC. Resume preparation advice, career books, selected company information are some of the main offerings other than the extensive job listings. Please note that OCC is also available via CompuServe.

U.S. Industry Outlook

Access: **gopher umslvma.umsl.edu**

Figure 6.25 The OCC opening menu

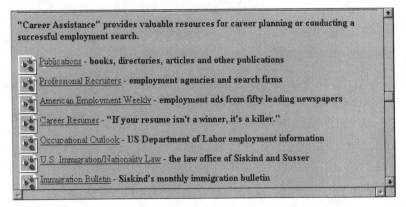

Figure 6.26 The OCC career assistance menu of offerings

Content: Statistics generated by the U.S. government regarding the future of your profession. For example, if you are a writer, you can locate statistics about the projected growth of all sectors of your profession, which in this case might include screen writing, fiction, magazines, and newspapers. You can also find statistics on income and speculation on future trends in the industry. You will find information about thousands of professions in this resource from the most obscure to the most popular. And if you don't find your profession or interest listed here, you will likely find a close relative.

COMPANY RESOURCES

When you see a position announced online that you're interested in, it behooves you to research the company carefully before sending in your resume and cover letter, just as you would in a traditional job search. In your research about the company, you may uncover that the company in question manufactures a product that you use, or that the company has offices in a state you want to move to. You may even find out that the company is on shaky ground financially, and decide *not* to apply for the job.

The more information you have, the better you're able to decide if this is a company you want to work for. And if you do land an interview, you'll want to be up on company activities so that you appear "with it" in your interview. If you are the only applicant who has something to say about the company's pet project, you increase your chances of making it onto the short list.

Information about companies abounds on the information superhighway. Unfortunately, at this time, you must either pay for the information by using a for-a-fee database through a commercial online service, or access what you need through tenacious—and time-consuming—browsing. Therefore, to save you both time and money, we've given you a head start with the following list of company information sites.

We chose these online sites based on which have the most to offer for one visit. This means that you can, in one stop, browse many links. This gives you a chance to see what's available online quickly. And remember, information you find on the Internet or the Web is free of extra database charges. If, for instance, your job as an analyst for a hi-tech company is being downsized out of existence, you can browse the company profiles at the Internet Business Directory site. Looking through the detailed profiles, you will discover which companies could benefit from your expertise. You'll also find contact names in the profiles. Then, it will be up to you to send in your resume and network your way into a job.

If you're looking for a specific company on the Web, *and* you have time to browse, do a search on the keyword *inc*. You will find every incorporated company with a listing on the Web. When we performed this search, we found more than 5,000 companies with a presence on the Net. And that number grows every day.

Internet Sites

Business and Financial Information on the Web

Access: **http://www.wharton.upenn.edu/./netsites/businfo.html**

Content: Meta-list. GNN (Global Network Navigator) Business Pages, AstraNet Business Information (business information available from Prodigy's Internet Information Service), Commercial Sites Index, and much more. You can browse for companies by following the links.

Career Mosaic

Access: **http://www.service.com:80/cm/**

Content: Job listings, plus excellent, in-depth company profiles. To explain how to utilize the wealth of resources available here, let's say that you are currently working in a small company as a computer systems analyst. It was a great place to start out, but now you want something more. You've worked with a lot of Sun Microsystems products, and you know some people who have worked with the company who seemed happy with their jobs. Now you're ready to start your research. A good place to start would be to read the extensive Sun Microsystems profile available on the Career Mosaic database. It's free—all you have to spend is the time reading. You'll learn about the company's history, goals, structure, and success (or failure). You'll even be given a contact address should you wish to apply for a job. Just click on Company Profiles at the menu.

EDGAR Dissemination Project

Access: **http://town.hall.org/edgar/general.html**

Content: This is a project managed by the New York University Stern School of Business. You have access through this Web site to companies' 1994–1995 filings to the Securities and Exchange Commission (SEC), including available annual reports and 10K reports. (A 10K is a detailed report companies are required by law to send to stockholders.) (Note: Only companies who have filed electronically with the SEC are accessible through EDGAR.) See Figures 6.27 and 6.28 for some samples from this source.

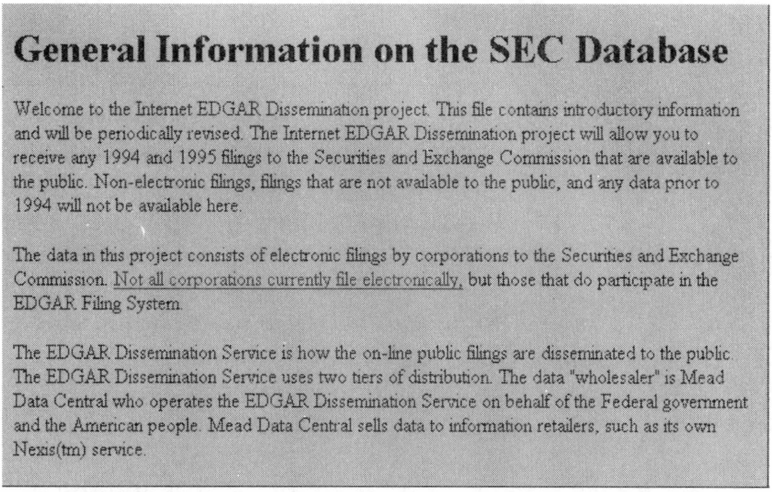

General Information on the SEC Database

Welcome to the Internet EDGAR Dissemination project. This file contains introductory information and will be periodically revised. The Internet EDGAR Dissemination project will allow you to receive any 1994 and 1995 filings to the Securities and Exchange Commission that are available to the public. Non-electronic filings, filings that are not available to the public, and any data prior to 1994 will not be available here.

The data in this project consists of electronic filings by corporations to the Securities and Exchange Commission. Not all corporations currently file electronically, but those that do participate in the EDGAR Filing System.

The EDGAR Dissemination Service is how the on-line public filings are disseminated to the public. The EDGAR Dissemination Service uses two tiers of distribution. The data "wholesaler" is Mead Data Central who operates the EDGAR Dissemination Service on behalf of the Federal government and the American people. Mead Data Central sells data to information retailers, such as its own Nexis(tm) service.

Figure 6.27 General information available through the EDGAR Dissemination Project

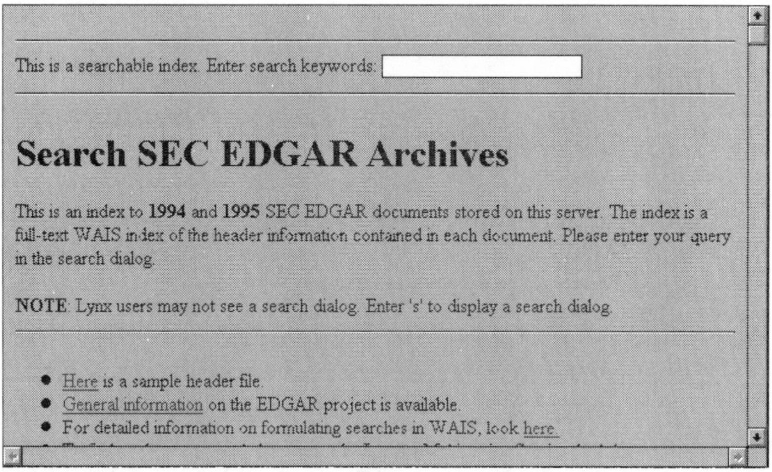

This is a searchable index. Enter search keywords:

Search SEC EDGAR Archives

This is an index to 1994 and 1995 SEC EDGAR documents stored on this server. The index is a full-text WAIS index of the header information contained in each document. Please enter your query in the search dialog.

NOTE: Lynx users may not see a search dialog. Enter 's' to display a search dialog.

- Here is a sample header file.
- General information on the EDGAR project is available.
- For detailed information on formulating searches in WAIS, look here.

Figure 6.28 This is the search screen of the Edgar database. To find out detailed information about a company, just fill in the blank with the company name and press Enter. (Note: Not all companies have information available through Edgar. Please see Edgar for details and master index of companies.)

Interactive Employment Network

Access: **http://www.espan.com**

Content: Profiles of sponsor companies. When you use the Interactive Employment Network, there is no charge to look for jobs and send in your resume to be placed on its system. Sponsoring companies pay a fee so that they can be "profiled" on the IEN. This means that detailed information about the company's products, organization, goals, and history are available online. From an employer's point of view, advertising on a Web site attracts top talent. And it gives you, the job seeker, easy online access to inside company information.

Internet Business Directory

Access: **http://ibd.ar.com/**

Content: Excellent resource for company profiles. Includes a Web Page resume database on which you can put your own HTML resume. If you are an individual browsing for company information online, there is no fee to you; listed companies pay the fees.

Online Career Center

Access: **http://www.iquest.net/occ/**

Content: Selected company profiles, all sponsors.

Open Market's Commercial Sites Index

Access: **http://www.directory.net**

Content: Companies listed, based on approval by the editor. Browse the companies alphabetically. Originally begun by Henry Houh of MIT, this fabulous list was taken over by Open Market, Inc., and is offered as a free service to Web users. (Open Market is a Cambridge, Massachusetts-based company specializing in electronic commerce.) As of this writing, there were 3,326 businesses listed on this database, including AT&T Home Page, Bank of America, Bank of Ireland, Citicorp, Club Med, Eaton Law Firm, and Allstate Motor. Also included in this database are listings for nonprofit organizations, cities, states, and government agencies.

Primenet

Access: **http://www.primenet.com/links/companies.html**

Content: A list of companies, organizations, and Internet commercial services. Examples include Berkeley Software Design, Inc., the Celestin Company, Farallon, Federal Express, IBM, Milne Jewelry Co., Silicon Graphics; many more.

Interesting Business Sites on the Web

Access: **http://www.rpi.edu/~okeefe/business.html**

Content: A select group of large and small companies on the Web. Pizza Hut, Compaq, General Electric, and College Pro were some of the ones we saw when we visited. Excellent links to other business sites on the Web.

Rocky Mountain Region Manufacturers Information Service

Access: **http://129.72.1761**

or

http://129.72.176.1/man-docs/man-query-info-sys.html

Content: Regional company locator. If you live in this area, this may be the only online service you need to access—and, it's free.

World Wide Web Yellow Pages

Access: **http://www.yellow.com**

Content: Selected business categories. Search by category; for example, *plumbing*. Yields name, number, and address. If you are looking for a company that specializes in your field or area of interest, this is a good resource to tap. If, for instance, you are trying to find all of the commercial advertising firms located in southern Florida, you could search the WWW Yellow Pages for *advertising*, and then scour the addresses to see if you find a match. Or, if you've heard about a company, but you don't know where it's located or the phone number, you can search the Yellow Pages for a possible match. Since the pages are national in scope, you save yourself the time it would take to look through numerous phone books in the library.

Commercial Online Service Sites

All of the listings you have seen so far are available for free. There are, however, several for-pay listings we don't want you to miss. Almost every online service has such databases available. An online encyclopedia, a selection of electronic newspapers, a medical guide, dictionaries, Dun and Bradstreet's Business Directory, and other general references are also staples of many services.

But other helpful references are available only on certain online services. This is the bane of competition in the information age—sometimes you have to subscribe to two services or more to get all of the reference information you want, simply because the online services want exclusivity to a particular resource. Two services that currently offer what we consider to be very attractive but exclusive business references are America Online and CompuServe. Of course, this may all change by the time you read this.

We stress again that these services cost extra (and sometimes they can be very pricey!), so check into the cost before you begin your online research. You can do this by accessing the area by keyword, and then by reading the help sections. (Reading the help sections does not carry a surcharge, and will, in the long run, save you a good deal of money.)

America Online

Access: Voice 800-827-6364

Content: *Hoover's Handbook* (information on over 500 major corporations, including a brief history of the corporation, earnings, locations, and corporate structure) and *Executive Desk Register of Publicly Held Corporations*. Keywords for searching: *Hoover, career*.

CompuServe

Access: Voice 800-848-8199

Content: Extensive company information. *Corporate Affiliations* (keyword: *affiliations*) offers profiles and reference information on most of the large U.S. public companies and their affiliates. *D&B Dun's Electronic Business Directory* (keyword: *dun-*

sebd) is a directory of information on more than 8.5 million professionals and businesses in the U.S., both public and private. Lists type of business, address and phone number, number of employees, and information about parent company. *D&B Dun's Market Identifiers* (keyword: *duns*) allows you to find complete company information about international companies. For really detailed information, go for *Disclosure II* (keyword: *disclosure)* which includes the 10K and detailed financial statements as well as owners, directors, and more.

≡≡≡ SOURCES OF EXPERTISE

In Chapter 4, we told you that Usenet is a way to locate and communicate with experts. In addition, increasingly, there are other ways being developed to tap into expert advice, including Internet "White Pages" and business directories.

To access these resources, simply use Internet search engines such as the Web Crawler (see Chapter 5 and later in this chapter) to type in a keyword related to the professional organizations, associations, or university departments you would like to make contact with. More often than not, you will find an expert's name this way.

Internet Sites

AT&T 800 Directory on the Internet

Access: **http://att.net/dir800**

Content: Toll-free numbers of people and businesses. Search by category or name. You would use this service to find people and companies nationwide. If, for example, there is a company you know you want to work for, you can look up the name on this directory. If the company is listed, you will have a toll-free contact number that you can call for more information. Another way to use this service is for verification. If someone advertises a position online, you can look here to see if there is an 800 number.

AmeriCom Long Distance Area Decoder

Access: **http://www.xmission.com/~americom/aclookup.html**

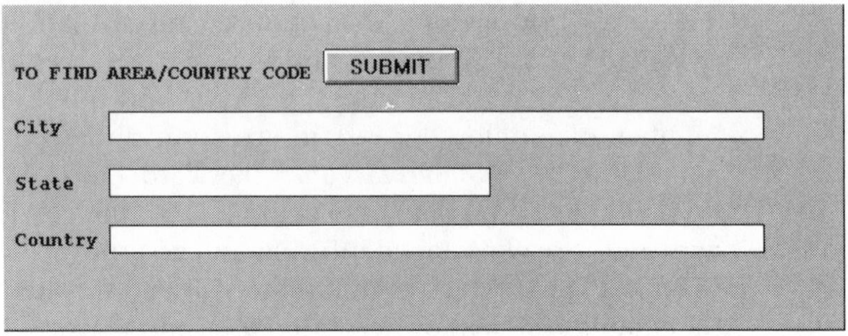

TO FIND AREA/COUNTRY CODE SUBMIT

City

State

Country

Figure 6.29 Area code searching on the Web

Content: This is a tool that will decode any city, area, or country code—it's a basic look-up service (see Figure 6.29).

Community of Science Web Server

Access: **http://best.gdb.org/**

Content: This is a service that helps you identify and locate researchers with interests and expertise similar to your own. You can even add yourself! For a sample, see Figure 6.30.

Great Organizations' Phone Books

Access: **gopher gopher.nd.edu**

Content: A gopher site listing hundreds of organizations, universities, labs, agencies, and corporations that have their phone books stored on the Web.

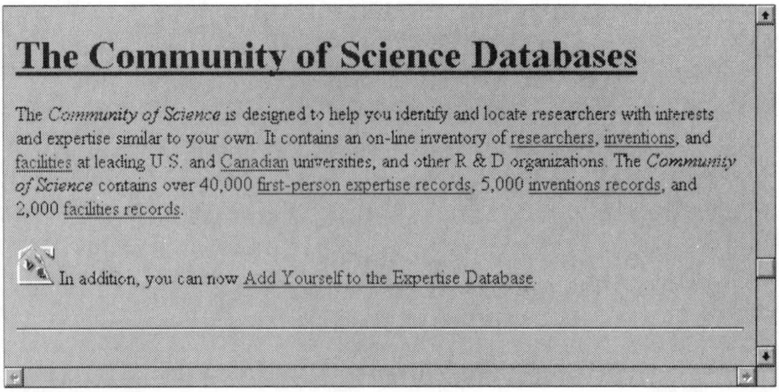

The Community of Science Databases

The *Community of Science* is designed to help you identify and locate researchers with interests and expertise similar to your own. It contains an on-line inventory of researchers, inventions, and facilities at leading U.S. and Canadian universities, and other R & D organizations. The *Community of Science* contains over 40,000 first-person expertise records, 5,000 inventions records, and 2,000 facilities records.

In addition, you can now Add Yourself to the Expertise Database.

Figure 6.30 A quick look at the Community of Science Web Server

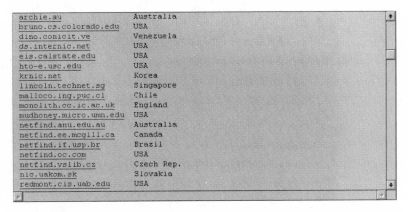

archie.au	Australia
bruno.cs.colorado.edu	USA
dino.conicit.ve	Venezuela
ds.internic.net	USA
eis.calstate.edu	USA
hto-e.usc.edu	USA
krnic.net	Korea
lincoln.technet.sg	Singapore
malloco.ing.puc.cl	Chile
monolith.cc.ic.ac.uk	England
mudhoney.micro.umn.edu	USA
netfind.anu.edu.au	Australia
netfind.ee.mcgill.ca	Canada
netfind.if.usp.br	Brazil
netfind.oc.com	USA
netfind.vslib.cz	Czech Rep.
nic.uakom.sk	Slovakia
redmont.cis.uab.edu	USA

Figure 6.31 Telnet addresses for accessing Netfind

Netfind

Access: Telnet to a host. See Figure 6.31 for hosts and host addresses.

Content: Netfind is an email lookup service that operates through a simple interface. To operate, telnet to one of the sites shown in Figure 6.31 and follow the instructions. Briefly, you go to a Telnet prompt from your Internet account (you will see a prompt at your opening menu). There, you type in one of the addresses you see in Figure 6.31 exactly as shown. Press Enter, and a screen of instructions will appear on your screen. If this does not work, at the telnet prompt, type "open" followed by one space and then the address. Press Return.

PC Phone List

Access: **http:// comp.sys.ibm.pc.harware.misc**

Content: An extensive list of computer industry phone numbers.

Who's Online

Access: **http://www.ictp.trieste.it/Canessa/entries/ entries.html**

Content: In-depth information about who is online, with some limitations. See Figure 6.32.

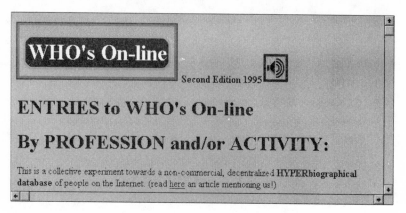

Figure 6.32 Information about the Who's Online service

X500 World Directory

Access: **Gopher umich.edu**

Content: A simple interface to a world directory of folks on the Internet.

Yahoo List of Organizations and Associations

Access: **http://akebono.stanford.edu/yahoo/economy/ organization/professional/**

Content: Created by David Filo and Jerry Yang, (both Ph.D. candidates in electrical engineering at Stanford University) this list boasts over 32,000 entries. We've listed just one portion of the Yahoo list, which links to the professional associations and organizations that have a presence on the Web. If you are looking for an expert, this is a good place to start looking.

Commercial Online Service Sites

CompuServe

Access: Voice 800-848-8199

Content: Phone File, keyword *phonefile.* An online phone book that gives you instant access to over 75 million U.S. households, and one that we can personally vouch for.

PROFESSION-SPECIFIC INFORMATION

Whatever you do for a living, trust us when we tell you that you will very likely find volumes—perhaps even libraries—of highly detailed profession-specific information about it online. It is an impossible task to keep up with the growth and changes constantly taking place in this area of online resources, so we've just listed many of the current hotspots from a variety of professional fields, plus meta-lists—you remember, those lists with links to other resources organized by subjects. There are hundreds of these lists, so we've chosen those we think will be of the most help to you as you look for a job.

Internet Meta-Lists

Clearinghouse for Subject-Oriented Resource Guides

Access: **http://www.lib.umich.edu/chhome.html**

Content: This is a repository of almost 200 guides to subjects on the Internet. Check here for information that relates to your profession. For example, there are guides for journalists, writers, librarians, scientists, etc. Each of these guides is a world unto itself.

Institute of Chartered Accountants of England and Wales, Accounting Information Service

Access: **http://www.ex.ac.uk/~BJSpaul/icaew/icaew.html**

Content: A large meta-list for professional accountants. Click on the Summa Project, and you will find yourself at a Web site for accounting academics, professionals, and students. This is the Summa Project, which is part of the International Accounting Network. Here you can take part in an "Accountants on the Web" workshop, or you can visit one of many information-packed sites, such as the Dow Jones page, the World Bank, Financenet, the European Accounting Association, the Currency Converter, the U.S. Institute of Management, and the IRS online.

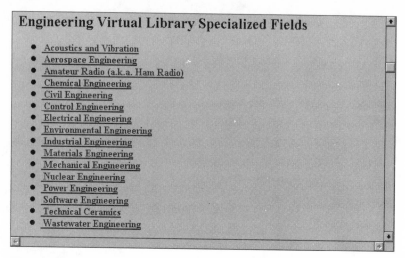

Figure 6.33 Specifics on the Engineering Meta-List

Engineering Meta-List

Access: **http:// epims1.gsfc.nasa.gov/engineering/ engineering.html**

Content: Every possible engineering field is covered in this meta-list. See Figure 6.33 for a list of links.

Humbul Gateway

Access: **http://sable.ox.ac.uk/departments/humanities/ international.html**

Content: Probably the best meta-list for the humanities. Figure 6.34 offers a peek at some of what's offered.

Infomine Meta-List

Access: **http://lib-www.ucr.edu/rivera/california**

Content: A meta-list for arts, humanities, and social science resources. One-stop Web-hopping—many links.

Medical Matrix: Guide to Internet Medical Resources

Access: **http://kuhttp.cc.ukans.edu/cwis/units/medcntr/la/ homepage.html**

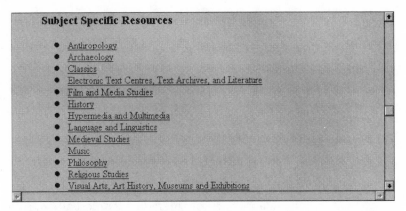

Figure 6.34 A peek at the Humbul Gateway humanities meta-list

Content: The very best medical meta-list available. Information for nurses and physicians.

Merit Gopher

Access: **gopher nic.merit.edu**

Content: This is a comprehensive collection of information in a gopher meta-list. You will find information about professions such as accounting, science, and medicine—but note that every resource will be available through a gopher.

Virtual Reference Desk

Access: **http://www.gnn.com/gnn/wic/refbook.ll.html**

Content: A good place to browse for all professional information. For example, you can find the CIA World Factbook, a geographic database, online phone books, dictionaries (computing, technical, German, English, French, slang) selected dissertations, Vanderbilt news archives, and online reference works. You can use resources like these to tweak your resume into shape, to tap into the latest research, and to get terms and definitions accurate before you go into a nerve-wracking interview.

Whole Internet Catalog

Access: **http://nearnet.gnn.com/wic/newrescat.toc.html**

Content: It's not an exaggeration to say that every possible profession has links in this wonderful meta-list.

World Wide Web Virtual Library

Access: **http://info.cern.ch/hypertext/DataSources/ bySubject/Overview.html**

Content: Don't skip this meta-list! The creators and maintainers have gone to extraordinary lengths to make it as complete as a library. You can find detailed information about the following subjects at this site: architecture, art, biotechnology, communications, conferences, design, education, engineering, history, law, medicine, politics, publishing, and sports—to mention only a few. The links you'll find are extensive. You can easily spend one hour in just one small area, so pick well!

Yahoo

Access: **http://akebono.stanford.edu/yahoo/**

Content: This is a very extensive, yet selective list of resources. You could spend hours exploring the links. Many professional resources available. Highly recommended. For example, you could access this site and choose the link Business. There are over 8,000 business links on this list, one of which leads to 8,000 corporations on the Web. Another link leads to employment sites on the Web (over 200 and expanding rapidly). And a reminder: This is the main address for the Yahoo list. We've given you the addresses for highly specialized portions of the list already. Here, you'll be able to roam at will, without us choosing your point of entry into the list.

Profession-Specific Sites

These sites have been listed alphabetically, not by profession. Note that because of the way the Web cross-links information, you will discover that each of these sites has great depth of information.

American Accounting Association

Access: **http://www.rutgers.edu/accounting/raw/aaa/ aaa.htm**

Content: For accountants.

American Philosophical Association

Access: **http://www.oxy.edu/apa/apa.html**

Content: Hume archives for philosophers.

Architecture and Building: Net Resources

Access: **gopher una.hh.lib.umich.edu**

or

http://www.uky.edu/artsource/bibliography/brown.html

Content: Anyone even remotely connected to these professions should take a look at these huge lists. Many links to other resources.

Astronomy Resources on the Web

Access: **http://anarky/stsci/edu/astroweb/net-www.html**

Content: Hundreds of links to astronomy and astronomy-related information. A spectacular list. Some examples: Radio Astronomy Group, Xerox Palo Alto Center, Whipple Observatory, Washington Area Astronomers Networking Group.

Bureau of the Census

Access: **http://www.census.gov/**

Content: Census figures. Good for professionals working as city planners, marketers, sales professionals—for anyone who needs in-depth knowledge of demographics.

Economic Bulletin Board

Access: **gopher una.hh.lib.umich.edu**

Content: Many links to vast economic resources.

Financenet: U.S. Government Internet Service

Access: **http://www.financenet.gov**

Content: Anything and everything to do with the finance professions.

Imaging Systems Laboratory (ISL)

Access: **http//www.cc.columbia.edu:80/~archpub/**

Content: A site maintained at the Columbia Graduate School of architecture. See Figure 6.35 for a sample. From this site you can browse cathedral drawings and construction sequences, follow links to other schools of architecture to snoop the latest trends and hot topics, or follow links to other architectural sites, such as the civil and construction engineering links that are available.

Chemistry Information

Access: **http://www.chemie.fa-berlin.de/index_e.html**

Content: International information for chemists. A huge list.

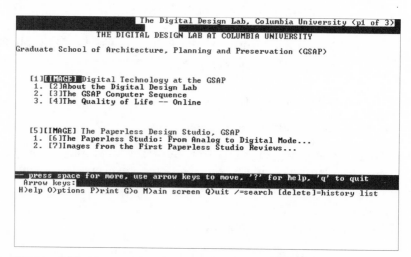

Figure 6.35 ISL as seen from Lynx, a text-based Web browser. Note how the graphics are marked with the word IMAGE.

Relativistic rocket equation (constant acceleration)

$$t \text{ (unaccelerated)} = c/a * \sinh(a*t/c)$$
$$d = c**2/a * (\cosh(a*t/c) - 1)$$
$$v = c * \tanh(a*t/c)$$

Figure 6.36 A rocket science equation from NASA

NASA

Access: **http://www.gsfc.nasa.gov/**

Content: Extremely high-level astronomy information, including a helpful listing of constants and equations. See the lovely equation in Figure 6.36.

National Institute of Allergy and Infectious Diseases

Access: **http://web.fie.com/web/fed/nih**

Content: A branch of the NIH, only this is on the Web.

National Institutes of Health (NIH)

Access: **gopher gopher.nih.gov**

Content: One of the most extensive medical listings available. Many menus for research projects, email addresses of professionals, information index of topics, etc. A must-stop for medical professionals.

National Science Foundation (NSF)

Access: **gopher stis.nsf.gov**

Content: An avalanche of information for scientists. See Figure 6.37.

Pharmacology

Access: **http://pharminfo.com/**

Content: Very useful drug database. The very latest information.

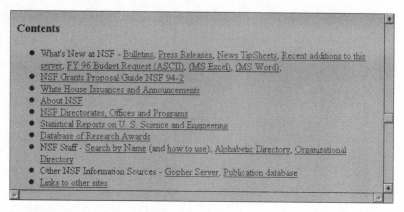

Contents

- What's New at NSF - Bulletins, Press Releases, News TipSheets, Recent additions to this server, FY 96 Budget Request (ASCII), (MS Excel), (MS Word),
- NSF Grants Proposal Guide NSF 94-2
- White House Issuances and Announcements
- About NSF
- NSF Directorates, Offices and Programs
- Statistical Reports on U. S. Science and Engineering
- Database of Research Awards
- NSF Staff - Search by Name (and how to use), Alphabetic Directory, Organizational Directory
- Other NSF Information Sources - Gopher Server, Publication database
- Links to other sites

Figure 6.37 A portion of the NSF gopher

Purdue University OWL

Access: **http://owl.trc.purdue.edu/**

Content: Excellent resource for journalists and writers. Information about writing, including discussions about outlining techniques, (necessary for any professional writer) and those tricky MLA and APA formats.

The Virtual Hospital

Access: **http://www2.osaka-med.ac.jp/iowa/virtualhospital.html**

Content: This is, literally, a "virtual hospital." A must-visit for medical professionals. Figure 6.38 has a partial list of topics covered.

Thomas

Access: **http://thomas.loc.gov**

Content: For all professionals who need to keep up on legislation regarding their industry. Full text of any and all bills introduced in Congress since 1992, and daily proceedings of the congressional record, all searchable by keyword and updated daily.

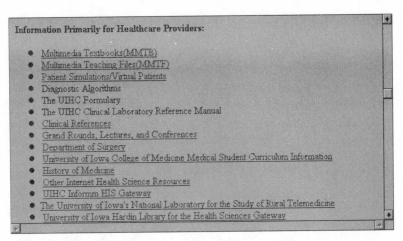

Information Primarily for Healthcare Providers:

- Multimedia Textbooks(MMTB)
- Multimedia Teaching Files(MMTF)
- Patient Simulations/Virtual Patients
- Diagnostic Algorithms
- The UIHC Formulary
- The UIHC Clinical Laboratory Reference Manual
- Clinical References
- Grand Rounds, Lectures, and Conferences
- Department of Surgery
- University of Iowa College of Medicine Medical Student Curriculum Information
- History of Medicine
- Other Internet Health Science Resources
- UIHC Informm HIS Gateway
- The University of Iowa's National Laboratory for the Study of Rural Telemedicine
- University of Iowa Hardin Library for the Health Sciences Gateway

Figure 6.38 Some of the topics covered at the Virtual Hospital site

Toll-Free Numbers for Health Information

Access: **http://nhic-nt.health.org/html/gen/html/gen.ex/ tollfree?descriptor='800'**

Content: Organizations you can contact free of charge for up-to-date medical information. See Figure 6.39.

- ABLEDATA
- Aerobics and Fitness Association of America
- Al-Anon Family Group Headquarters
- Alzheimer's Association
- American Academy of Pediatrics (AAP)
- American Board of Medical Specialties
- American Cancer Society
- American Diabetes Association
- American Institute for Cancer Research
- American Osteopathic Association
- American Social Health Association
- American Society For Dermatologic Surgery
- American Society of Plastic and Reconstructive Surgeons.
- Amyotrophic Lateral Sclerosis Association

Figure 6.39 A snapshot of the organizations you can contact on the Toll-Free Numbers Directory

U.S. Geological Survey

Access: **http://info.er.usgs.gov/network/science/earth/index.html**

Content: Climatology, earth science, earthquakes, environmental, volcanology, oceanography, GIS, hydrology—all are covered in this very extensive information site. Many resources.

U.S. Institute of Management

Access: **http:// starbase.ingress.com.ioma**

Content: Information for professionals involved in management. Many other links to business-related information.

White House Information

Access: **http://www.whitehouse.gov**

Content: Policy briefings, speeches, executive orders, Congressional testimony, much more. See Figure 6.40 for a sample of what you can find at this Web site. Useful for many disciplines; it's always important to stay up on the latest goings-on in our government.

Commercial Profession-Specific Sites

Commercial online services, as a group or separately, offer an incalculable wealth of professional information. Unfortu-

2. Topical Releases

- Browse briefings on economic policy.
- Browse briefings on environmental policy.
- Browse briefings on foreign affairs.
- Browse briefings on jobs.
- Browse releases on healthcare.
- Browse releases on science and technology [1993, 1994].

Figure 6.40 A small sample of what you can find at the White House Information site

nately, it is beyond the scope of this book to list the individual attributes of each. If you have just signed on to a commercial online service and still have questions as to how to tap into the professional resources of your particular service, you'll find plenty of help simply by logging on to your account. If you have not signed on to one of these services yet, but want to, refer to Chapter 7 for the toll-free numbers of America Online, CompuServe, Prodigy, GEnie, and Delphi.

RELOCATING? DO IT TECHNO-STYLE

Your company is relocating its headquarters, and you're faced with moving to a new part of the country—or world. Or the job market in your profession has dried up where you live. Or your spouse has a great opportunity in another city and now you've got to look for work there, too. Or, you're just sick of where you live and want a fresh start in a new place. Whatever the reason for relocating, online technology can help answer your questions, find out about where you're going, and how to do it the most efficiently.

Internet Sites

CIA World Factbook

Access: **http://www.ic.gov/94fact/fb94toc/fb94toc.html**

Content: Now you can make use of those tax dollars. This factbook is filled with precise and helpful information on every country on the globe. The countries are analyzed by many criteria—a must-see.

City Net

Access: **http://www.city.net/**

Content: If you only access this one page, you'll probably find every shred of relocation information you need. Pictures, restaurants, you name it. There is simply no better resource for finding city or community information in the United States or abroad. Figures 6.41, 6.42, and 6.43 give you an idea of the scope of this network.

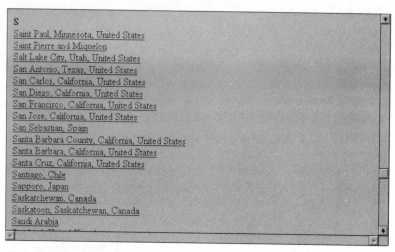

Figure 6.41 City Net's city page links

Country Studies/Area Handbooks

Access: **http://lcweb.loc.gov/homepage/country.html**

Content: Analyses of Egypt, Indonesia, Israel, Japan, the Philippines, Singapore, Somalia, South Korea, and the areas formerly known as Yugoslavia. Incredibly detailed and scholarly,

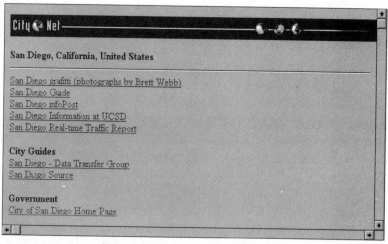

Figure 6.42 San Diego's opening page

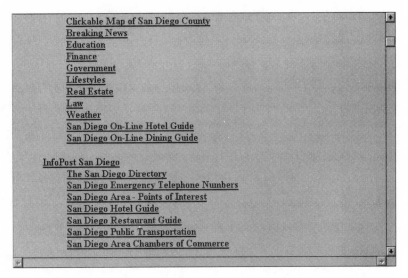

Clickable Map of San Diego County
Breaking News
Education
Finance
Government
Lifestyles
Real Estate
Law
Weather
San Diego On-Line Hotel Guide
San Diego On-Line Dining Guide

InfoPost San Diego
The San Diego Directory
San Diego Emergency Telephone Numbers
San Diego Area - Points of Interest
San Diego Hotel Guide
San Diego Restaurant Guide
San Diego Public Transportation
San Diego Area Chambers of Commerce

Figure 6.43 Offering available via the San Diego city page

these studies were prepared by social scientists working for the Federal Research Division of the Library of Congress. The guides describe each foreign country in every way, particularly as relating to the culture.

Freenets U.S and Abroad

Access: **http://herald.usask.ca/~scottp/freewww.html**

Content: A linked list of all Web freenets. Remember that freenets contain unparalleled information on local communities. See Figure 6.44 for a sample.

GNN Travel Centre

Access: **http://gnn.com/gnn/meta/travel**

Content: Features currency exchange rates, traveler's reading room. Much information about planning a trip, including travel guides, health notes, languages, lodging, packing and travel tips, important phone numbers, transportation, and maps.

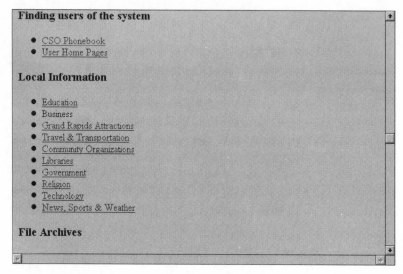

Figure 6.44 A look at the Grand Rapids freenet offerings

Railroad-Related Internet Resources

Access: **http://www-cse.ucsd.edu/users/bowdidge/ railroad/rail-home.html**

Content: Lists extensive rail information—times, ticket prices—at specific cities in the U.S. and abroad.

Toll-Free Airline Phone Numbers

Access: **gopher cs4sun.cs.ttu.edu**

Content: A list of all commercial airlines and their toll-free numbers.

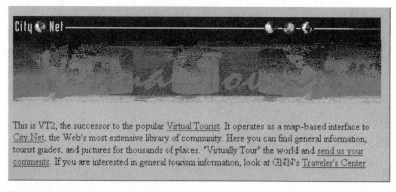

Figure 6.45 VT2's opening page

VT2 (successor to Virtual Tourist)

Access: **http://wings.buffalo.edu/world/vt2**

Content: Virtual Tourist 2 is a part of the City Net, discussed previously. It offers a point-and-click interface to maps of the world and detailed information about the destinations. Figure 6.45 is the opening page. From the map in Figure 6.46, you can access the list of countries shown in Figure 6.47. A quick take on the offerings for Ireland is shown in Figure 6.48.

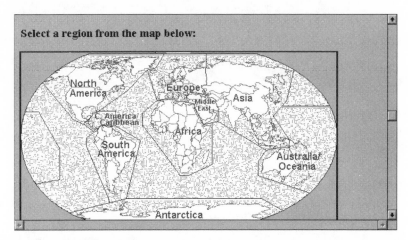

Figure 6.46 The Virtual Map available through VT2

Afghanistan	Eritrea	Luxembourg	Slovenia
Argentina	Estonia	Macau	Somalia
Aruba	Ethiopia	Malaysia	South Africa
Australia	Finland	Mauritius	South Korea
Austria	France	Mexico	Spain
Bangladesh	Germany	Moldova	Sri Lanka
Barbados	Ghana	Morocco	Suriname
Belgium	Greece	Nepal	Sweden
Bermuda	Guatemala	Netherlands	Switzerland
Bosnia and Herzegovina	Hong Kong	New Zealand	Taiwan
Brazil	Hungary	Norway	Thailand
British Virgin Islands	Iceland	Pakistan	Trinidad and Tob
Bulgaria	India	Panama	Tunisia
Canada	Indonesia	Peru	Turkey
Cayman Islands	Iran	Philippines	Turks and Caicos
Chile	Ireland	Poland	Ukraine
China	Israel	Portugal	United Kingdom
Croatia	Italy	Republic of Macedonia	United States
Cyprus	Japan	Romania	Uruguay
Czech Republic	Jordan	Russia	Vatican City
Denmark	Kuwait	Saudi Arabia	Venezuela
Ecuador	Latvia	Singapore	Yugoslavia
Egypt	Lithuania	Slovakia	

Figure 6.47 The list of countries covered by City Net

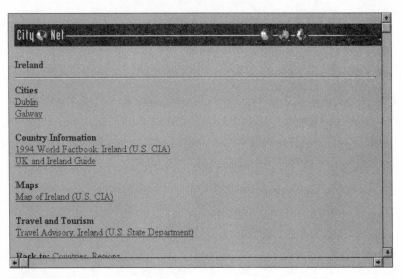

Figure 6.48 The results of following one link in City Net. Clicking on any underlined link leads you immediately to more information displayed graphically or textually.

Yahoo List

Access: **http://akebono.stanford.edu/yahoo/ regional_inform ation/**

Content: This portion of the Yahoo meta-list provides maps and detailed regional information. A super starting point that gives a different spin from City Net.

≡ CONCLUSION

In this chapter we have given you the addresses and names of some of our favorite Internet resources. These spots will give you a great start as you begin to develop your own career trail through the online data forest. And as you cut through the thickets, remember to use your search tools, because they're the fastest and most efficient way to make your own way through the Internet.

Where the Jobs Are

Welcome to a comprehensive online job list that tells you where to look for jobs and post resumes on the World Wide Web, the Internet, commercial online services, bulletin boards, and more. This list will save you from literally hundreds of hours of hunting and pecking online. Obviously, no printed list of this sort can ever be complete because of the rapid growth of online services, but this one will show you where the current hotspots are. In addition, because we know that the list will need to be updated, we tell you how to do this at the end of this chapter.

When we first compiled this list in mid-1994, there were hundreds of listings. When we updated this list just prior to completion of this book, the number of online job listings had grown by a whopping 2,000 additional addresses. And most of that growth occurred on the World Wide Web.

Which brings us to an important point for job seekers. A year ago, you could have gone online to find a job and not missed anything by not perusing the Web sites at all. Juicy spots via Telnet, gopher, and commercial online services would've kept you busy. Now, while those sites are still attractive and useful, you'll miss out on many valuable job resources if you ignore the Web.

PUT YOUR SIGHTS ON WEB SITES

The World Wide Web is now *the* place to look for jobs. In fact, the Web is home to the *very best job offerings available* because almost every major corporation, university, and college in the United States—and many abroad—have very high-speed connections to the Web. And once on the Web, almost no one goes back to a basic Internet connection. As of early 1995, most of these organizations used the Web exclusively to post anything. Admittedly, this smacks of elitism for those of us sitting at home with our little PCs and slower connection speeds. But remember that soon, just as the Internet became mainstream, the Web too will become mainstream.

Meanwhile, do whatever you can to get a Web connection. Also don't forget about using Lynx, a text-only Web browser you can access through public sites with a simple computer setup. (That is, if you don't have windows or a SLIP account.)

ZEROING IN ON YOUR PROFESSION

As you look through these job listings, your area of interest may not be readily visible, but keep looking! After searching through thousands of listings, we can assure you that you can—and will—find job gems hiding in the unlikeliest places. So the best advice is to keep your options—and eyes—open. As mentioned in Chapter 4 on networking, browse all sorts of obtuse job lists, and be prepared to be surprised. For example, if you're not a mathematician, you may not think of looking in the Mathematical Society's listings for a job. But maybe you ought to. Mathematicians need more than just number crunchers to get their work done. They need administrators to manage them, landscapers to design and take care of their building grounds, accountants to keep the books, data entry clerks to input data, editors to make their newsletter sparkle . . . well, you get the idea.

HOW THIS LIST IS ORGANIZED

The Internet portion of the job list follows this order:

♦ Job-related sites available via the World Wide Web.

- ◆ Usenet job sites. Usenet contains very important job lists and is accessible through so many services.
- ◆ Gopher listings.
- ◆ Telnet listings.
- ◆ Freenet/community net listings.

The next section of the list contains sites available via employment bulletin boards, commercial online services, and independent online employment databases.

The Joys of Overlap

We've mentioned before that the online services overlap. It bears repeating that Usenet is now accessible not just from the Internet, but from most commercial online service providers, too. Gopher, currently only available from the Internet or from a service like Delphi or BIX, will soon be available from some of the commercial online service providers.

And this isn't the only kind of overlap that occurs in the electronic world. Because so much of the Internet is currently in the process of shifting to the World Wide Web, there are many sites that have more than one major electronic address. For example, the Online Career Center (OCC) is now available via gopher and the Web—and both are important sites. However, the Web version of the OCC is much more attractive, easier to use, and has additional help for job seekers. The gopher version of OCC contains the important job information and resume information, but in text-only form.

Because the Web is the future focus of online technology, we have decided to list any site that has a Web address, plus another address like a gopher or FTP, as a Web site first, with a cross-reference to the other service. For example, the Online Career Center is listed as a major Web site, and under the Web section of this job list, you will find a detailed description of the OCC and its services. At the end of the listing, you will find a cross-reference to the OCC's gopher address. In the gopher section of the list, you will find OCC's gopher address, a very brief description, and a reference back to the Web section for details.

Details, Details, Details

The job listings contain several elements (depending on availability) to help you get the most from the list, including:

♦ Electronic address.

♦ Approximate number of jobs listed, when available. In all cases, the number given should be interpreted as that quantity or fewer (based on information gathered January 1995).

♦ Types of jobs (technical, managerial, etc.).

♦ How frequently the list is updated, if available.

♦ Whether the list is fee-based (most of the job lists in this book are free of charge).

♦ Whether the list posts just job openings or also accepts resumes and has discussions about jobs.

♦ Any rules you need to be aware of for the list.

♦ If the list is available via another service or means.

For the very best job lists, be on the lookout for the sunburst icon, which indicates job search hotspots.

If you have access to both a Web account and a basic Internet account, you may be wondering which is the better way to access "overlapping" services such as the Online Career Center. It's simple: if you are using a PC and are most concerned about saving time, try the basic connection, which is much faster for PC users. In an overlapped service, you know you're not missing anything, so you may as well save time.

But if you are concerned about your ability to navigate, then stick with your Web connection. Even though you will not get to where you are going as quickly, you will not get lost, thanks to the easy interface.

If you are accessing the Internet from a high-speed line, (perhaps from a university or a corporation) then by all means use the Web connection to take advantage of the easy graphical interface.

We cannot make any guarantees about the services or information on any of these lists, so please use common sense as you
look through them. For example, recently, someone put a message on many of the job lists asking for money in exchange for
a booklet about the supposedly greatest home-based business
ever. This is the kind of message you should ignore.

JOB RESOURCES AVAILABLE VIA THE WORLD WIDE WEB

This list is organized in sections, as follows:

♦ In the first section, you'll find the best, general job
searching areas on the Web.

♦ In the second section, you'll find the best industry- or
organization-specific job searching areas on the Web.

♦ In the third section, you'll find companies that list job
openings on the Web.

♦ The fourth section briefly covers universities.

♦ Finally, a miscellaneous section wraps up the listings that
don't fit comfortably anywhere else.

Remember, this is not a comprehensive list, but you will find
the very best of what is available. If you need help navigating
the Web, refer to Chapter 5. If you don't currently have Web
access, you'll want to get it!

General Job Listings Sites on the Web

National/International

Career Mosaic

Access: **http://www.service.com:80/cm/**

This is one of the sleekest members of the Big Five, which are
the top mega-hotspots of all online services. Career Mosaic
bears the distinction of being one of the first employment spots
on the Web. It has grown steadily to become a place you should
browse for ideas, no matter what your profession. Currently,
companies such as the ones shown in Figure 7.1 post their job

Figure 7.1 A small portion of the high-profile companies setting up shop at the Career Mosaic Web site

vacancies here. The number of jobs available varies from 100 to many more.

Career Taxi

Access: **http://www.iquest.net/Career_Taxi/taxi.html**

Career Taxi maintains a link to the Online Career Center for its job listings. Be aware that Career Taxi is graphics-heavy, and you may want to turn off your image loading if you're using Netscape or Mosaic.

Contract Employment Weekly (CE Weekly)

Access: **http://www.ceweekly.wa.com**

The purpose of CE Weekly is to "furnish subscribers, as fast as possible, with information about immediate and anticipated job openings throughout the U.S., Canada, and overseas . All jobs appearing in CE Weekly are temporary technical jobs that are usually higher paying than similar direct jobs."

CyberDyne CS

Access: **http://www.demon.co.uk/cyberdyne/cyber.html**

This is a U.K.-based service that will put you in touch with top recruiter's openings in Australia, Asia, Africa, Europe, and more. If you want to move overseas, don't miss this site.

Direct Marketing World's Job Center

Access: **http://mainsail.com/jobsinfo.html**

This site, as of December 23, 1994, has turned out to be a very hot place to visit, with job openings ranging from home page designer to restaurant manager—this site has it all. Take a look for yourself.

E-Span's Interactive Employment Network (IEN)

Access: **http://www.espan.com**

This is perhaps the biggest of the Big Five of the job listing and resume posting sites on all of the online services. To say that E-Span is busy is an understatement: It is getting well *over 100,000 accesses per week on its Web site alone.* The service is free to job seekers, the setup is very user-friendly, and there are super job hunting resources in addition to job postings. This site has so many lines that you'll have little to no difficulty connecting. Monitor this site regularly for the jobs you want—they're up-dated *every day.* Don't miss it. Look at Figures 7.2–7.3 for a smattering of what IEN looks like.

Employment Edge Control

Access: **http://sensemedia.net/employment.edge**

This is a brand new service that promises to be a fabulous resource for job seekers (see Figure 7.4). When we checked, there were many jobs listed for a varied group of professions. This site is getting accessed a lot, which is always a good sign.

Welcome! E-SPAN's Interactive Employment Network (IEN) provides current, authoritative resources for the job seeker and--in the near future--for the employer. Hypertext links enable direct postings of resumes to the database, and speed access to job search tips, employment listings, salary guides, career fair calendars, a comment section, and more.

Figure 7.2 Opening menu of E-Span

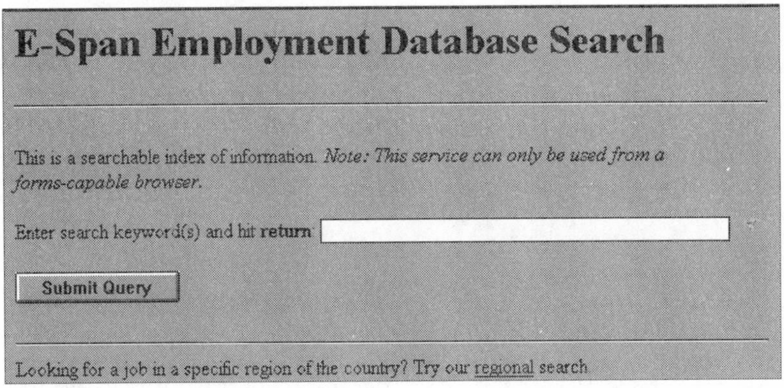

E-Span Employment Database Search

This is a searchable index of information. *Note: This service can only be used from a forms-capable browser.*

Enter search keyword(s) and hit **return**

[Submit Query]

Looking for a job in a specific region of the country? Try our regional search

Figure 7.3 You can use keywords to search E-Span's employment database.

Biggest areas of interest are: accounting, auditing, engineering, legal, management, and programming.

FedWorld

Access: **http://www.fedworld.gov**

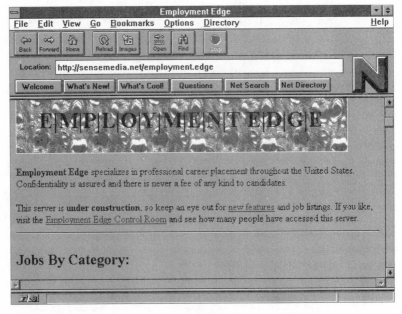

Figure 7.4 The opening screen of Employment Edge

This is a Web site for government job listings of many types. There are about 3,000 jobs available through FedWorld. To apply, look at the phone number and address listed under each separate job listing. Be aware that the jobs contain little actual salary information; they are referenced by "government service levels" such as GS-9.

HeartMosaic

Access: **http://www.geo.net:8500/**

This is the Web version of the telnet and gopher site. Heart "specializes in facilitating the connection between recruiters and candidates." The Web site links to their Telnet site as of this writing.

 ### Online Career Center

Access: **http://www.iquest.net/occ/** or
http://www.iquest.net/occ/HomePage.html

This is an intensely busy Web site. In December 1994, the site was accessed once every four seconds. You may have to access the OCC at odd hours to gain access. (Odd translates to after the 7 to 11 p.m. rush and before business hours.) But the wait will be worth it. This is another of the Big Five job searching sites on the Web and Internet. The reason it's so hot is because you can post your resume and know that employers will see it. You also can browse jobs by state, city, keyword, and more. It's job searching worth staying up for.

Papyrus Media Careers Online

Access: **http://www.Britain.EU.net/vendor/jobs/main.html**

Papyrus Media specializes in listing international jobs. As this is a relatively new service, there were only a few jobs listed when we visited this site.

The Job Board

Access: **http://www.fsu.edu/Jobs.html**

This is actually a server maintained at Florida State University. In general, we haven't mixed university sites with any other job listing sites, but the Job Board has so many fabulous links to other information that we made an exception. By accessing the Job Board, you can link to the Online Career Center, Med-search, Margaret Riley's Job List, the Job Bank from the University of Texas, FedWorld at Dartmouth, and a host of other compelling job lists. When other services are busy, this one's a good one to check out.

The Monster Board

Access: **http://ageninfo.tamu.edu/jobs.html**

This is a commercial site operated by ADION Information Services Technology, a large recruitment advertising agency in New England. The Monster Board offers an overview of employers along with their easy-to-search job listings. If you're browsing the Web using Mosaic, you can fill out an application online. The number of job openings varies from 50 and up, depending on what vacancies the companies have available.

Regional

Job Web

Access: **html://www.jobweb.com/jobweb.html**

Click on Monster Board.

This site is a free service provided to Chicago-area companies (see Figure 7.5). You can enter a resume online or update a previously uploaded resume.

Web Sites by Organization

ACM Sigmod

Access: **http://bunny.cs.uiuc.edu/jobs**

Type: academic and computer

ACM stands for Association for Computing Machines. There are chapters throughout the United States. Most of the jobs you'll find listed are in academia, but keep a lookout for a few corporate computing jobs.

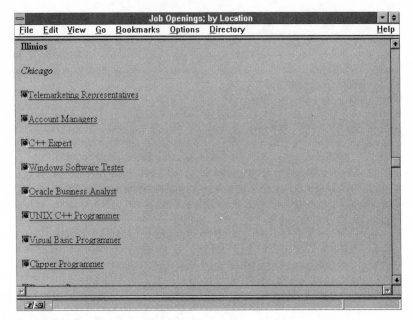

Figure 7.5 A great Web site based in the windy city

Academe This Week

Access: **http://chronicle.merit.edu**

Type: academic

Academe This Week is the ultimate job-listing haven for academics. If you want to find a fellowship, nab a juicy grant, or land a position at a university, look here. There is a link on this server to jobs outside of academe, however, that may be worth your browsing time even if you aren't inclined to be a professor.

American Astronomical Society

Access: **http://blackhole.aas.org/JobRegister/aas.jobs.html**

Type: astronomy

These are fabulous positions for starry-eyed academics and other professional astronomers.

American Marketing Association

Access: **http://www.mba.wfu.edu/b2b.html**

Type: marketing

Job listings relevant to business-to-business marketing professionals.

Bionet

Access: **http://net.bio/ageinfo.tamu.edu:80/jobs.html**

Type: healthcare

This is a Web version of the Gopher site. Scroll down the page and click on Bionet.

Broad

Access: **http://www.bus.msu.edu/news.htm**

Type: business

Who named this Web site anyhow? This server links to the Online Career Center, jobs in Michigan, and the Usenet group misc.jobs.offered. There are also links to the MBA listserver and Business Library listserver.

CLRnet

Access: **http://www.clr.toronto.edu:1080/VIRTUALLIB/ jobs.html**

Type: architecture, landscape architecture

There were only a few jobs listed in this Web site when we visited it, and they are primarily in academia. The home page also includes career information for careers in architecture.

Career Magazine

Access: **http://www.careermag.com/careermag/**

Type: lists recruiters

If you can look past their self-promotional copy, this service can help you find an executive recruiter in the fields of accounting, banking, finance, computer, engineering, environmental, food, hospital, retail, generalist, graphic arts, printing, publishing, insurance, legal, manufacturing, medical, health care, and sales and marketing.

Corporation for Public Broadcasting (CPB)

Access: **http://www.cpb.org/home.html**

Type: television and radio

The CPB lists job openings by state. To get to the list, click on The CPB Jobline. Many jobs available.

Franklin Search Group, Inc.

Access: **http://www.gate.net/bio-techjobs**

Type: biotechnology

This is a marvelous site for anyone in biotech, as you can see from Figure 7.6. There are job openings, information about resume preparation, and career counseling.

GIS Jobs Clearinghouse

Access: **http://walleye.forestry.umn.edu:70/0/www/ rsgisinfo/jobs.html**

Type: forestry

This is the Web version of the Geographic Information System's job openings. When you actually go to look at the job list,

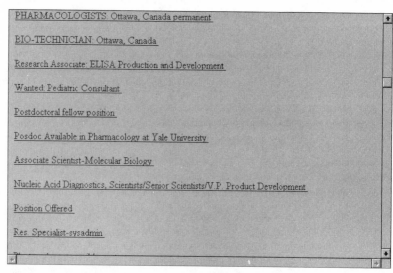

Figure 7.6 Franklin Search Group site

you will get transferred to a gopher. The gopher does look better via the Web, but if you have a slow connection, you may want to just access the job list through gopher.

 ### G-Web

Access: **http://www.cinenet.net/GWEB/index.html**

Type: animators

If you have a BFA or related degree, visit this board for inspiration and a possible great job. If you are an computer animator, this is a must-see. G-Web is an electronic trade journal for computer animators. They have a super job listing site, too. When we checked, there were jobs for a senior animator to work on the first all-digital major motion picture for Sony Pictures, a 3D modeler for 3DO, a CGI animator for Turner Features, and many more.

Job Board

Access: **http://www.io.org:80/~jwsmith/jobs.html**

Type: hi-tech only

Read the rules for resumes before uploading your resume to this site. It prefers to see very short resumes with a short cover letter. Despite the rather cranky emphasis on rules here, jobs with excellent salaries and within the highest echelon of technical positions are listed here. It's worth enduring the grump factor for. P.S. Don't confuse this with the university site of the same name.

Nonprofit/Fundraising Jobnet

Access: **http://www.nando.net/philant/philant.html**

Type: positions in nonprofit sector and in fundraising.

This Web site is beginning to heat up—nonprofit organizations offer some very lucrative and plum jobs to reach for.

Opto-Link SPIE

Access: **http://www.spie.org/web/employment/
employ_home.html**

Type: scientific and engineering

This is a great place for anyone working with optics to visit. A well-maintained, well-structured board.

Mathematics and Statistics Job Announcements

Access: **http://math.umbc.edu/misc.html**

Type: mathematics and statistics

The majority of jobs listed here require top-notch qualifications in statistics.

MedSearch America

Access: **http://www.medsearch.com**

Type: medical

This is a spot where people working in the medical industries can look for openings. Gopher available as well; see gopher listing for address.

NPR Home Page (National Public Radio)

Access: **http://www.npr.org/index.html**

Type: job listings related to broadcasting.

Everything and anything related to radio is what you'll find here: jobs for new reporters, producers, editors, engineers, and correspondents. See Figure 7.7 for examples. Job listings only; this is not the place to post resumes.

NREL

Access: **http://nrelinfo.nrel.gov:70/1s/people/jobs/data**

Type: administrative, other

This site has about 100 upper-level contracting and professional jobs listed. See its Web site listing for resume details. Figure 7.8 shows examples of jobs available here.

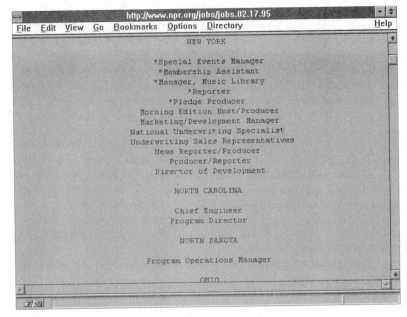

Figure 7.7 A quick take on NPR's job listings

Physics Jobs Announcements

Access: **http://xxx.lanl.gov/announce/Jobs**

This site is a boon for physicists. There aren't hundreds of jobs listed, but those that do get posted here are usually of a very high caliber.

SAGE (System Administrator's Guild)

Access: **http://www.usenix.org/about_sage.html**

Type: Unix systems administrators

This is not a job list per se, but it does contain job descriptions to help systems administrators craft their lengthy resumes. A great job search resource.

Starlink News Items

Access: **http://ast.leeds.ac.uk./news.html**

Type: astronomy

Current NREL Job Postings

- SENIOR COUNSEL
- PUBLIC AFFAIRS ADMINISTRATOR
- INTERNATIONAL PROGRAM DIRECTOR
- SENIOR MIS ANALYST/PROGRAMMER
- ASSOC. TECHNICAL COMMUNICATOR
- COMMUNICATIONS COORDINATOR
- VISUAL DEVELOPMENT MARKETING SPECIALIST
- PUBLICATIONS DEVELOPMENT LEAD
- STAFF BASIS DATABASE ENGINEER
- STAFF COMPUTER SCIENTIST
- COMPUTER USER SUPPORT ANALYST
- NETWORK ENGINEER

Figure 7.8 NREL job listings in January 1995

This server is for professional astronomers, or for those who yearn to be one. The jobs listed in Figure 7.9 will give you a clear idea of the highly specialized professionals who will bene-fit from gazing at this Web site.

TKO Personnel, Inc.

Access: **http://www.internet-is.com/tko/**

Type: bicultural technical and sales

This could also have been listed under Companies. But, for anyone looking for a bicultural job in the U.S. or Asia-Pacific, this site is unbeatable. (By *bicultural* we mean Japanese, Chinese, and Korean.) The job vacancies listed usually include high-echelon stuff, such as senior technical support manager (in Japan), site manager (in Singapore), sales manager (Japan), and more.

Veterinary Job Opportunities

Access: **http://www.ovcnet.voguelph.ca/jobs.ovc/list.html**

Type: veterinary

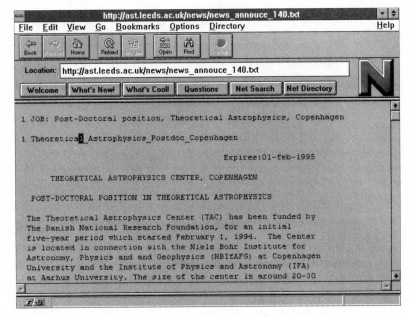

Figure 7.9 A handful of jobs for people who do their best work at night

What can we say? If you want to work with animals or animal sales, this is the spot for you. Many job listings along with some summer employment opportunities.

Young Scientists Network

Access: **http://snorri.chem.washington.edu:80/ysnarchive**

Type: scientists

Job archives list as well as job resource list with great links.

Zycad Job Page

Access: **http://www.zycad.com:80/jobs/**

Type: marketing

This is a new site, so not that many jobs listed, and seem to be in the area of marketing, with a few in engineering.

Companies with Job Listings on the Web

Companies are hopping on the Web so fast that we expect the listing of companies with home pages (complete with links to their job openings) to skyrocket. To keep up with new listings, perform a keyword search using the company's name on a Web search engine. The companies we've listed post from 1 to 20 job openings on the average. Many are technical, but, as we've mentioned before, if you are interested in working for a particular company and you aren't in a technical field, check to see if they have other openings as well before you write them off.

For more information about companies with careermosaic.com in their Web addresses, read the complete company listing in Career Mosaic. Other major online sites listing company profiles include the Interactive Employment Network (E-Span), the Online Career Center, and The Monster Board.

Altera Corporation

Access: **http://www.careermosaic.com/cm/altera**

Type: high-density logic devices

San Jose-based company. Forward resumes to kitp@altera.com. Positions include: applications engineers, product marketing engineer, layout designers, and many more.

Amdahl Corporation

Access: **http://www.amdahl.com/**

Click on Employment.

Type: large-scale data processing technology, open systems, and software developments

Headquartered in Sunnyvale, CA.

Send resumes via email to: **jobs@amdahl.com**

Andersen Consulting

Access: **http://www.ac.com/recruit/welcome.html**

This corporation boasts 150 offices in 46 countries and more than 29,000 employees. There are opportunities in almost every country on the globe. See its Web listing for details on applying.

Auspex Systems

Access: **http://www.auspex.com/Welcome.html**

Click on Job Openings.

Type: high-performance/reliability network data servers and advances network services

Headquartered in Santa Clara, CA. Positions available worldwide.

BBN Internet Services Corporation

Subsidiary of Bolt Beranek and Newman, Inc.

Access: **http://www.helpwanted.com/bbnhome.html**

Type: opportunities for network nerds

This is the company that developed ARPANET 25 years ago. Now, they have NEARNET in New England and BARRNET in California. Headquartered in Cambridge, MA.

Send email to: **rpayne@bbn.com**

BTG Inc.

Access: **http://www.btg.com/jobs/jobmenu.html**

Type: open systems, reusable software, system management

Headquartered in Vienna, VA, but positions open nationwide, including in Hawaii. See Figure 7.10 for examples.

Cambridge Scientific Computing, Inc.

Access: **http://www.camsci.com**

Click on Positions Available.

Type: software for chemists

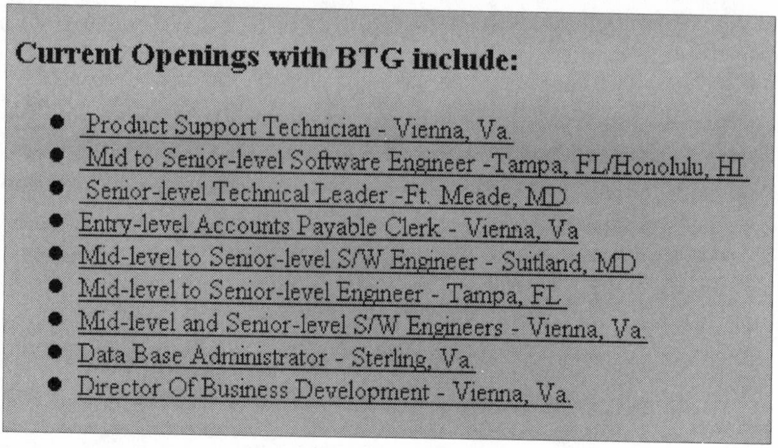

Current Openings with BTG include:

- Product Support Technician - Vienna, Va.
- Mid to Senior-level Software Engineer -Tampa, FL/Honolulu, HI
- Senior-level Technical Leader -Ft. Meade, MD
- Entry-level Accounts Payable Clerk - Vienna, Va.
- Mid-level to Senior-level S/W Engineer - Suitland, MD
- Mid-level to Senior-level Engineer - Tampa, FL
- Mid-level and Senior-level S/W Engineers - Vienna, Va.
- Data Base Administrator - Sterling, Va.
- Director Of Business Development - Vienna, Va.

Figure 7.10 Jobs available via BTG, Inc.

Headquartered in Cambridge, MA.

Send resumes to: **info@camsci.com**

Chemical Bank

Access: **http://www.careermosaic.com/cm/chemical-bank**

Type: networking, software, financial

This is a broad-based financial institution.

Send resumes to: **tgibbon@hodes.com**

Cisco Systems

Access: **http://cio.cisco.com/public/Employment.html**

Type: hardware/software for LANs

There are opportunities in sales, LANs manufacturing, and software at this San Jose, CA-based company, as seen in Figure 7.11.

Send resumes to: **jobs@cisco.com**

ClariNet Communications Corp.

Access: **http://www.clarinet.com/**

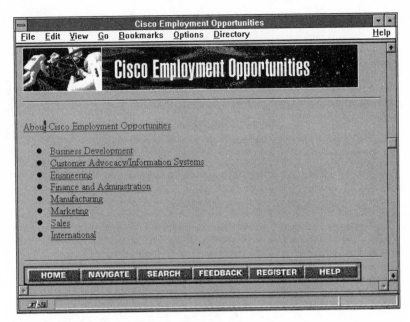

Figure 7.11 Jobs at Cisco Systems

Click on Job Opportunities at Clarinet.

Type: electronic publishers

Headquartered in San Jose, CA, there are opportunities for systems administrators and software developers.

Send resumes to: **hr@clarinet.com**

Compaq Computer Corporation

Access: **http://www.iquest.net/Career_Taxi/compaq/ Compaq.html**

Click on Employment Opportunities.

Type: computers, peripherals, software, entertainment, multi-media.

Headquartered in Houston, there are opportunities in information management, sales, marketing, and manufacturing.

Send resumes to: **careerpaq@compaq.com**

DeLorme Mapping

Access: **http://www.delorme.com./home.htm**

Click on Employment Page.

Type: mapping software and databases

Job openings for project managers, software engineers, database administrators, and programmers.

Send resumes to: **jobs@delorme.com**

eWorld

Access: **http://www.eworld.com/Welcome.html**

Click on Job Listings.

Type: part of Apple Computer

Many opportunities in marketing, system management, publishing, and software programming. Headquartered in Cupertino, CA.

Send resumes to: **jobs@eworld.com**

Fidelity Investments

Access: **http://www.helpwanted.com/fidelhp.html**

Type: computer science jobs in financial setting

Positions available for directors, managers, database administrators, applications specialists, and system administrators. Positions mainly in Boston or Marlborough, MA.

Send resumes to: **staffing@fidelity-inv.com**

Forrester Research, Inc.

Access: **http://www.forrester.com/misc/employment.html**

Type: analysts

Opportunities for brainy analysts (impact of technology on large companies, consumers, and public policy) as well as in sales.

Analysts, send resumes to: **gcolony@forrester.com**

Sales, send resumes to: **jschwartz@forrester.com**

IPC Technologies, Inc.

Access: **http://www.ipc.tech.com/~jobs/joblist.html**

Lists primarily computer positions open within the company. Respond to jobs@ipctech.com, Stormy Hamilton, Technical Recruiter.

Integrated Computer Solutions, Inc.

Access: **http://www.ics.com**

Click on Employment at ICS.

Type: software development tools

Headquartered in Cambridge, MA, there are opportunities for writers, product managers, sales professionals, and software engineers.

Send resume to: **jobs@ics**

Infonet Services Corporation

Access: **http://www.info.net/Public/infonet-toc.html**

Click on Employment Opportunities.

Type: communications network and support

Headquartered in El Segundo, CA, opportunities for financial analysts, technical staff, product area managers, and computer scientists. See Web site listing for resume details.

Intel

Access: **http://www.intel.com/intel/index.html**

Click on Working at Intel.

Click on Opportunities at Intel.

Type: semiconductors

Many sites; California, New Mexico, Oregon, Puerto Rico, England, Germany, Ireland, Japan. Positions for administrators, engineers. Read "The Intel Employment Management System" available on the Web site. After you read the manual, send resumes to jobs@intel.com. Resumes are placed directly into a resume tracking system.

Intermetrics

Access: **http://www.inmet.com/index.html**

Click on Employment Opportunities.

Type: software development and systems integrations.

Positions available for general administrators and software developers in Maryland, Washington DC, and California. Some offices in U.K. and Japan. See Web site for other resume information.

Intuit, Inc.

Access: **http://www.careermosaic.com/cm/intuit.html**

Type: developer of Quicken and Turbo Tax software

Positions available for sales professionals, software developers, and administrators. See Web site for resume information.

Metricom

Access: **http://www.metricom.com/Welcome.html**

Click on Jobs Available.

Type: wireless data communications

Headquartered in Los Gatos, CA, positions available for various technical professionals.

Send resumes to: **alan@metricom.com**

NEC

Access: **http// web.nec.com/index.html**

Click on Company Overview.

Click on Employment Opportunities.

Type: communications, computers, and semiconductors

Job locations are in Herndon, VA; Irving, TX; and Hillsboro, OR. When we checked this listing, there were opportunities for software developers and network analysts.

Send resumes to: **jobmaster@nec.com**

National Semiconductors

Access: **http://www.commerce.net/directories/participants/ns/job. html**

Type: hi-tech

Positions available for business planners, failure analysis engineers, tax analysts, corporate contract associates, business analysts, and communications coordinators. Positions in Texas, California, Maine, Utah.

Netscape Communication Corporation

Access: **http://www.netscape.com/help-wanted/index.html**

Type: Internet software

Openings for Windows programmers, network engineers, hypermedia experts.

Send resumes to: **(department head)@ mcom.com**

NeXT Computer

Access: **http://www.next.com/HumanResources/**

Type: computer

Many opportunities for computer experts as well as marketing, sales, and temps. Headquartered in Redwood City, CA.

Send resumes to: **resumes@next.com**

PeopleSoft

Access: **http://www.peoplesoft.com/**

Type: business applications

Headquartered in Walnut Creek, CA. Positions in sales, marketing, administration, software development.

Prudential Insurance and Financial

Access: **http://www.helpwanted.com/prudent.html**

Type: marketing services in areas such as CDs, money market, and mutual funds

Check site for jobs info.

Email resumes to: **yss@yss.com**

Santa Cruz Operation (SCO)

Access: **http://www.sco.com/Company/Jobs/jobs.html**

Type: open systems software sales

Positions in marketing, product management, sales, service, software development, and systems administration.

Send resumes in ASCII format only to: **susanbe@sco.com**

Symantec

Access: **http://www.careermosaic.com/cm/symantec/**

Type: software

Many opportunities for technical, sales, and marketing managers.

Send resumes to: **itaft@symantec.com**

Tangram Enterprise Solutions

Access: **http://www.tesi.com/employ.htm**

Type: communications software

Opportunities for engineers, consulting analysts, district sales managers, programmers.

The Internet Access Company, Inc.

Access: **http://www.tiac.net/staff/open.html**

Type: Internet service provider

Opportunities for telephone sales, Internet tutors.

Transaction Information Systems, Inc.

Access: **http://www.tisny.com/tis/hotjobs.html**

Type: technical

Jobs for architects, business analysts, manufacturing.

Send resumes to: **resumes@tisny.com**

TRW

Access: **http://www.helpwanted.com/trwhp.html**

Type: designs and manufactures precision-molded plastics and assembled components

Plants are in Westminster, MA, and Roseville, MI. Positions for design engineers and administrators.

Send resumes to: **Jobspro@yss.com**

Union Bank

Access: **http://www.careermosaic.com/cm/union_bank/ub1.html**

Type: banking

Positions available in community banking, specialized lending, and other financial fields. For resume information, see Web site.

US West

Access: **http://www.careermosaic.com/cm/uswest**

Type: wide area networks

Positions in marketing, network engineering.

Send resumes to: **ameeker@acs.uswest.com**

Your Software Solutions

Access: **http://helpwanted.com/**

Click on Search Jobs in YSS Jobs Database.

Opportunities for copy writers, C++ developers, mainly technical.

Miscellaneous

Mother of all BBS

Access: **http://www.cs.colorado.edu/cgi-bin/grepitp**

This site may have a less than elegant name, but it is nevertheless a great job listing site. You can upload your resumes to this site as well as browse the 650-plus job openings.

JOBS VIA USENET NEWSGROUPS

All lists in this section can be accessed via Usenet with the exception of some of the regional newsgroups—which you can still reach by telnet to a public gopher site. Or, you can access Usenet through a Web browser like Netscape, which you learned how to use in Chapter 5.

Be aware that the number of jobs given in the entries in this list represent activity for one month in early 1995 and will no doubt be different when you explore these same sites. So, if you log in to misc.jobs.offered and find 10,000 jobs or more listed instead of 5,000, as shown here, it's just further testimony to the constantly changing and updating that's always going on at these sites. By the time you read this, there will be new job lists available, some of the inactive lists will boom, and others will have thinned out. Watch for these changes, and be flexible.

Global Newsgroups

The newsgroups in this section reach across the entire network. Groups are listed alphabetically, by hierarchy.

misc.jobs.misc

A general discussion group about jobs and job searching

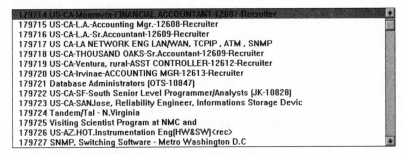

```
179714 US-CA-Monrovia-FINANCIAL ACCOUNTANT-12607-Recruiter
179715 US-CA-L.A.-Accounting Mgr.-12608-Recruiter
179716 US-CA-L.A.-Sr.Accountant-12609-Recruiter
179717 US CA-LA NETWORK ENG LAN/WAN, TCPIP , ATM , SNMP
179718 US-CA-THOUSAND OAKS-Sr.Accountant-12609-Recruiter
179719 US-CA-Ventura, rural-ASST CONTROLLER-12612-Recruiter
179720 US-CA-Irvinae-ACCOUNTING MGR-12613-Recruiter
179721 Database Administrators (OTS-10847)
179722 US-CA-SF-South Senior Level Programmer/Analysts (JK-10828)
179723 US-CA-SANJose, Reliability Engineer, Informations Storage Devic
179724 Tandem/Tal - N.Virginia
179725 Visiting Scientist Program at NMC and
179726 US-AZ.HOT.Instrumentation Eng(HW&SW)<rec>
179727 SNMP, Switching Software - Metro Washington D.C
```

Figure 7.12 A portion of misc.jobs.offered, one of the largest news-groups containing job notices.

500

Type: discussion only

Note: Do not post resumes on this list.

misc.jobs.offered

A listing of jobs available worldwide

5,000

Type: many technical; mostly professional. See Figure 7.12 for examples.

Post: job openings only

misc.jobs.entry

Entry-level jobs listing

100

Type: graduate fellowships and entry-level technical jobs. Examples: electrical engineer, occupational trainer, entry-level visual basic programmer.

Post: only entry-level positions available

misc.jobs.resume

Postings of electronic resumes in ASCII format

3,000

Type: varied. Resume postings from all fields, though primarily professional. Economist, technical writer, publications director, engineer, radio announcer are examples from posts in January.

Post: resumes in ASCII only. Most resumes are no more than 1 to 2 pages.

Regional Newsgroups

The newsgroups listed here are based in specific regions of a country or areas in the United States. Again, remember that you may not be able to reach some of these newsgroups directly.

Foreign Regional Groups

aus.jobs

Jobs in Australia and New Zealand

50

Type: varied. A mix of technical and general professional. Examples from list are openings for engineers, life insurance analysts, illustrators, public relations and marketing specialists, and bookkeepers.

Post: jobs only

Note: Includes a FAQ file. Read before posting. Note that prices quoted in job offers are in Australian or New Zealand currency.

ab.jobs

Jobs in Alberta, Canada

50

Type: primarily technical; for example, technical writer, engineer, and "web surfer."

Post: job openings only

bln.jobs

Berlin jobs

50

Type: varied, with an emphasis on technical. Examples: occupational trainee, Clipper programmer.

Post: job openings and resumes

Note: The articles in this newsgroup are written primarily in German.

can.jobs

Jobs available in Canada

300

Type: varied. On the days we browsed this list we found job openings for medical imagers, managers, microbiologists, and graphic artists, among others.

Post: primarily jobs, though there seem to be a few resumes sprinkled in the job listings

Note: The jobs listed were primarily for the Vancouver and Toronto areas.

de.markt.jobs

Jobs in Germany

100

Type: varied, though many for computer experts.

Post: primarily job openings, some resumes

Note: The articles in this newsgroup are almost exclusively in German.

de.mrkt.jobs.d

A discussion group about jobs in Germany

Type: N/A

Post: This is a discussion group only. Do not post resumes on this list.

Note: The discussions are in German.

dk.jobs

Jobs in Denmark

10

Type: varied. Listed in January were technical and managerial positions such as PC supervisor, MS office "producktmand."

Post: jobs only

Note: In Dutch.

fr.jobs.demandes

Jobs wanted in France

10

Type: varied

Post: resumes

Note: The articles in this newsgroup are written in French.

fr.jobs.offres

Jobs in France

10

Type: primarily technical, for example, research engineers.

Post: job openings only

Note: In French.

kw.jobs

Kitchener-Waterloo, Ontario, Canada jobs

10

Type: technical. Jobs primarily from Northern Digital were posted when we browsed.

Post: job openings only

ont.jobs

Jobs in Ontario, Canada

50

Type: balanced list of offerings, from technical to other professional. Examples: occupational trainee, communications specialist, Lotus Notes.

Post: job openings only

Note: At least half of this list is in French.

tor.jobs

Jobs in Toronto and Ontario, Canada

100

Type: varied. Mac developer, communications specialist, and a telecommuting position are examples of some jobs available on the list.

Post: job openings only

uk.jobs.offered

Jobs in the United Kingdom

100

Type: varied, with some telecommuting positions. See Figure 7.13 for a sample.

Post: job openings only

Note: Most jobs offered are in the U.K., but a few in the United States have slipped into this group.

uk.jobs.wanted

Jobs wanted in the United Kingdom

50

Type: varied. Resumes for accounts payable, technical writer are examples of resumes posted here.

Post: resumes only

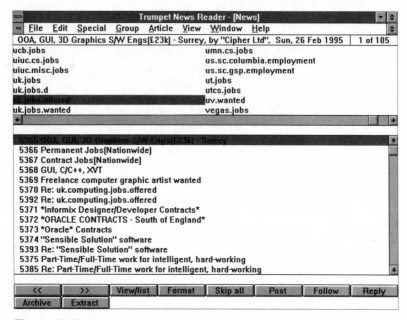

Figure 7.13 Listings from *uk.jobs.offered*

za.ads.jobs

Jobs available in South Africa

10

Type: primarily technical. Examples from January listings: Internet surfer, electronic editor, systems engineer.

Post: resumes, job openings

Regional United States Newsgroups

atl.jobs

Atlanta-based jobs

100

Type: varied, a blend of technical and other. Listings are for openings such as: marketing/promotions director, administrative assistant, C++ developers, software engineers, and research and design physics majors.

Post: job openings only

Atl.resumes

Atlanta resumes

50

Type: varied; see **stl.jobs**.

Post: resumes only

Austin.jobs

Jobs in Austin, Texas

50

Type: primarily technical; see Figure 7.14 for samples.

Post: jobs or a summary

Note: Includes a FAQ posting which gives explicit directions on how to post to this list. The preference is for short entries summarizing interests and experience versus a resume. Anything not posted in ASCII is frowned upon.

az.jobs

Jobs in Arizona

50

Type: varied. Many executive recruiters use this list. Some jobs listed during our last stop here were for a technical writer, a stockbroker, and a PC communications expert.

Post: job openings and resumes.

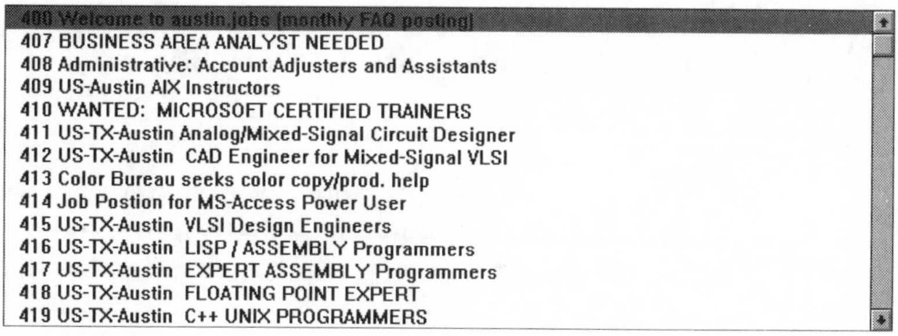

```
400 Welcome to austin.jobs (monthly FAQ posting)
407 BUSINESS AREA ANALYST NEEDED
408 Administrative: Account Adjusters and Assistants
409 US-Austin AIX Instructors
410 WANTED: MICROSOFT CERTIFIED TRAINERS
411 US-TX-Austin Analog/Mixed-Signal Circuit Designer
412 US-TX-Austin  CAD Engineer for Mixed-Signal VLSI
413 Color Bureau seeks color copy/prod. help
414 Job Postion for MS-Access Power User
415 US-TX-Austin  VLSI Design Engineers
416 US-TX-Austin  LISP / ASSEMBLY Programmers
417 US-TX-Austin  EXPERT ASSEMBLY Programmers
418 US-TX-Austin  FLOATING POINT EXPERT
419 US-TX-Austin  C++ UNIX PROGRAMMERS
```

Figure 7.14 A portion of *austin.jobs*

```
23693 US-CA-SF-South Senior Level Programmer/Analysts (JK-10828)
 23694 US-CA-SF-South Senior EDI Analsyts (JK-10829)
 23695 US-CA-Fairfield HelpDesk/QA Professionals (LS-10809)
 23696 US-CA-SF Programmer/Analysts (CI-10820)
 23697 US-CA-Berkeley Systems Administrators (NS-10832)
 23698 US-CA-SF Senior Programmer/Analysts (JR-10851)
 23699 US-CA-Oakland Senior DBMS Software Engineer  #1036AF - DEI recruiter
 23700 US-CA-SF-South Oracle Database Developers (RS-10853)
 23701 US-CA-SF-East Network Engineers/Support (OTSI-10855)
 23702 US-CA-Sacramento Programmer/Analysts/UNIX/Cobol/Informix (CI-10856)
 23703 US-CA-Milpitas Video Systems Engineers (DB-10817)
 23704 UNIX kernel / virtual memory / multiprocessors - Sunnyvale, CA
 23705 USA.IBM MAINFRAME OPPORTUNITIES
 23706 USA. CLIENT SERVER OPPORTUNITIES
```

Figure 7.15 Job openings posted in January on *ba.jobs.contract*

ba.jobs.contract

San Francisco Bay area contract jobs

500

Type: very sophisticated technical positions, as you can see from Figure 7.15.

Post: job openings only

ba.jobs.misc

Miscellaneous positions in San Francisco Bay area

100

Type: varied. More of a discussion group than a pure job posting list. For a job opening, *ba.jobs.offered* is a much better place to look.

Post: jobs, comments, resumes

ba.jobs.offered

Positions offered in the San Francisco Bay area

1,000

Type: many technical, but some nontechnical as well. Examples include: medical imaging, UNIX programmer, Spanish teacher, graphics designer, telemarketers, multimedia, network design engineer.

Post: jobs only

balt.jobs

Jobs available in the Baltimore-Washington D.C. area.

50

Type: technical, financial, and other. Examples: residential mortgage banker, UNIX programmer, MS Windows expert, security.

Post: job openings only

chi.jobs

Chicago jobs

100

Type: varied. Examples: credit union branch supervisor, contractor, multimedia developer, manager.

Post: job openings only

cmh.jobs

10

Type: varied. The jobs ranged from technical to managerial for entire United States.

Post: job openings only

conn.jobs.offered

Connecticut jobs

50

Type: primarily technical with a few others. Examples: customer relations, accountant, tax preparers.

Post: job openings only

dc.jobs

Jobs in Washington D.C. and the surrounding area.

300

```
2472 US-TX-Dallas - Visual Basic Prgmr.
2473 US-TX-Dallas - Sr DB/2 Prgmr. Analyst
2474 US-TX-Dallas - C/POS/DOS/OS/2
2475 US-TX-Dallas - R E Acctg Systems Software Analyst/Tester Q & A $35K
2476 US-TX-Dallas - Automation Analysts
2477 US-TX-Dallas - Dun & Bradstreet Analysts
2478 Worldwide opportunities - Banking - Hogan/Systematics/AS400 Programmers
2479 US-TX-Dallas - Smalltalk Object-Oriented Programmer Mid-$50s
2480 US-TX-Dallas - C Programmer Mid-$40s
2481 US-TX-Dallas - Marketing Director/LAN Products
2482 US-TX-Dallas - AS400 Programmer
2483 US-TX-Dallas - AS400/BPCS
2484 US-TX-Dallas - COBOL/Image/HP3000
2485 Europe-Portugal - AS400 Banking
```

Figure 7.16 A slice of the jobs available via the Usenet group *dfw.jobs*

Type: primarily nontechnical: sales, mortgage consultants, insurance analysts, factory liaison manager.

Post: job openings or resumes

dfw.jobs

Dallas/ Fort Worth jobs

350

Type: primarily technical and banking. Examples: AS400 engineer, banker. See Figure 7.16.

Post: job openings only

fl.jobs

Jobs available in Florida

100

Type: technical with a few others. Examples: therapist, technical programmer, contract consulting, Solaris, data storage analyst.

Post: job openings only

houston.jobs.offered

Positions available in Houston, Texas.

50

Type: varied

Note: This list included more part-time offers than other lists. Example: part-time Object programmer.

Post: job openings only

houston.jobs.wanted

Positions wanted in Houston, Texas

10

Type: varied. Examples: international trade, administrative, biochemist, and scientist.

Post: resumes only

ia.jobs

Jobs in Iowa

10

Type: sales

Post: job openings only

Note: This newsgroup is the only one we saw in which many of the employers were offering to "fly people home on the weekends" as part of the job package.

il.jobs.misc

Positions available in Illinois.

10

Type: varied. Examples were ConAgra positions, MS Windows support.

Post: job openings or helpful advice

Note: Harry's Job Search BBS and Internet Hot List is available on this newsgroup as of January 1995. Good resources.

Il.jobs.offered

Illinois jobs

50

Type: varied: insurance, management, and teacher are three examples.

Post: job openings only

il.jobs.resumes

Resumes of people seeking employment in Illinois.

10

Type: varied

Post: resumes only

in.jobs

Indiana jobs

10

Type: only one job was posted when we browsed this list, for a manager of electronic advertising.

Post: job listings only

 la.jobs

Los Angeles jobs

100

Type: a 50–50 blend of technical, nontechnical. See Figure 7.17 for examples.

Post: job openings only

la.wanted.jobs

Los Angeles jobs wanted

10

Type: varied

Post: resumes only

mi.jobs

Michigan job listings

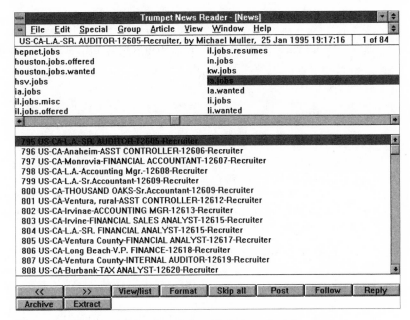

Figure 7.17 A quick look at jobs offered on *la.jobs*

50

type: primarily automotive. See Figure 7.18 for examples.

Post: job openings only

Note: This was the only list we found with extensive automotive industry openings.

milw.jobs

Milwaukee, Wisconsin jobs

Figure 7.18 Jobs listed on *mi.jobs*

50

Type: varied. Example: psychologist, computer programmer.

Post: job openings only

ne.jobs

Jobs available in the New England region

100

Type: financial and technical, other. Examples include listings for a senior application engineer, financial analyst, Autocad developer, and product communication strategist.

Post: job openings only

nm.jobs

Jobs in New Mexico, primarily in Albuquerque

10

Type: technical; CAD engineer, for example.

Post: job openings only

nyc.jobs.contract

Contract jobs in New York City

100

Type: many financial, some technical, publishing. Examples: financial planners, brokers, engineers, and QA testers, among many others.

nyc.jobs.misc

Discussion group of jobs and work in New York City

50

Type: discussion

nyc.jobs.offered

Jobs in New York City

100

Type: varied. Examples: technical services manager, project manager, programmer, OLE developer.

nyc.jobs.wanted

Jobs wanted in New York City

10

Type: nontechnical, such as publishing, drafting.

Post: resumes only

pgh.jobs.offered

Jobs in Pittsburgh, Pennsylvania

10

Type: sales and management.

Post: job openings only

pgh.jobs.wanted

Jobs wanted in Pittsburgh, Pennsylvania

10

Type: varied

Post: resumes only

sdnet.jobs

Jobs in San Diego with overlap to Orange County

100

Type: technical

Post: job openings only

seattle.jobs.offered

100

Type: varied. Positions for artists, computer operators, trainers, course developers, and UNIX gurus were posted, along with many others.

Post: job openings only

seattle.jobs.wanted

Jobs wanted in Seattle

50

Type: varied, many from recent graduates.

Post: resumes only

triangle.jobs

Jobs in the Raleigh, North Carolina area. Some overlap in other parts of North Carolina.

50

Type: technical, such as computer consultants, network engineers, Oracle programmers.

Post: job openings only

Job Lists from Other Hierarchies

Several other newsgroups exist that are organized under a miscellaneous set of hierarchies. Here they are.

 bionet.jobs

This is a listing of a wide variety of jobs in the biological sciences.

100

Type: biology-related. Examples: occupational trainees, forest biometrician, x-ray technician, forensics.

Post: job openings only

bionet.jobs.wanted

People who are seeking work and or research opportunities in biology and related professions.

50

Type: related—not restricted—to biology. We found resumes from English teachers, forestry majors, researchers.

Post: resumes

Bionet.women-in-bio

Biology discussion group for women.

10

Type: biology-related, usually requiring advanced degrees.

Post: This is not a true job list per se, but often contains job postings in the field of biology. It is a good list to monitor.

biz.jobs.offered

List of commercial postings.

750

Type: business-oriented, with some technical positions, as you can see in Figure 7.19. Examples from a recent sweep: object trainer, auditor, secretary.

Post: job openings only

Note: If you are looking for a list that is less technically oriented, this list is for you.

```
21620 US-CA-Ventura, rural-ASST CONTROLLER-12612-Recruiter
21621 US-CA-Irvinae-ACCOUNTING MGR-12613-Recruiter
21622 Database Administrators [OTS-10847]
21623 US-CA-SF-South Senior Level Programmer/Analysts [JK-10828]
21624 LAN Consultants NYC, PHILA
21625 US-CA-Irvine-FINANCIAL SALES ANALYST-12615-Recruiter
21626 US-CA-L.A.-SR. FINANCIAL ANALYST-12615-Recruiter
21627 US-CA-Ventura County-FINANCIAL ANALYST-12617-Recruiter
21628 US-CA-Long Beach-V.P. FINANCE-12618-Recruiter
21629 US-CA-Ventura County-INTERNAL AUDITOR-12619-Recruiter
21630 US-CA-Burbank-TAX ANALYST-12620-Recruiter
21631 US-CA-L.A.-CASH MANAGEMENT ANALYST-12621-Recruiter
21632 US-CA-L.A.-FINANCIAL ANALYST-12622-Recruiter
21633 US-NY-NYC Senior Analysts [DB-10807]
```

Figure 7.19 Listings from *biz.jobs.offered*

dod.jobs

Department of Defense jobs, and more

5,000

Type: varied. See Figure 7.20 for examples.

Post: job openings only

Note: The Office of Personnel Management (OPM) and Department of the Interior (DOI) cross-post thousands of jobs. In Figures 7.20 and 7.21, you'll see a figure of the bureaus that are covered in this newsgroup. This is a Usenet jewel.

hepnet.jobs

high energy and nuclear physics

10

Type: very technical.

Post: job openings only

Note: Primarily posts jobs available on the East coast.

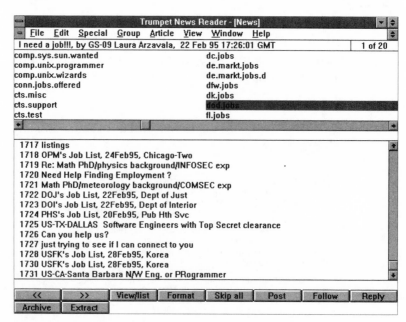

Figure 7.20 Jobs at DOD

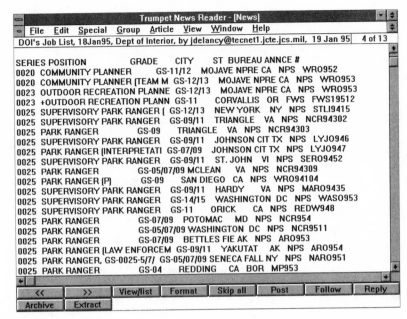

Figure 7.21 Bureaus listing jobs on *dod.jobs*

hsv.jobs

Positions in the health services industry.

10

Type: professional health, with some related technical. Examples: therapist, dBASE programmer.

Post: job openings only

prg.jobs

programming jobs

10

Type: technical.

Post: job openings only

vmsnet.employment

Moderated job list of DEC VAX/VMS and DECNET computer systems users.

10

Type: technical, some healthcare.

Post: job openings only

═══ JOB LISTS VIA GOPHER

This list is current as of January 1995, but because many of the sites previously available via Gopher have shifted completely to the World Wide Web, you'll no doubt find some empty gopher holes by the time you log on to these sites. Fortunately, if you do come across such a vacancy, you will usually find the new Web address listed there for you.

Academe This Week (Chronicle of Higher Education)

Posts job listings from the current edition of *The Chronicle of Higher Education*. Listings are organized by job terms, geographic location, or keywords. This is the best source for finding college or university positions. Also, some research positions are posted here by independent companies. See the entry under Web Resources for more information.

Access: **gopher chronicle.merit.edu**

Academic Physician and Scientist (Also listed as APS)

This gopher lists academic medical teaching positions for over 125 medical schools and related institutions in the United States. Jobs are searchable by state, specialty, and WAIS.

Access: **gopher aps.acad-phy-sci.com**

Email: **info@acad-phy-sci.com**

Academic Position Network

The Academic Position Network is a prime tool for job seekers interested in faculty, administrative, and staff positions. The network also lists openings for fellowship and graduate assistant positions. The service is free, and it is arranged by country, state, and institution. See Web Resources for more details.

Access: **gopher wcni.cis.umn.edu**

AMI: A Friendly Public Interface

This gopher lists positions from several colleges and universities along with other companies and professional organizations. A good jumping off point for further job lead investigation.

Access: **gopher gopher.mountain.net**

American Mathematical Society

Lists positions for top-flight mathematicians. See listing under Web Resources for more details.

Access: **gopher e-math.ams.com**

American Physiological Association

Lists jobs for physiologists. There is no charge for browsing jobs, but there is a $50.00 charge for listing a job.

Access: **gopher gopher.uth.tmc.edu**

BIONET

Access: **gopher net.bio.net**

BIOSCI

A large listing of jobs related to the biological sciences. In addition to jobs for biomedical researchers and professors, there are also many jobs for biomedical engineers.

Access: **gopher net.bio.net**

CITE Job Bank

The CITE Job Bank lists jobs in chronological order. When you first pull down the menu, you will see a list of numbers followed by cryptic jargon. Don't be put off—just choose a number and press Enter, and a job listing will appear on your screen. Jobs are for positions at various universities.

Access: **gopher gopher.utexas.edu**

Note: This gopher address is for the Job Bank at the University of Texas at Austin, a spectacular resource in itself. To get to CITE, choose CITE job bank at the menu.

Gopher Jewels

Gopher Jewels is the gopher connecting the University of Southern California campuses. It is a particularly well-constructed gopher, and a good place to begin a job search, with connections to job listings from around the world. For those with gopher access only, this is another excellent jumping off point. To get to the job listings, choose the menu Personal Development menu option.

Access: **gopher cwis.usc.edu**

International Career Employment Network (ICEN)

Based at the International Center at Indiana University, this center receives career information and job notices from around the world. ICEN is provided as a free service, and it is in menu form.

Access: **gopher**, or send a message to **INTLCENT@indiana.edu** and say "Subscribe ICEN."

Job Openings in the Federal Government

This is a megasite for anyone looking for a job with the federal government. Thousands of jobs are listed here in many federal agencies. But before you break into the job lists, read the help files (as of this writing, called "Miscellaneous Information Useful to Job Applicants.") See Web Resources for complete details about this resource.

Access: **gopher dartcms1.dartmouth.edu**

Jobs in Education Research, Evaluation, and Measurement

This job list originates from ERIC, a prime resource tool for educators the world over. Any job related to the research aspect of education you will find here: jobs for statisticians, research positions, educational theorists, and more.

Access: **gopher vmsgopher.cva.edu**

Library of Congress

This gopher, named Marvel, lists jobs available at the Library of Congress. It also offers menu items that allow you to jump to and search many other job listing sites. See Web Resources for more details.

Access: **gopher marvel.loc.gov**

Martin Marietta Energy Systems, Oak Ridge, TN

This is a rich resource for all job seekers. Marietta lists resumes of their employees who are being affected by the recent spate of downsizing in Marietta's corporate structure. These are some of the top resumes around, and well worth browsing for ideas. Beyond employee resumes, there are postings for positions available. At last check, this gopher looked like it was about to be abandoned for Marietta's new Web site. See listing under Web Resources for Web address.

Access: **gopher1.ctd.ornl.gov**

MedSearch America

This gopher lists job openings for people working in the biotech and healthcare industries. Job seekers can post resumes. See Web Resources for more details.

Access: **gopher gopher.medsearch.com**

Metropolitan Tuscon Electronic Communications Network (Metcom)

Metcom is a community-based network that offers listings of jobs in Arizona, a job calendar of events, and a menu that includes job sources in the federal government and a list of all university job listings. The types of jobs listed for the Arizona section include offerings as varied as Police Dispatcher for $10.75/hour to Director of Environmental Management for $73,000/annually. The service provides excellent links and contact names.

Access: via **gopher** or call 602-791-4241 for local access from Tuscon.

Online Career Center (MSEN Inc.)

The Online Career Center is a not-for-profit online employment service. The center, which lists vast numbers of jobs as well as offers career guidance, is free of charge. Jobs are organized by state, region, keyword, type, and country. Job seekers can input an electronic resume online with an unlimited number of keywords. In addition to job listings, job hunting resources, such as germaine books, are listed. See Web Resources for complete details.

Access: via **gopher Msen.com**

≡ JOB RESOURCES VIA TELNET

We hate to say this yet again, but many Telnet sites have now moved to —you guessed it—the World Wide Web. But, don't count Telnet resources out, yet. Telnet is still a marvelous resource for job seekers because Telnet can connect you to the job-rich freenets and community nets sprouting up all across the United States.

When you attempt to Telnet, and you get the response "unable to connect to host," this means that the connection is busy, and that you'll need to check back later. If you get the response back "unable to locate host," then check the address you typed very carefully. Telnet addresses must be completely accurate. As of February 1995, all Telnet addresses in this list connected to fully functioning services.

Career Connections On-Line Information System (HEART)

HEART, which stands for Human Resources Electronic Advertising and Recruitment Tool, is a free, menu-driven system. Companies pay to list their jobs and company profiles on this system. The jobs are organized by title and geographic location. When you first log on to this system, you will be asked to create a user profile, as seen in Figure 7.22. You'll need to give your name, address, and phone number. In return, you'll get to browse the jobs listings and be able to apply for a job online (Figure 7.23). Note the special area for new graduates (Figure 7.24). Note: HEART has recently begun sponsoring online job

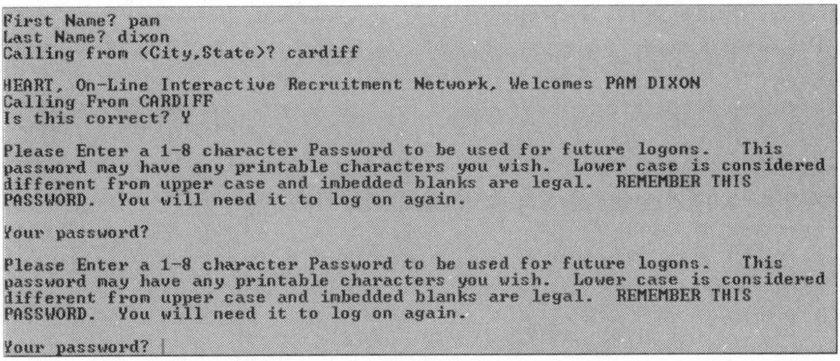

```
First Name? pam
Last Name? dixon
Calling from <City,State>? cardiff

HEART, On-Line Interactive Recruitment Network, Welcomes PAM DIXON
Calling From CARDIFF
Is this correct? Y

Please Enter a 1-8 character Password to be used for future logons.  This
password may have any printable characters you wish.  Lower case is considered
different from upper case and imbedded blanks are legal.  REMEMBER THIS
PASSWORD.  You will need it to log on again.

Your password?

Please Enter a 1-8 character Password to be used for future logons.  This
password may have any printable characters you wish.  Lower case is considered
different from upper case and imbedded blanks are legal.  REMEMBER THIS
PASSWORD.  You will need it to log on again.

Your password? |
```

Figure 7.22 HEART's entry screen which you fill out online

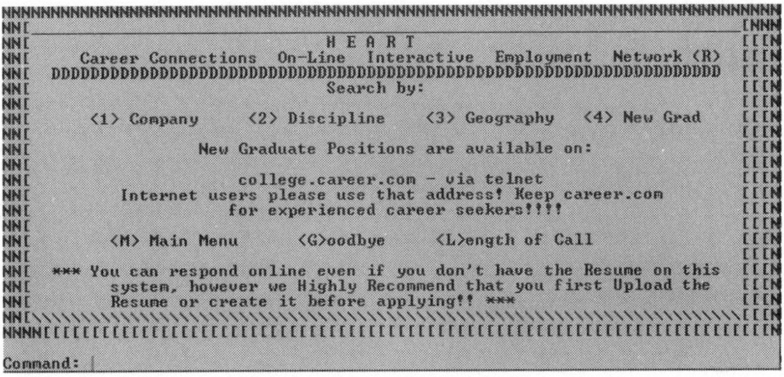

```
NNNNNNNNNNNNNNNNNNNNNNNNNNNNNNNNNNNNNNNNNNNNNNNNNNNNNNNNNNNNNNNNNNNNNNNNNN
NN[                                                                    [NNN
NN[_____[[NN
NN[                           H E A R T                                [[[N
NN[      Career Connections  On-Line  Interactive  Employment  Network <R>  [[[N
NN[ DDDDDDDDDDDDDDDDDDDDDDDDDDDDDDDDDDDDDDDDDDDDDDDDDDDDDDDDDDDDDDDDDDDDDD [[[N
NN[                           Search by:                                [[[N
NN[                                                                    [[[N
NN[      <1> Company     <2> Discipline    <3> Geography   <4> New Grad  [[[N
NN[                                                                    [[[N
NN[              New Graduate Positions are available on:               [[[N
NN[                                                                    [[[N
NN[                   college.career.com - via telnet                  [[[N
NN[            Internet users please use that address! Keep career.com  [[[N
NN[                  for experienced career seekers!!!!                 [[[N
NN[                                                                    [[[N
NN[      <M> Main Menu      <G>oodbye     <L>ength of Call             [[[N
NN[                                                                    [[[N
NN[ *** You can respond online even if you don't have the Resume on this  [[[N
NN[     system, however we Highly Recommend that you first Upload the    [[[N
NN[     Resume or create it before applying!! ***                       [[[N
NN[\\\\\\\\\\\\\\\\\\\\\\\\\\\\\\\\\\\\\\\\\\\\\\\\\\\\\\\\\\\\\\\\\\\[[[N
NNNN[[[[[[[[[[[[[[[[[[[[[[[[[[[[[[[[[[[[[[[[[[[[[[[[[[[[[[[[[[[[[[[[[[[[[[[[N

Command: |
```

Figure 7.23 HEART's professional career menu

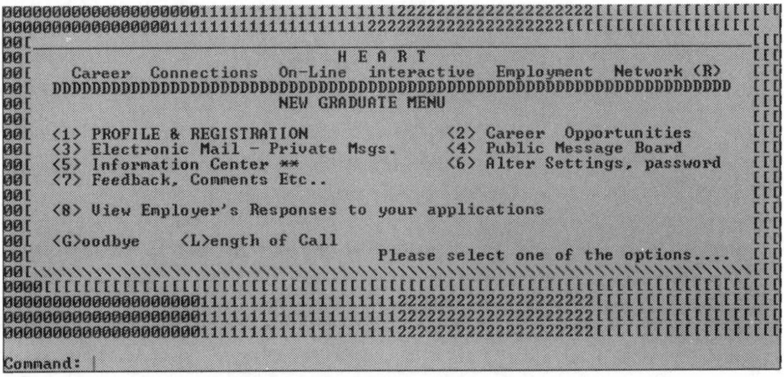

```
00000000000000000000001111111111111111111122222222222222222222[[[[[[[[[[[[[[[[[0
00000000000000000000001111111111111111111122222222222222222222[[[[[[[[[[[[[[[[[
00[                                                                    [[[
00[_____[[[
00[                           H E A R T                                [[[
00[      Career  Connections  On-Line  interactive  Employment  Network <R>  [[[
00[ DDDDDDDDDDDDDDDDDDDDDDDDDDDDDDDDDDDDDDDDDDDDDDDDDDDDDDDDDDDDDDDDDDDDDDDDDD
00[                        NEW GRADUATE MENU                             [[[
00[                                                                    [[[
00[  <1> PROFILE & REGISTRATION              <2> Career  Opportunities  [[[
00[  <3> Electronic Mail - Private Msgs.     <4> Public Message Board    [[[
00[  <5> Information Center **               <6> Alter Settings, password [[[
00[  <7> Feedback, Comments Etc..                                        [[[
00[                                                                    [[[
00[  <8> View Employer's Responses to your applications                [[[
00[                                                                    [[[
00[  <G>oodbye    <L>ength of Call                                      [[[
00[                              Please select one of the options....    [[[
00[\\\\\\\\\\\\\\\\\\\\\\\\\\\\\\\\\\\\\\\\\\\\\\\\\\\\\\\\\\\\\\\\\\[[[
0000[[[[[[[[[[[[[[[[[[[[[[[[[[[[[[[[[[[[[[[[[[[[[[[[[[[[[[[[[[[[[[[[[[[[[[[[[
00000000000000000000001111111111111111111122222222222222222222[[[[[[[[[[[[[[[[[
00000000000000000000001111111111111111111122222222222222222222[[[[[[[[[[[[[[[[[0
00000000000000000000001111111111111111111122222222222222222222[[[[[[[[[[[[[[[[[0

Command: |
```

Figure 7.24 HEART's new graduate menu

fairs. Their last one boasted 425 participants chatting online to professional recruiters. Look for more of these in the future!

Access: **telnet college.career.com** or IP **198.207.167.3**

Federal Job Opportunity Board (FJOB)

This is a good alternate site for browsing job openings in the federal government if you find that FedWorld (next entry) is too busy, but be aware that the listings aren't as complete or as well-organized.

Access: **telnet://fjob.mail.opm.gov** or IP **198.78.46.10**

FedWorld: The U.S. Government Bulletin Board

This is the ultimate resource for anyone looking for a job in the United States government. It is listed here as a cross-reference because it is a prime Telnet resource, but it is best accessed via the Web. The gopher and Telnet access is often very busy. If, however, you have only gopher or Telnet access, the best time to access FedWorld is in the early morning, before 8:00 a.m. EST.

See Web Resources for complete details.

Access: **telnet:// fedworld.doc.gov** or IP **192.239.92.201**

Informatrix

Informatrix contains a very large set of databases for most professions. It is set up very much like a bulletin board in that you must register with them to access the system.

Access: **telnet:// informatrix.com** or IP **204.213.232.3**

Login: **imsi**

NISS

NISS stands for National Information Services and Systems. This is a system maintained in the U.K.. There aren't hundreds of jobs available here, but if you are looking for a job overseas it wouldn't be a bad idea to check here. When you Telnet,

```
                        JOB VACANCIES
  G1   Introduction and Submission Details        <02-NOV-94>
  G2   Computing                                  <02-FEB-95>
  G3   Maths and Sciences                         <31-JAN-95>
  G4   Engineering, Technology and Business       <02-FEB-95>
  G5   Medicine                                   <30-JAN-95>
  G6   Languages and Literature                   <24-JAN-95>
  G7   Arts                                       <empty>
  G8   Social Sciences, Law and Education         <26-JAN-95>
  G9   Geography and History                      <19-JAN-95>
  G10  Theology, Philosophy and Psychology        <31-JAN-95>
  G11  Library and Librarianship                  <24-JAN-95>
  G12  Administrative Staff                       <24-JAN-95>
  G13  Miscellaneous                              <empty>
  G20  Overseas - Association of Commonwealth Univs.[M] <25-JAN-95>
  G30  Short-term Research Opportunities
  G40  New Graduates
  G50  PFUE/YII Graduate recruitment scheme       <24-JAN-95>
```

Figure 7.25 A sample of jobs available through NISS

choose option AA for the Bulletin Board System. See Figure 7.25 for a sample of NISS' job listings.

Access: **telnet://niss.ac.uk** or IP **193.63.76.1**

Supernet Int'l

At press time, this site was under construction. According to the note, the Supernet will be back online soon, better than before. The good thing about this Telnet site is that large corporations such as IBM and Intel list jobs here.

Access: **telnet:// supernet.ans.net** or **Telnet://hpcwire.ans.net**

Login: **hpcwire**

≡ BULLETIN BOARD SYSTEMS WITH JOB RESOURCES

Bulletin board systems (BBSs), are great for unearthing regional or local job information, but keep in mind that unless you live in the base locale of the BBS, you will incur long distance phone charges (some BBSs have Telnet capability, which is noted).

This list of BBSs was culled from more than 1,500, and represents what we consider to be the cream of the crop. Unfortunately, of all online features, bulletin boards tend to be the most changeable, so don't be surprised at the differences you find when you log on.

A couple of pieces of advice for you to be aware of before you explore these boards:

♦ Check area codes *before* you call, so you don't add to your long distance charges with mistakes.

♦ When you dial up a BBS, usually you will be asked to fill out personal or professional information. The boards listed here all have a policy of privacy, which means all such information will be kept confidential unless you request otherwise. For additional protection, you can send a note to the sysop of the board you're interested in and express your concerns and request that none of your personal data be used for mailing lists or anything else.

♦ When you get ready to dial a BBS, set your modem to a timeout delay for 60 seconds or more. It takes just over 30 seconds to call and connect to a long-distance BBS, and if your modem is set to a 30-second timeout (a standard default) you won't have time to connect.

♦ After you've connected to a BBS, wait! Don't press the Enter key. The screen will come up on its own. If you do press Enter, you will probably get unreadable machine code. To remedy this, hang up, dial again, and don't press *anything* until you see a menu come up on your screen.

Enough talk—let's hit the boards!

AVADS-BBS

Modem: 800-366-3321

This is the Automated Vacancy Announcement Information Center, which lists job information from the Department of the Interior. Like the other online areas carrying these job announcements, this BBS is packed with about 3,000 job openings. If you do not have access to the Internet, this is a fabulous place to look for a government job.

CAPACCESS Career Center

Modem: 202-785-1523

See the listing Capital Access in the Telnet section for details. If you have Telnet capability, you can access this BBS without making a long distance phone call.

Career Link, Inc.

Modem: 602-973-2002

Career Link has recently revamped itself to include *only overseas or U.S-based with international travel* job listings. Currently, the database contains 1,300 jobs, and new jobs are added at the rate of 135 per week. The sysops of this board have set a goal of maintaining the best international job BBS available. The great thing about this BBS is the way the information is set up—it is very easy to access and to navigate. When you call the number listed above, you will have free access to about 450 real jobs, but they are not kept as current as the weekly updated database. For complete database access, there is a fee required, but if you are looking for a job overseas, this board is a must-visit.

DICE National Network

Modem: 201-242-4166
           214-782-0960
           408-737-9339
           515-280-3423
           708-782-0960

As you can surmise from the access numbers, DICE operates from several cities in the U.S. This is a good board to visit if you

```
                        Enter your selection:   o
Date: 02-FEB-95     System Time: 21:32:04       Time Online Today: 0 minutes

            Data Processing Independent Consultant's Exchange
          ╔══════════════════════════════════════════════════╗
          ║             Region Selection Menu                ║
          ╚══════════════════════════════════════════════════╝
      # of Jobs
   1 =>    49  in -> New England Region        <CT, MA, ME, NH, RI, VT>
   2 =>   414  in -> North Atlantic Region     <NJ, NY, PA>
   3 =>    50  in -> Middle Atlantic Region    <DE, MD, VA, WV, WASH DC>
   4 =>   242  in -> South Atlantic Region     <AL, FL, GA, KY, MS, NC, SC, TN>
   5 =>   240  in -> Midwest Region            <IA, IL, IN, KS, MI, MN, MO, ND
                                                NE, OH, SD, WI>
   6 =>    41  in -> South Central Region      <AR, LA, OK, TX>
   7 =>    51  in -> Mountain Region           <AZ, CO, ID, MT, NM, NV, UT, WY>
   8 =>    78  in -> North Pacific Region      <AK, HI, OR, WA>
   9 =>  2400  in -> Northern California
  10 =>    85  in -> Southern California
  11 =>     1  in -> International Region       X ... Exit, Return to Main Menu

                        Enter your selection: |
```

Figure 7.26 A sample of DICE BBS

```
After you login, you will be at the ECCO*BBS Main Menu. Select the option
Opportunities. From the Opportunities menu select Job Area and select one
one of the following:

    0 - National Opportunities <default>
    2 - Permanent Opportunities
    3 - Contract Opportunities <try this first>

  You MUST Change Job Area to see listed positions ! ! ! ! !

Now, selecting List will allow you to see all postings in the Job area you
have chosen. If you see a job description that interests you, select
[V]iew from the listing screen for further details on that position.
Opportunities may also be Searched for on [K]eywords such as COBOL, VMS,
NOVELL etc. and then [V]iewed.

You can now easily [M]ark indvidual listings for batch [D]ownload right
from the listings screen. If your communications package supports it,
we suggest using the Zmodem protocol for downloads.

-Pause- [C]ontinue, [N]onStop, [S]top? |
```

Figure 7.27 ECCO BBS

are looking for hi-tech job openings. A description of DICE can be seen in Figure 7.26. When you enter DICE, you will be asked to fill out a questionnaire that will help employers find you by keyword.

ECCO BBS

Modem: 212-580-4510
           312-404-8685
           415-331-7227

ECCO stands for East Coast Consulting Opportunities. This is another BBS that emphasizes hi-tech positions. Figure 7.27 shows a sample of what ECCO looks like online. If you live in New York, Northern California, or Chicago, you can get an Internet email address for free.

Employment Board

Modem: 619-689-1348 or 619-993-9319

This is not the busiest employment board you can access but it does have an interesting employment database called ERISS, which gives statistics for every imaginable profession from pay averages to employment outlook. There is a job openings database, too, but to access it you have to give your date of birth. This put us off—but maybe you won't mind as much as we did. Jobs are primarily for California.

```
┌─────────────────────────────────────────────────────────────┐
│                     FirstStep(sm) Menu              Node # 1  │
│   Date: 02-02-95          Time: 22:43       System Call # 9,352│
├─────────────────────────────────────────────────────────────┤
│  <R>ead Messages [Ex: 'R A L'    <Q>uick Scan for messages    │
│    reads all msgs last to first] <QWK>for msgs for Off-line reader│
│  <E>nter messages, Briefs        <TS> - Search Msgs for key words│
│    and attach Resume file            [Example: 'ts a cobol']  │
│  <J>oin or <A>bandon conferences <U>pload a File              │
│  <D>ownload Resumes/Help files   <F>iles available for downloading│
│  ...........................................................  │
│  Read <B>ulletins                Read <NEWS> about this system.│
│  ...........................................................  │
│  <M> Toggle color on/off         <U>iew your status/statistics│
│  <X> Toggle expert mode on/off   See <I>nitial logon screen again│
│  An<S>wer script questionnaires  Set your <T>ransfer protocol │
│  Page <O>perator for help        Set # of lines <P>er screen  │
│  <DOOR> Currently Restricted     <W> Change initial settings  │
│  ...........................................................  │
│    <C>omment to sysop    <Charge> your Subscription   <G>oodbye│
└─────────────────────────────────────────────────────────────┘
```

Figure 7.28 FirstStep's opening menu

FirstStep

Modem: 404-642-0665

Simply put, this is one of the best managed and organized BBSs around. It links to Usenet employment newsgroups, and is planning on adding an online employment database and Telnet capability. In Figure 7.28, you will see FirstStep's opening screen.

JOBS-BBS

Modem: 503-281-6808

If ever there were an ultimate employment BBS, this is it. This board is updated *every day* and offers job seekers thousands of national job openings.

Online Opportunities

Modem: 610-873-7170

You can put your resume on this BBS for free, but to access the job listings there is a fee. This BBS is extremely busy.

The Resume File

Modem: 805-575-6521

A fabulous BBS with thousands of national job listings, and a very busy BBS.

≡ JOB OPENINGS VIA COMMERCIAL ONLINE SERVICES

Each of the following commercial online services offers at least some online employment information. We are listing the services' voice numbers, as they often will send you free or low-cost setup materials.

America Online

Access: Voice 800-827-6364

America Online offers access to E-Span as well as links to Help Wanted U.S.A. There are some other areas of career information available. Examples: Career Guidance Services, Occupational Profiles Database, Employer Contacts Database, and resume and cover letter templates.

CompuServe

Access: Voice 800-848-8990

CompuServe, in addition to carrying E-Span, offers very comprehensive career discussion groups that post jobs, offer specialized job advice, and allow members to post resumes. There are too many professional forums to list comprehensively, but here's a sampling: Education Forum, Astronomy Forum, Journalism Forum, Legal Forum, Entrepreneurs/Small Business Forum, Computer Consultants Forum. As CompuServe is the most professionally oriented of all the commercial online services, it is worth a trial browse-through.

Delphi

Access: Voice 800-695-4005

Delphi has one big benefit: Internet access. Beyond that, there are some business groups that may be helpful for job searchers such as Business Forum and Business Wire.

eWorld

Access: Voice 800-775-4556

If you haven't heard of eWorld, you're probably not a Macintosh user. For job seekers, it's a great place to at least browse. Some very high-level career experts hang out online. Also, look for more career services to come online in '95.

GEnie

Access: Voice 800-638-9636

GEnie contains many helpful career tools, including access to E-Span, career counselors, and career information. Examples: Workplace Roundtable, Dr. Job, Business Resource Directory, Law Center, and more. There are also many good professional forums available on GEnie such as Medical RT, Law RT, and Education RT.

Lexus/Nexus

Access: Voice 800-227-4908

This is a very expensive service. If you have access already, you may be interested in the employment section for legal professionals available through Lexus.

Microsoft Network

Access: Microsoft General Number only: 800-426-9400

As we went to press, there was not a contact number available for this service-to-be. We have, however, spoken with the people involved in building the career section of this online service, and it promises to be competitive with CompuServe's extensive career services. To find the phone number, call directory assistance at 800 555-1212 and ask for Microsoft Network. If they're up and running, they'll be listed there.

OS/2 Warp

Access: Voice 800-426-4329 or **http://www.ibm.com**

This is IBM's mega-network that you can connect to if you purchase the OS/2 system. This system will give you Internet access. And, if you want to put up a home page, for a fee they will write it, set it up, and store it for you. No career services such as forums are offered, but this network and configuration has already won many awards for its smooth setup and easy navigation.

Prodigy

Access: Voice 800-776-3449

Prodigy has a sprinkling of job search and career services, but its best offering to job seekers, as of this writing, is Web access.

INDEPENDENT EMPLOYMENT DATABASES

Independent employment databases are for-pay, and for that reason, we have chosen to list only two here. Too many of these sprout up and then die off within the space of one year—along with your money. We caution you to check out references, research how long the database has been in business, and ask to see success statistics before you subscribe to any for-pay database.

Help-Wanted U.S.A.

Access: **http:/www.webcom.com/~career/hwusa.html**

or

gopher://garnet.msen.com:906z/11/

Skill Search

Access: **http://www.internet-is.com:80/skillsearch**

At time of writing, membership costs $65.00 and an additional $15.00 upon each anniversary of enrollment.

UPDATING THIS LIST

The best way to update this list is to log on the Internet or the World Wide Web and browse the *meta-lists* (lists that launch you to other resources) that are available. Each list has its own flavor; and you'll want to browse all of them as no single list is absolutely complete.

The other—more laborious—way to update this list is to perform keyword searches in Veronica or on Web search engines. The keywords you should use are:

CAREER
JOBS
EMPLOYMENT
RESUME

These keywords will pull up many documents, some new, some old. Reserve this course of action until after you've checked the meta-lists, as the process of checking each site garnered from a keyword search is long and tedious.

Here are some of the meta-lists we like:

Catapult

Access: **http://www.wm.edu/catapult/catapult.html**

The Catapult is a blessedly concise list of jobs and job resources with many excellent links.

Job Info at Yahoo

Access: **http://mtmis1.mis.semi.harris.com/jobs.html**

This is a huge list of job resources. Not a bad place to begin looking. Figure 7.29 reveals a slice of Yahoo.

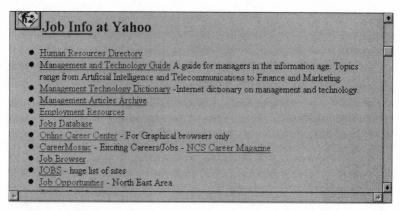

Figure 7.29 A vignette of Yahoo's list

Peter's Page O' Jobs

Access: **http://sahara.bu.edu:4021/Career/jobs.html**

If you need a starting point to the Web, this is it. Includes many links to sites on this list. See Figure 7.30 for an example of what this site looks like.

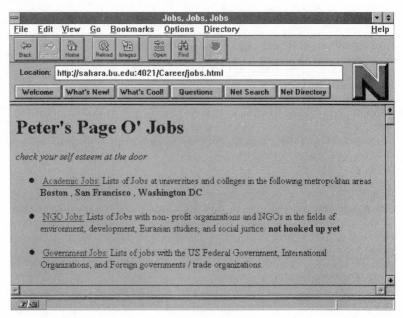

Figure 7.30 Peter's Page O' Jobs. A useful, albeit tongue-in-cheek, list

Getting Yourself Online

This appendix is composed primarily of a resource called the PDIAL List, the Public Dialup Internet Access List. Compiled by Peter Kaminski, the list contains the names, numbers, and service details of most Internet service providers that offer public access dial-in capabilities and outgoing Internet access (FTP, telnet, and more). Most of them also offer email and Usenet news, and other services. Chances are, you'll find a provider near you.

The PDIAL list is printed in this appendix in its entirety (with the permission of Peter Kaminski), as you will find it online, but don't assume you have to approach it in a top-down fashion. In fact, we recommend that you flip to the entry numbered -06- in the list's contents. That section, titled "What the PDIAL Is," can help to familiarize you with this valuable Internet resource.

Following the PDIAL list you will find the names—organized by state and country—of the freenets and community nets available as of March 1995.

Before you get started, though, here are some guidelines to help make your online travel turbulence-free:

- ♦ Buy the fastest modem available. Already, 14,400 bps (that's bits per second data transmission speed) modems are waning in popularity. Faster modems of 28,800 bps and higher are the most popular now. The faster your modem, the more time you save online.

♦ Get on the Web. If you use a PC, you must be running Microsoft Windows to run a graphical interface to the Web. Aim for 8MG of memory as a minimum, and 100MG or more of disk space (the more memory and disk space, the faster you'll be online). On a Macintosh, the same requirements apply for speed and memory.

♦ When you call a service provider on the PDIAL list, ask what kind of technical support is offered. Are experts available to walk you through every step of getting on-line? There should be, and it shouldn't cost an arm and a leg, either.

♦ Make sure that your service provider gives you the software and the instructions you need to get online. Each system is slightly different, and Internet providers set up their services individually, using their favorite software. You shouldn't have to guess your way through your first online journeys.

♦ Before you sign up with a service, ask these questions:

Do you have Web access? If so, what kind? (SLIP or PPP connection or just Lynx)?

Do you have Telnet, FTP, Usenet news, Gopher, and email?

What other Internet services do you offer?

Is it clear from the opening menu how I access the Internet?

Can you help me get online and get my computer set up correctly? How much does this cost?

If I get in trouble on your system, is there a way for me to get help?

You will usually find that Internet providers are very sensitive to the needs of new users and are very helpful. All you need to do at this point is choose a service you like from the PDIAL list and start calling.

THE PDIAL LIST

Although the copyright date you see here is for 1993, the PDIAL list was actually updated in January 1995. To get future updates, access the following Web address:

http://www.pdial.com/

```
         The Public Dialup Internet Access List (PDIAL)
         ===============================================
              File PDIAL015.TXT — 09 December 1993
```

Copyright 1992-1993 Peter Kaminski. Do not modify. Freely distributable
for non-commercial purposes. Please contact me if you wish to distribute
commercially or in modified form.

I make no representations about the suitability or accuracy of this document
for any purpose. It is provided "as is" without express or implied warranty.
All information contained herein is subject to change.

Contents:

-00- Quick Start!
-01- Area Code Summary: Providers With Many Local Dialins (1-800, PDN)
-02- Area Code Summary: US/Canada Metro and Regional Dialins
-03- Area Code Summary: International Dialins
-04- Alphabetical List of Providers
-05- What *Is* The Internet?
-06- What The PDIAL Is
-07- How People Can Get The PDIAL (This List)
-08- Appendix A: Other Valuable Resources
-09- Appendix B: Finding Public Data Network (PDN) Access Numbers
-10- Providers: Get Listed in PDIAL!

Subject headers below are formatted so this list may be read as a
digest by USENET newsreaders that support digests. Example commands:
rn, "control-G" skips to next section; nn, "G%" presents as a digest.

Or, just skip to desired section by searching for the desired section
number string (e.g. "-01-") from the list above.

From: PDIAL -00-
Subject: Quick Start!
THE INTERNET is a global cooperative information network which can give
you instant access to millions of people and terabytes of data. Providers
listed in the PDIAL provide inexpensive public access to the Internet
using your regular modem and computer.

[Special note: the PDIAL currently lists only providers directly connected
to the Internet. Much of the Internet can still be explored through
systems with only Internet email and USENET netnews connections, but you
need to check other BBS lists to find them.]

GET A GUIDE: I highly recommend obtaining one of the many good starter or
guide books to the Internet. Think of them as travel guides to a new and

different country, and you wouldn't be far off. See section -08- below
for more details.

CHOOSING A PROVIDER: Phone charges can dominate the cost of your access to
the Internet. Check first for providers with metro or regional dialins
that are a local call for you (no per-minute phone charges). If there
aren't any, move on to comparing prices for PDN, 800, and direct-dial long
distance charges. Make sure to compare all your options. Calling long
distance out-of-state or across the country is often cheaper than calling
30 miles away.
If you're not in North America and have no local provider, you may still
be able to use one of the providers listed as having PDN access. Contact
the individual providers with PDN access (see listings below) to find out.

INFORMATION CHANGES: The information listed in the PDIAL changes and
expands rapidly. If this edition is more than 2 months old, consider
obtaining a new one. You can use the Info Deli email server, which
will provide you with updates and other information. Choose from the
commands below and just email them to <info-deli-server@netcom.com>.

   "Send PDIAL" — receive the current PDIAL
   "Subscribe PDIAL" — receive new editions of the PDIAL automatically
   "Subscribe Info-Deli-News" — news of Info Deli changes and additions

See section -07- below for more details and other ways to obtain the
PDIAL.

CHECK IT OUT: Remember, the PDIAL is only a summary listing of the
resources and environment delivered by each of the various providers.
Contact the providers that interest you by email or voice phone and make
sure you find out if they have what you need.

Then GO FOR IT! Happy 'netting!

From: PDIAL -01-
Subject: Area Code Summary: Providers With Many Local Dialins (1-800, PDN)

       800 class cns crl csn dial-n-cerf-usa hookup.net IGC jvnc OARnet
       PDN delphi holonet hookup.net IGC michnet millennium novalink portal
       PDN psi-world-dial psilink tmn well world

"PDN" means the provider is accessible through a public data network
(check the listings below for which network); note that many PDNs
listed offer access outside North America as well as within North
America. Check with the provider or the PDN for more details.

"800" means the provider is accessible via a "toll-free" US phone
number. The phone company will not charge for the call, but the
service provider will add a surcharge to cover the cost of the 800
service. This may be more expensive than other long-distance options.

From: PDIAL -02-
Subject: Area Code Summary: US/Canada Metro and Regional Dialins

If you are not local to any of these providers, it's still likely you
are able to access those providers available through a public data
network (PDN). Check the section above for providers with wide area
access.

       201 jvnc-tiger
       202 CAPCON clarknet express michnet tmn
       203 jvnc-tiger
       205 nuance
       206 eskimo GLAIDS halcyon netcom nwnexus olympus
       212 echonyc maestro mindvox panix pipeline

```
213 crl dial-n-cerf kaiwan netcom
214 metronet netcom
215 jvnc-tiger PREPnet
216 OARnet wariat
217 prairienet
301 CAPCON clarknet express michnet tmn
302 ssnet
303 cns csn netcom nyx
305 gate.net
310 class crl dial-n-cerf kaiwan netcom
312 InterAccess mcsnet netcom xnet
313 michnet MSen
401 anomaly ids jvnc-tiger
403 PUCnet UUNET-Canada
404 crl netcom
407 gate.net
408 a2i netcom portal
410 CAPCON clarknet express
412 PREPnet telerama
415 a2i class crl dial-n-cerf IGC netcom portal well
416 hookup.net UUNET-Canada uunorth
419 OARnet
503 agora.rain.com netcom teleport
504 sugar
508 anomaly nearnet northshore novalink
510 class crl dial-n-cerf holonet netcom
512 realtime
513 fsp OARnet
514 CAM.ORG UUNET-Canada
516 jvnc-tiger
517 michnet
519 hookup.net UUNET-Canada uunorth
602 crl Data.Basix evergreen indirect
603 MV nearnet
604 UUNET-Canada
609 jvnc-tiger
613 UUNET-Canada uunorth
614 OARnet
616 michnet
617 delphi nearnet netcom northshore novalink world
619 cg57 class crash.cts.com cyber dial-n-cerf netcom
703 CAPCON clarknet express michnet netcom tmn
704 concert Vnet
707 crl
708 InterAccess mcsnet xnet
713 blkbox nuchat sugar
714 class dial-n-cerf express kaiwan netcom
717 PREPnet
718 maestro mindvox netcom panix pipeline
719 cns csn oldcolo
804 wyvern
810 michnet MSen
814 PREPnet
815 InterAccess mcsnet xnet
817 metronet
818 class dial-n-cerf netcom
905 UUNET-Canada
906 michnet
907 alaska.edu
908 express jvnc-tiger
910 concert
916 netcom
919 concert Vnet
```

These are area codes local to the dialups, although some prefixes in the
area codes listed may not be local to the dialups. Check your phone book
or with your phone company.

From: PDIAL -03-
Subject: Area Code Summary: International Dialins

If you are not local to any of these providers, there is still a chance
you are able to access those providers available through a public data
network (PDN). Check section -01- above for providers with wide area
access, and send email to them to ask about availability.

```
+44 (0)81 Demon dircon ibmpcug
      +49 Individual.NET
   +49 23 ins
  +49 069 in-rhein-main
  +49 089 mucev
    +61 2 connect.com.au
    +61 3 connect.com.au
     +301 Ariadne
   +353·1 IEunet
```

From: PDIAL -04-
Subject: Alphabetical List of Providers

Fees are for personal dialup accounts with outgoing Internet access;
most sites have other classes of service with other rate structures as
well. Most support email and netnews along with the listed services.
"Long distance: provided by user" means you need to use direct dial
long distance or other long distance services to connect to the provider.

```
<< a2i >>
name ——-> a2i communications
dialup ——-> 408-293-9010 (v.32bis), 415-364-5652 (v.32bis), 408-293-9020
               (PEP); login 'guest'
area codes ——> 408, 415
local access -> CA: West and South SF Bay Area
long distance -> provided by user
services ——-> shell (SunOS UNIX and MS-DOS), ftp, telnet, irc, feeds,
               domains and host-less domains, virtual ttys, gopher
fees ——-> $20/month or $45/3 months or $72/6 months
email ——-> info@rahul.net
voice ——-> 408-293-8078 voicemail
ftp more info -> ftp.rahul.net:/pub/BLURB

<< agora.rain.com >>
name ——-> RainDrop Laboratories
dialup ——-> 503-293-1772 (2400) 503-293-2059 (v.32, v.32 bis) 'apply'
area codes ——> 503
local access -> OR: Portland, Beaverton, Hillsboro, Forest Grove, Gresham,
          .    Tigard, Lake Oswego, Oregon City, Tualatin, Wilsonville
long distance -> provided by user
services ——-> shell, ftp, telnet, gopher, usenet
fees ——-> $6/month (1 hr/day limit)
email ——-> info@agora.rain.com
voice ——-> n/a
ftp more info -> agora.rain.com:/pub/gopher-data/agora/agora

<< alaska.edu >>
name ——-> University Of Alaska Southeast, Tundra Services
dialup ——-> 907-789-1314
area codes ——> 907
local access -> All Alaskan sites with local UACN access — Anchorage,
               Barrow, Fairbanks, Homer, Juneau, Keni, Ketchikan, Kodiak,
               Kotzebue, Nome, Palmer, Sitka, Valdez
long distance -> provided by user
```

```
services ——-> Statewide UACN Mail, Internet, USENET, gopher, Telnet, FTP
fees ——-> $20/month for individual accounts, discounts for 25+ and 50+
                 to public, gov't and non-profit organizations.
email ——-> JNJMB@acad1.alaska.edu
voice ——-> 907-465-6453
fax ——-> 907-465-6295
ftp more info -> n/a


<< anomaly >>
name ——-> Anomaly - Rhode Island's Gateway To The Internet
dialup ——-> 401-331-3706 (v.32) or 401-455-0347 (PEP)
area codes ——> 401, 508
local access -> RI: Providence/Seekonk Zone
long distance -> provided by user
services ——-> shell, ftp, telnet, SLIP
fees ——-> Commercial: $125/6 months or $200/year; Educational: $75/6
                 months or $125/year
email ——-> info@anomaly.sbs.risc.net
voice ——-> 401-273-4669
ftp more info -> anomaly.sbs.risc.net:/anomaly.info/access.zip


<< Ariadne >>
name ——-> Ariadne - Greek Academic and Research Network
dialup ——-> +301 65-48-800 (1200 - 9600 bps)
area codes ——> +301
local access -> Athens, Greece
long distance -> provided by user
services ——-> e-mail, ftp, telnet, gopher, talk, pad(EuropaNet)
fees ——-> 5900 drachmas per calendar quarter, 1 hr/day limit.
email ——-> dialup@leon.nrcps.ariadne-t.gr
voice ——-> +301 65-13-392
fax ——-> +301 6532910
ftp more info -> n/a


<< blkbox >>
name ——-> The Black Box
dialup ——-> (713) 480-2686 (V32bis/V42bis)
area codes ——> 713
local access -> TX: Houston
long distance -> provided by user
services ——-> shell, ftp, telnet, SLIP, PPP, UUCP
fees ——-> $21.65 per month or $108.25 for 6 months
email ——-> info@blkbox.com
voice ——-> (713) 480-2684
ftp more info -> n/a


<< CAM.ORG >>
name ——-> Communications Accessibles Montreal
dialup ——-> 514-931-7178 (v.32 bis), 514-931-2333 (2400bps)
area codes ——> 514
local access -> QC: Montreal, Laval, South-Shore, West-Island
long distance -> provided by user
services ——-> shell, ftp, telnet, gopher, wais, WWW, irc, feeds, SLIP,
                 PPP, AppleTalk, FAX gateway
fees ——-> $25/month Cdn.
email ——-> info@CAM.ORG
voice ——-> 514-931-0749
ftp more info -> ftp.CAM.ORG


<< CAPCON >>
name ——-> CAPCON Library Network
dialup ——-> contact for number
area codes ——> 202, 301, 410, 703
local access -> District of Columbia, Suburban Maryland & Northern Virginia
long distance -> various plans available/recommended; contact for details
```

```
services ----> menu, archie, ftp, gopher, listservs, telnet, wais, whois,
                  full day training and 'CAPCON Connect User Manual'
fees -------> $35 start-up + $150/yr + $24/mo for first account from an
                  institution; $35 start-up + $90/yr + $15/mo for additional
                  users (member rates lower); 20 hours/month included,
                  additional hours $2/hr
email ------> capcon@capcon.net
voice ------> 202-331-5771
fax -------> 202-797-7719
ftp more info -> n/a


<< cg57 >>
name ------> E & S Systems Public Access *Nix
dialup -----> 619-278-8267 (V.32bis, TurboPEP), 619-278-8267 (V32)
                  619-278-9837 (PEP)
area codes --> 619
local access -> CA: San Diego
long distance -> provided by user
services ----> shell, ftp, irc, telnet, gopher, archie, bbs (UniBoard)
fees -------> bbs (FREE), shell - $30/3 months, $50/6 months, $80/9
                  months, $100/year
email ------> steve@cg57.esnet.com
voice ------> 619-278-4641
ftp more info -> n/a


<< clarknet >>
name ------> Clark Internet Services, Inc. (ClarkNet)
dialup -----> 410-730-9786, 410-995-0271, 301-596-1626, 301-854-0446,
                  301-621-5216 'guest'
area codes --> 202, 301, 410, 703
local access -> MD: Baltimore; DC: Washington; VA: Northern VA
long distance -> provided by user
services ----> shell, menu, ftp, telnet, irc, gopher, hytelnet, www, WAIS,
                  SLIP/PPP, ftp space, feeds (UUCP & uMDSS), dns, Clarinet
fees -------> $23/month or $66/3 months or $126/6 months or $228/year
email ------> info@clark.net
voice ------> Call 800-735-2258 then give 410-730-9764 (MD Relay Svc)
fax -------> 410-730-9765
ftp more info -> ftp.clark.net:/pub/clarknet/fullinfo.txt


<< class >>
name ------> Cooperative Library Agency for Systems and Services
dialup -----> contact for number; NOTE: CLASS serves libraries and
                  information distributors only
area codes --> 310, 415, 510, 619, 714, 818, 800
local access -> Northern and Southern California or anywhere (800) service
                  is available
long distance -> 800 service available at $6/hour surcharge
services ----> menus, mail, telnet, ftp, gopher, wais, hytelnet, archie,
                  WWW, IRC, Unix shells, SLIP, etc.  Training is available.
fees -------> $4.50/hour + $150/year for first account + $50/year each
                  additional account + $135/year CLASS membership.  Discounts
                  available for multiple memberships.
email ------> class@class.org
voice ------> 800-488-4559
fax -------> 408-453-5379
ftp more info -> n/a


<< cns >>
name ------> Community News Service
dialup -----> 719-520-1700 id 'new', passwd 'newuser'
area codes --> 303, 719, 800
local access -> CO: Colorado Springs, Denver; continental US/800
long distance -> 800 or provided by user
services ----> UNIX shell, email, ftp, telnet, irc, USENET, Clarinet,
                  gopher, Commerce Business Daily
fees -------> $2.75/hour; $10/month minimum + $35 signup
```

```
email ——--> service@cscns.com
voice ——--> 719-592-1240
ftp more info -> cscns.com


<< concert >>
name ———-> CONCERT-CONNECT
dialup ———-> contact for number
area codes ——-> 704, 910, 919
local access —-> NC: Asheville, Chapel Hill, Charlotte, Durham, Greensboro,
                  Greenville, Raleigh, Winston-Salem, Research Triangle Park
long distance -> provided by user
services ——-> UUCP, SLIP
fees ——-> SLIP: $150 educational/research or $180 commercial for first
                  60 hours/month + $300 signup
email ——--> info@concert.net
voice ——--> 919-248-1999
ftp more info -> ftp.concert.net


<< connect.com.au >>
name ——-> connect.com.au pty ltd
dialup ——-> contact for number
area codes ——-> +61 3, +61 2
local access —-> Australia: Melbourne, Sydney
long distance -> provided by user
services ——-> SLIP, PPP, ISDN, UUCP, ftp, telnet, NTP, FTPmail
fees ——-> AUS$2000/year (1 hour/day), 10% discount for AUUG members;
                  other billing negotiable
email ——--> connect@connect.com.au
voice ——--> +61 3 5282239
fax ———--> +61 3 5285887
ftp more info -> ftp.connect.com.au


<< crash.cts.com >>
name ——-> CTS Network Services (CTSNET)
dialup ——-> 619-637-3640 HST, 619-637-3660 V.32bis, 619-637-3680 PEP
                  'help'
area codes ——-> 619
local access —-> CA: San Diego, Pt. Loma, La Jolla, La Mesa, El Cajon, Poway,
                  Ramona, Chula Vista, National City, Mira Mesa, Alpine, East
                  County, new North County numbers, Escondido, Oceanside, Vista
long distance -> provided by user
services ——-> Unix shell, UUCP, Usenet newsfeeds, NNTP, Clarinet, Reuters,
                  FTP, Telnet, SLIP, PPP, IRC, Gopher, Archie, WAIS, POPmail,
                  UMDSS, domains, nameservice, DNS
fees ——-> $10-$23/month flat depending on features, $15 startup,
                  personal $20-> /month flat depending on features, $25
                  startup, commercial
email ——--> info@crash.cts.com (server), support@crash.cts.com (human)
voice ——--> 619-637-3637
fax ——--> 619-637-3630
ftp more info -> n/a


<< crl >>
name ——-> CR Laboratories Dialup Internet Access
dialup ——-> 415-389-UNIX
area codes ——-> 213, 310, 404, 415, 510, 602, 707, 800
local access —-> CA: San Francisco Bay area + San Rafael, Santa Rosa, Los
                  Angeles, Orange County; AZ: Phoenix, Scottsdale, Tempe, and
                  Glendale; GA: Atlanta metro area; continental US/800
long distance -> 800 or provided by user
services ——-> shell, ftp, telnet, feeds, SLIP, WAIS
fees ——-> $17.50/month + $19.50 signup
email ——--> info@crl.com
voice ——--> 415-381-2800
ftp more info -> n/a
```

```
<< csn >>
name ———> Colorado SuperNet, Inc.
dialup ———> contact for number
area codes —> 303, 719, 800
local access —> CO: Alamosa, Boulder/Denver, Colorado Springs, Durango, Fort
                    Collins, Frisco, Glenwood Springs/Aspen, Grand Junction,
                    Greeley, Gunnison, Pueblo, Telluride; anywhere 800 service
                    is available
long distance -> provided by user or 800
services ———> shell or menu, UUCP, SLIP, 56K, ISDN, T1; ftp, telnet, irc,
                    gopher, WAIS, domains, anonymous ftp space, email-to-fax
fees ———> $1/hour off-peak, $3/hour peak ($250 max/month) + $20
                    signup, $5/hr surcharge for 800 use
email ———-> info@csn.org
voice ———-> 303-273-3471
fax ———-> 303-273-3475
ftp more info -> csn.org:/CSN/reports/DialinInfo.txt
off-peak ———> midnight to 6am

<< cyber >>
name ———> The Cyberspace Station
dialup ———> 619-634-1376 'guest'
area codes —> 619
local access —> CA: San Diego
long distance -> provided by user
services ———> shell, ftp, telnet, irc
fees ———> $15/month + $10 startup or $60 for six months
email ———-> help@cyber.net
voice ———-> n/a
ftp more info -> n/a

<< Data.Basix >>
name ———> Data Basix
dialup ———> 602-721-5887
area codes —> 602
local access —> AZ: Tucson
long distance -> provided by user
services ———> Telnet, FTP, NEWS, UUCP; on-site assistance
fees ———> $25 monthly, $180 yearly; group rates available
email ———-> info@Data.Basix.com (automated); sales@Data.Basix.com (human)
voice ———-> 602-721-1988
ftp more info -> Data.Basix.COM:/services/dial-up.txt

<< Demon >>
name ———> Demon Internet Systems (DIS)
dialup ———> +44 (0)81 343 4848
area codes —> +44 (0)81
local access —> London, England
long distance -> provided by user
services ———> ftp, telnet, SLIP/PPP
fees ———> GBPounds 10.00/month; 132.50/year (inc 12.50 startup
                    charge).  No on-line time charges.
email ———-> internet@demon.co.uk
voice ———-> +44 (0)81 349 0063
ftp more info -> n/a

<< delphi >>
name ———> DELPHI
dialup ———> 800-365-4636 'JOINDELPHI password:INTERNETSIG'
area codes —> 617, PDN
local access —> MA: Boston; KS: Kansas City
long distance -> Sprintnet or Tymnet: $9/hour weekday business hours, no
                    charge nights and weekends
services ———> ftp, telnet, feeds, user groups, wire services, member
                    conferencing
fees ———> $10/month for 4 hours or $20/month for 20 hours + $3/month
                    for Internet services
```

```
email ——-> walthowe@delphi.com
voice ——-> 800-544-4005
ftp more info -> n/a

<< dial-n-cerf >>
name ——-> DIAL n' CERF or DIAL n' CERF AYC
dialup ——> contact for number
area codes —> 213, 310, 415, 510, 619, 714, 818
local access -> CA: Los Angeles, Oakland, San Diego, Irvine, Pasadena, Palo
                   Alto
long distance -> provided by user
services ——> shell, menu, irc, ftp, hytelnet, gopher, WAIS, WWW, terminal
                   service, SLIP
fees ——> $5/hour ($3/hour on weekend) + $20/month + $50 startup OR
                   $250/month flat for AYC
email ——-> help@cerf.net
voice ——-> 800-876-2373 or 619-455-3900
ftp more info -> nic.cerf.net:/cerfnet/dial-n-cerf/
off-peak ——> Weekend: 5pm Friday to 5pm Sunday

<< dial-n-cerf-usa >>
name ——-> DIAL n' CERF USA
dialup ——> contact for number
area codes —> 800
local access -> anywhere (800) service is available
long distance -> included
services ——> shell, menu, irc, ftp, hytelnet, gopher, WAIS, WWW, terminal
                   service, SLIP
fees ——> $10/hour ($8/hour on weekend) + $20/month
email ——-> help@cerf.net
voice ——-> 800-876-2373 or 619-455-3900
ftp more info -> nic.cerf.net:/cerfnet/dial-n-cerf/
off-peak ——> Weekend: 5pm Friday to 5pm Sunday

<< dircon >>
name ——-> The Direct Connection
dialup ——> +44 (0)81 317 2222
area codes —> +44 (0)81
local access -> London, England
long distance -> provided by user
services ——> shell or menu, UUCP feeds, SLIP/PPP, ftp, telnet, gopher,
                   WAIS, Archie, personal ftp/file space, email-to-fax
fees ——> Subscriptions from GBPounds 10 per month, no on-line
                   charges. GBPounds 7.50 signup fee.
email ——-> helpdesk@dircon.co.uk
voice ——-> +44 (0)81 317 0100
fax ——--> +44 (0)81 317 0100
ftp more info -> n/a

<< echonyc >>
name ——-> Echo Communications
dialup ——> (212) 989-8411 (v.32, v.32 bis) 'newuser'
area codes —> 212
local access -> NY: Manhattan
long distance -> provided by user
services ——> shell, ftp, telnet, gopher, archie, wais, SLIP/PPP
fees ——> Commercial: $19.95/month; students/seniors: $13.75/month
email ——-> horn@echonyc.com
voice ——-> 212-255-3839
ftp more info -> n/a

<< eskimo >>
name ——-> Eskimo North
dialup ——> 206-367-3837 300-14.4k, 206-362-6731 for 9600/14.4k,
                   206-742-1150 World Blazer
area codes —> 206
local access -> WA: Seattle, Everett
```

```
long distance -> provided by user
services ----> shell, ftp, telnet
fees ------> $10/month or $96/year
email ------> nanook@eskimo.com
voice ------> 206-367-7457
ftp more info -> n/a


<< evergreen >>
name ------> Evergreen Communications
dialup ----> (602) 955-8444
area codes --> 602
local access -> AZ
long distance -> provided by user or call for additional information
services ----> ftp, telnet, gopher, archie, wais, www, uucp, PPP
fees ------> individual: $239/yr; commercial: $479/yr; special
                     educational rates
email ------> evergreen@libre.com
voice ------> 602-955-8315
fax -------> 602-955-5948
ftp more info -> n/a


<< express >>
name ------> Express Access - A service of Digital Express Group
dialup ----> 301-220-0462, 410-766-1855, 703-281-7997, 714-377-9784,
                     908-937-9481 'new'
area codes --> 202, 301, 410, 703, 714, 908
local access -> Northern VA, Baltimore MD, Washington DC, New Brunswick NJ,
                     Orange County CA
long distance -> provided by user
services ----> shell, ftp, telnet, irc, gopher, hytelnet, www, Clarinet,
                     SLIP/PPP, archie, mailing lists, autoresponders, anonymous
                     FTP archives
fees ------> $25/month or $250/year
email ------> info@digex.net
voice ------> 800-969-9090, 301-220-2020
ftp more info -> n/a


<< fsp >>
name ------> Freelance Systems Programming
dialup ----> (513) 258-7745 to 14.4 Kbps
area codes --> 513
local access -> OH: Dayton
long distance -> provided by user
services ----> shell, ftp, telnet, feeds, email, gopher, archie, SLIP, etc.
fees ------> $20 startup and $1 per hour
email ------> fsp@dayton.fsp.com
voice ------> (513) 254-7246
ftp more info -> n/a
<< gate.net >>
name ------> CyberGate, Inc
dialup ----> 305-425-0200
area codes --> 305, 407
local access -> South Florida, expanding in FL
long distance -> provided by user
services ----> shell, UUCP, SLIP/PPP, leased, telnet, FTP, IRC, archie,
                     gopher, etc.
fees ------> $17.50/mo on credit card; group discounts; SLIP/PPP:
                     $17.50/mo + $2/hr
email ------> info@gate.net or sales@gate.net
voice ------> 305-428-GATE
fax -------> 305-428-7977
ftp more info -> n/a


<< GLAIDS >>
name ------> GLAIDS NET (Homosexual Network)
dialup ----> 206-322-0621
area codes --> 206
```

```
local access -> WA: Seattle
long distance -> provided by user
services -----> BBS, Gopher, ftp, telnet
fees ------> $10/month.  Scholarships available. Free 7 day trial.
                Visitors are welcome.
email ------> tomh@glaids.wa.com
voice ------> 206-323-7483
ftp more info -> GLAIDS.wa.com


<< halcyon >>
name ------> Halcyon
dialup -----> 206-382-6245 `new', 8N1
area codes --> 206
local access -> Seattle, WA
long distance -> provided by user
services -----> shell, telnet, ftp, bbs, irc, gopher, hytelnet
fees ------> $200/year, or $60/quarter + $10 start-up
email ------> info@halcyon.com
voice ------> 206-955-1050
ftp more info -> halcyon.com:/pub/waffle/info


<< holonet >>
name ------> HoloNet
dialup -----> 510-704-1058
area codes --> 510, PDN
local access -> Berkeley, CA
long distance -> [per hour, off-peak/peak] Bay Area: $0.50/$0.95; PSINet A:
                $0.95/$1.95; PSINet B: $2.50/$6.00; Tymnet: $3.75/$7.50
services -----> ftp, telnet, irc, games
fees ------> $2/hour off-peak, $4/hour peak; $6/month or $60/year minimum
email ------> info@holonet.net
voice ------> 510-704-0160
ftp more info -> holonet.net:/info/
off-peak -----> 5pm to 8am + weekends and holidays


<< hookup.net >>
name ------> HookUp Communication Corporation
dialup -----> contact for number
area codes --> 800, PDN, 416, 519
local access -> Ontario, Canada
long distance -> 800 access across Canada, or discounted rates by HookUp
services -----> shell or menu, UUCP, SLIP, PPP, ftp, telnet, irc, gopher,
                domains, anonymous ftp space
fees ------> Cdn$14.95/mo for 5 hours; Cdn$34.95/mo for 15 hrs;
                Cdn$59.95/mo for 30 hrs; Cdn$300.00/yr for 50 hrs/mo;
                Cdn$299.00/mo for unlimited usage
email ------> info@hookup.net
voice ------> 519-747-4110
fax ------> 519-746-3521
ftp more info -> n/a


<< ibmpcug >>
name ------> UK PC User Group
dialup -----> +44 (0)81 863 6646
area codes --> +44 (0)81
local access -> London, England
long distance -> provided by user
services -----> ftp, telnet, bbs, irc, feeds
fees ------> GBPounds 15.50/month or 160/year + 10 startup (no time
                charges)
email ------> info@ibmpcug.co.uk
voice ------> +44 (0)81 863 6646
ftp more info -> n/a


<< ids >>
name ------> The IDS World Network
dialup -----> 401-884-9002, 401-785-1067
```

```
area codes --> 401
local access -> East Greenwich, RI; northern RI
long distance -> provided by user
services ----> ftp, telnet, SLIP, feeds, bbs
fees -------> $10/month or $50/half year or $100/year
email ------> sysadmin@ids.net
voice ------> 401-884-7856
ftp more info -> ids.net:/ids.net


<< IEunet >>
name -------> IEunet Ltd., Ireland's Internet Services Supplier
dialup -----> +353 1 6790830, +353 1 6798600
area codes --> +353 1
local access -> Dublin, Ireland
long distance -> provided by user, or supplied by IEunet
services ----> DialIP, IPGold, EUnet Traveller, X400, X500, Gopher, WWW,
               FTP, FTPmail,SLIP/PPP, FTP archives
fees -------> IEP25/month Basic
email ------> info@ieunet.ie, info@Ireland.eu.net
voice ------> +353 1 6790832
ftp more info -> ftp.ieunet.ie:/pub


<< IGC >>
name -------> Institute for Global Communications/IGC Networks (PeaceNet,
              EcoNet, ConflictNet, LaborNet, HomeoNet)
dialup -----> 415-322-0284 (N-8-1), 'new'
area codes --> 415, 800, PDN
local access -> CA: Palo Alto, San Francisco
long distance -> [per hour, off-peak/peak] SprintNet: $2/$7; 800: $11/$11
services ----> telnet, local newsgroups for environmental, peace/social
               justice issues; NO ftp
fees -------> $10/month + $3/hr after first hour
email ------> support@igc.apc.org
voice ------> 415-442-0220
ftp more info -> igc.apc.org:/pub


<< indirect >>
name -------> Internet Direct, Inc.
dialup -----> 602-274-9600 (Phoenix); 602-321-9600 (Tucson); 'guest'
area codes --> 602
local access -> AZ: Phoenix, Tucson
long distance -> provided by user
services ----> Shell/menu, UUCP, Usenet, NNTP, FTP, Telnet, SLIP, PPP, IRC,
               Gopher, WAIS, WWW, POP, DNS, nameservice, QWK (offline
               readers)
fees -------> $20/month (personal); $30/month (business)
email ------> info@indirect.com (automated); support@indirect.com (human)
voice ------> 602-274-0100 (Phoenix), 602-324-0100 (Tucson)
ftp more info -> n/a


<< Individual.NET >>
name -------> Individual Network e.V. (IN)
dialup -----> contact for number
area codes --> +49
local access -> Germany: Berlin, Oldenburg, Bremen, Hamburg, Krefeld, Kiel,
               Duisburg, Darmstadt, Dortmund, Hannover, Ruhrgebiet, Bonn,
               Magdeburg, Duesseldorf, Essen, Koeln, Paderborn, Bielefeld,
               Aachen, Saarbruecken, Frankfurt, Braunschweig, Dresden, Ulm,
               Erlangen, Nuernberg, Wuerzburg, Chemnitz, Muenchen,
               Muenster, Goettingen, Wuppertal, Schleswig, Giessen,
               Rostock, Leipzig and other
long distance -> provided by user
services ----> e-mail, usenet feeds, UUCP, SLIP, ISDN, shell, ftp, telnet,
               gopher, irc, bbs
fees -------> 15-30 DM/month (differs from region to region)
email ------> in-info@individual.net
voice ------> +49 2131 64190 (Andreas Baess)
```

```
fax ———-> +49 2131 605652
ftp more info -> ftp.fu-berlin.de:/pub/doc/IN/


<< in-rhein-main >>
name ———> Individual Network - Rhein-Main
dialup ———> +49-69-39048414, +49-69-6312934 (+ others)
area codes —-> +49 069
local access —> Frankfurt/Offenbach, Germany
long distance -> provided by user
services ———> shell (Unix), ftp, telnet, irc, gopher, uucp feeds
fees ———> SLIP/PPP/ISDN: 40 DM, 4 DM / Megabyte
email ———-> info@rhein-main.de
voice ———-> +49-69-39048413
ftp more info -> n/a


<< ins >>
name ———> INS - Inter Networking Systems
dialup ———> contact for number
area codes —-> +49 23
local access —> Ruhr-Area, Germany
long distance -> provided by user
services ———> e-mail,uucp,usenet,slip,ppp,ISDN-TCP/IP
fees ———> fees for commercial institutions and any others:
                uucp/e-mail,uucp/usenet:$60/month; ip:$290/month minimum
email ———-> info@ins.net
voice ———-> +49 2305 356505
fax ———-> +49 2305 25411
ftp more info -> n/a


<< InterAccess >>
name ———> InterAccess
dialup ———> 708-671-0237
area codes —-> 708, 312, 815
local access —> Chicagoland metropolitan area
long distance -> provided by user
services ———> ftp, telnet, SLIP/PPP, feeds, shell, UUCP, DNS, ftp space
fees ———> $23/mo shell, $26/mo SLIP/PPP, or $5/mo +$2.30/hr
email ———-> info@interaccess.com
voice ———-> (800) 967-1580
fax ———-> 708-671-0113
ftp more info -> interaccess.com:/pub/interaccess.info


<< jvnc >>
name ———> The John von Neumann Computer Network - Tiger Mail & Dialin'
                Terminal
dialup ———> contact for number
area codes —-> 800
local access —> anywhere (800) service is available
long distance -> included
services ———> email and newsfeed or terminal access only
fees ———> $19/month + $10/hour + $36 startup (PC or Mac SLIP software
                included)
email ———-> info@jvnc.net
voice ———-> 800-35-TIGER, 609-897-7300
fax ———-> 609-897-7310
ftp more info -> n/a


<< jvnc-tiger >>
name ———> The John von Neumann Computer Network - Dialin' Tiger
dialup ———> contact for number
area codes —-> 201, 203, 215, 401, 516, 609, 908
local access —> Princeton & Newark, NJ; Philadelphia, PA; Garden City, NY;
                Bridgeport, New Haven, & Storrs, CT; Providence, RI
long distance -> provided by user
services ———> ftp, telnet, SLIP, feeds, optional shell
fees ———> $99/month + $99 startup (PC or Mac SLIP software included —
                shell is additional $21/month)
```

```
email ——-> info@jvnc.net
voice ——-> 800-35-TIGER, 609-897-7300
fax ——-> 609-897-7310
ftp more info -> n/a


<< kaiwan >>
name ——-> KAIWAN Public Access Internet Online Services
dialup ——-> 714-539-5726, 310-527-7358
area codes —> 213, 310, 714
local access —> CA: Los Angeles, Orange County
long distance -> provided by user
services ——-> shell, ftp, telnet, irc, WAIS, gopher, SLIP/PPP, ftp space,
                feeds, dns, 56K leasd line
fees ——-> $15.00/signup + $15.00/month or $30.00/quarter (3 month) or
                $11.00/month by credit card
email ——-> info@kaiwan.com
voice ——-> 714-638-2139
ftp more info -> kaiwan.com:/pub/KAIWAN


<< maestro >>
name ——-> Maestro
dialup ——-> (212) 240-9700 'newuser'
area codes —> 212, 718
local access —> NY: New York City
long distance -> provided by user
services ——-> shell, ftp, telnet, gopher, wais, irc, feeds, etc.
fees ——-> $15/month or $150/year
email ——-> info@maestro.com (autoreply); staff@maestro.com,
                rkelly@maestro.com, ksingh@maestro.com
voice ——-> 212-240-9600
ftp more info -> n/a


<< mcsnet >>
name ——-> MCSNet
dialup ——-> (312) 248-0900 V.32, 0970 V.32bis, 6295 (PEP), follow prompts
area codes —> 312, 708, 815
local access —> IL: Chicago
long distance -> provided by user
services ——-> shell, ftp, telnet, feeds, email, irc, gopher, hytelnet, etc.
fees ——-> $25/month or $65/3 months untimed, $30/3 months for 15
                hours/month
email ——-> info@genesis.mcs.com
voice ——-> (312) 248-UNIX
ftp more info -> genesis.mcs.com:/mcsnet.info/
<< metronet >>
name ——-> Texas Metronet
dialup ——-> 214-705-2901/817-261-1127 (V.32bis),214-705-2929(PEP),'info'
                or 214-705-2917/817-261-7687 (2400) 'signup'
area codes —> 214, 817
local access —> TX: Dallas, Fort Worth
long distance -> provided by user
services ——-> shell, ftp, telnet, SLIP, PPP, uucp feeds
fees ——-> $5-$45/month + $10-$30 startup
email ——-> info@metronet.com
voice ——-> 214-705-2900, 817-543-8756
fax ——-> 214-401-2802 (8am-5pm CST weekdays)
ftp more info -> ftp.metronet.com:/pub/metronetinfo/


<< michnet >>
name ——-> Merit Network, Inc. — MichNet project
dialup ——-> contact for number or telnet hermes.merit.edu and type
                'help' at 'Which host?' prompt
area codes —> 202, 301, 313, 517, 616, 703, 810, 906, PDN
local access —> Michigan; Boston, MA; Wash. DC
long distance -> SprintNet, Autonet, Michigan Bell packet-switch network
services ——-> telnet, SLIP, PPP, outbound SprintNet, Autonet and Ann Arbor
                dialout
```

```
fees ———> $35/month + $40 signup ($10/month for K-12 & libraries in
              Michigan)
email ———-> info@merit.edu
voice ———> 313-764-9430
ftp more info -> nic.merit.edu:/


<< millennium >>
name ———> Millennium Online
dialup ———> contact for numbers
area codes ——> PDN
local access -> PDN private numbers available
long distance -> PDN
services ———> shell, ftp, telnet, irc, feeds, gopher, graphical bbs
              (interface required)
fees ———> $10 monthly/.10 per minute domestic .30 internationally
email ———-> jjablow@mill.com
voice ———> 800-736-0122
ftp more info -> n/a


<< mindvox >>
name ———> MindVOX
dialup ———> 212-989-4141 'mindvox' 'guest'
area codes ——> 212, 718
local access -> NY: New York City
long distance -> provided by user
services ———> conferencing system ftp, telnet, irc, gopher, hytelnet,
              Archives, BBS
fees ———> $15-$20/month.  No startup.
email ———-> info@phantom.com
voice ———> 212-989-2418
ftp more info -> n/a


<< MSen >>
name ———> MSen
dialup ———> contact for number
area codes ——> 313, 810
local access -> All of SE Michigan (313, 810)
long distance -> provided by user
services ———> shell, WAIS, gopher, telnet, ftp, SLIP, PPP, IRC, WWW,
              Picospan BBS, ftp space
fees ———> $20/month; $20 startup
email ———-> info@msen.com
voice ———> 313-998-4562
fax ———-> 313-998-4563
ftp more info -> ftp.msen.com:/pub/vendor/msen


<< mucev >>
name ———> muc.de e.V.
dialup ———> contact for numbers
area codes ——> +49 089
local access -> Munich/Bavaria, Germany
long distance -> provided by user
services ———> mail, news, ftp, telnet, irc, gopher, SLIP/PPP/UUCP
fees ———> From DM 20.— (Mail only) up to DM 65.— (Full Account with
              PPP)
email ———-> postmaster@muc.de
voice ———->
ftp more info -> ftp.muc.de:public/info/muc-info.*


<< MV >>
name ———> MV Communications, Inc.
dialup ———-> contact for numbers
area codes ——> 603
local access -> Many NH communities
long distance -> provided by user
services ———> shell, ftp, telnet, gopher, SLIP, email, feeds, dns,
              archives, etc.
```

```
fees  ———> $5.00/mo minimum + variable hourly rates.  See schedule.
email ——-> info@mv.com
voice ———> 603-429-2223
ftp more info -> ftp.mv.com:/pub/mv


<< nearnet >>
name  ———> NEARnet
dialup ———> contact for numbers
area codes —> 508, 603, 617
local access —> Boston, MA; Nashua, NH
long distance -> provided by user
services ———> SLIP, email, feeds, dns
fees  ———> $250/month
email ——-> nearnet-join@nic.near.net
voice ———-> 617-873-8730
ftp more info -> nic.near.net:/docs


<< netcom >>
name  ———> Netcom Online Communication Services
dialup ———> 206-547-5992, 214-753-0045, 303-758-0101, 310-842-8835,
             312-380-0340, 404-303-9765, 408-241-9760, 408-459-9851,
             415-328-9940, 415-985-5650, 503-626-6833, 510-274-2900,
             510-426-6610, 510-865-9004, 617-237-8600, 619-234-0524,
             703-255-5951, 714-708-3800, 818-585-3400, 916-965-1371
area codes —> 206, 213, 214, 303, 310, 312, 404, 408, 415, 503, 510,
             617, 619, 703, 714, 718, 818, 916
local access —> CA: Alameda, Irvine, Los Angeles, Palo Alto, Pasadena,
             Sacramento, San Diego, San Francisco, San Jose, Santa Cruz,
             Walnut Creek; CO: Denver; DC: Washington; GA: Atlanta; IL:
             Chicago; MA: Boston; OR: Portland; TX: Dallas; WA: Seattle
long distance -> provided by user
services ———> shell, ftp, telnet, irc, WAIS, gopher, SLIP/PPP, ftp space,
             feeds, dns
fees  ———> $19.50/month + $20.00 signup
email ——-> info@netcom.com
voice ———> 408-554-8649, 800-501-8649
fax  ———-> 408-241-9145
ftp more info -> ftp.netcom.com:/pub/netcom/


<< northshore >>
name  ———> North Shore Access
dialup ———> 617-593-4557 (v.32bis, v.32, PEP) 'new'
area codes —> 617, 508
local access —> MA: Wakefield, Lynnfield, Lynn, Saugus, Revere, Peabody,
             Salem, Marblehead, Swampscott
long distance -> provided by user
services ———> shell (SunOS UNIX), ftp, telnet, archie, gopher, wais, www,
             UUCP feeds
fees  ———> $9/month includes 10 hours connect, $1/hr thereafter, higher
             volume discount plans also available
email ——-> info@northshore.ecosoft.com
voice ———> 617-593-3110 voicemail
ftp more info -> northshore.ecosoft.com:/pub/flyer


<< novalink >>
name  ———> NovaLink
dialup ———> (800) 937-7644 'new' or 'info', 508-754-4009 2400, 14400
area codes —> 508, 617, PDN
local access —> MA: Worcester, Cambridge, Marlboro, Boston
long distance -> CPS: $1.80/hour 2400, 9600; SprintNet $1.80/hour nights and
             weekends
services ———> ftp, telnet, gopher, shell, irc, XWindows, feeds, adult,
             user groups, FAX, Legends of Future Past
fees  ———> $12.95 sign-up (refundable and includes 2 hours), + $9.95/mo
             (includes 5 daytime hours) + $1.80/hr
email ——-> info@novalink.com
```

```
voice ———-> 800-274-2814
ftp more info -> ftp.novalink.com:/info


<< nuance >>
name ———-> Nuance Network Services
dialup ———-> contact for number
area codes ——> 205
 local access —> AL: Huntsville
long distance -> provided by user
services ———-> shell (Unix SVR4.2), ftp, telnet, gopher, SLIP, PPP, ISDN
fees ———-> personal $25/mo + $35 start-up, corporate: call for options
email ———-> staff@nuance.com
voice ———-> 205-533-4296 voice/recording
ftp more info -> ftp.nuance.com:/pub/NNS-INFO


<< nuchat >>
name ———-> South Coast Computing Services, Inc.
dialup ———-> (713) 661-8593 (v.32) - (713) 661-8595 (v.32bis)
area codes ——> 713
local access —> TX: Houston metro area
long distance -> provided by user
services ———-> shell, ftp, telnet, gopher, Usenet, UUCP feeds, SLIP,
                dedicated lines, domain name service, FULL time tech support
fees ———-> dialup - $3/hour, UUCP - $1.50/hour or $100/month unlimited,
              dedicated - $120, unlimited access
email ———-> info@sccsi.com
voice ———-> 713-661-3301
ftp more info -> sccsi.com:/pub/communications/*


<< nwnexus >>
name ———-> Northwest Nexus Inc.
dialup ———-> contact for numbers
area codes ——> 206
local access —> WA: Seattle
long distance -> provided by user
services ———-> UUCP, SLIP, PPP, feeds, dns
fees ———-> $10/month for first 10 hours + $3/hr; $20 start-up
email ———-> info@nwnexus.wa.com
voice ———-> 206-455-3505
ftp more info -> nwnexus.wa.com:/NWNEXUS.info.txt


<< nyx >>
name ———-> Nyx, the Spirit of the Night; Free public internet access
                provided by the University of Denver's Math & Computer
                Science Department
dialup ———-> 303-871-3324
area codes ——> 303
local access —> CO: Boulder/Denver
long distance -> provided by user
services ———-> shell or menu; semi-anonymous accounts; ftp, news, mail
fees ———-> none; donations are accepted but not requested
email ———-> aburt@nyx.cs.du.edu
voice ———-> login to find current list of volunteer 'voice' helpers
ftp more info -> n/a


<< OARnet >>
name ———-> OARnet
dialup ———-> send e-mail to nic@oar.net
area codes ——> 614, 513, 419, 216, 800
local access —> OH: Columbus, Cincinnati, Cleveland, Dayton
long distance -> 800 service
services ———-> email, ftp, telnet, newsfeed
fees ———-> $4.00/hr to $330.00/month; call for code or send email
email ———-> nic@oar.net
voice ———-> 614-292-8100
fax ———-> 614-292-7168
ftp more info -> n/a
```

```
<< oldcolo >>
name ———> Old Colorado City Communications
dialup ———> 719-632-4111 'newuser'
area codes ——> 719
local access —> CO: Colorado Springs
long distance -> provided by user
services ———> shell, ftp, telnet, AKCS, home of the NAPLPS conference
fees ———> $25/month
email ———> dave@oldcolo.com / thefox@oldcolo.com
voice ———> 719-632-4848, 719-593-7575 or 719-636-2040
fax ———> 719-593-7521
ftp more info -> n/a

<< olympus >>
name ———> Olympus - The Olympic Peninsula's Gateway To The Internet
dialup ———> contact voice number below
area codes ——> 206
local access —> WA:Olympic Peninsula/Eastern Jefferson County
long distance -> provided by user
services ———> shell, ftp, telnet, pine, hytelnet
fees ———> $25/month + $10 startup
email ———> info@pt.olympus.net
voice ———> 206-385-0464
ftp more info -> n/a

<< panix >>
name ———> PANIX Public Access Unix
dialup ———> 212-787-3100 'newuser'
area codes ——> 212, 718
local access —> New York City, NY
long distance -> provided by user
services ———> shell, ftp, telnet, gopher, wais, irc, feeds
fees ———> $19/month or $208/year + $40 signup
email ———> alexis@panix.com, jsb@panix.com
voice ———> 212-877-4854 [Alexis Rosen], 212-691-1526 [Jim Baumbach]
ftp more info -> n/a

<< pipeline >>
name ———> The Pipeline
dialup ———> 212-267-8606 'guest'
area codes ——> 212, 718
local access —> NY: New York City
long distance -> provided by user
services ———> Windows interface or shell/menu; all IP services
fees ———> $15/mo. (inc. 5 hrs) or $20/20 hrs or $35 unlimited
email ———> info@pipeline.com, staff@pipeline.com
voice ———> 212-267-3636
ftp more info -> n/a

<< portal >>
name ———> The Portal System
dialup ———> 408-973-8091 high-speed, 408-725-0561 2400bps; 'info'
area codes ——> 408, 415, PDN
local access —> CA: Cupertino, Mountain View, San Jose
long distance -> SprintNet: $2.50/hour off-peak, $7-$10/hour peak; Tymnet:
                $2.50/hour off-peak, $13/hour peak
services ———> shell, ftp, telnet, IRC, UUCP, feeds, bbs
fees ———> $19.95/month + $19.95 signup
email ———> cs@cup.portal.com, info@portal.com
voice ———> 408-973-9111
ftp more info -> n/a
off-peak ———> 6pm to 7am + weekends and holidays
<< prairienet >>
name ———> Prairienet Freenet
dialup ———> (217) 255-9000 'visitor'
area codes ——> 217
local access —> IL: Champaign-Urbana
```

```
long distance -> provided by user
services ———> telnet, ftp, gopher, IRC, etc.
fees ———> Free for Illinois residents, $25/year for non-residents
email ———-> jayg@uiuc.edu
voice ———-> 217-244-1962
ftp more info -> n/a


<< PREPnet >>
name ———> PREPnet
dialup ———> contact for numbers
area codes —> 215, 412, 717, 814
local access —> PA: Philadelphia, Pittsburgh, Harrisburg
long distance -> provided by user
services ———> SLIP, terminal service, telnet, ftp
fees ———> $1,000/year membership.  Equipment-$325 onetime fee plus
                $40/month
email ———-> prepnet@cmu.edu
voice ———-> 412-268-7870
fax ———-> 412-268-7875
ftp more info -> ftp.prepnet.com:/prepnet/general/


<< psilink >>
name ———> PSILink - Personal Internet Access
dialup ———> North America: send email to classa-na-numbers@psi.com and
                classb-na-numbers@psi.com; Rest of World: send email to
                classb-row-numbers@psi.com
area codes —> PDN
local access —>
long distance -> [per hour, off-peak/peak] PSINet A: included; PSINet B:
                $6/$2.50; PSINet B international: $18/$18
services ———> email and newsfeed, ftp
fees ———> 2400: $19/month; 9600: $29/month (PSILink software included)
email ———-> all-info@psi.com, psilink-info@psi.com
voice ———-> 703-620-6651
fax ———-> 703-620-4586
ftp more info -> ftp.psi.com:/


<< psi-world-dial >>
name ———> PSI's World-Dial Service
dialup ———> send email to numbers-info@psi.com
area codes —> PDN
local access —>
long distance -> [per hour, off-peak/peak] V.22bis: $1.25/$2.75; V.32:
                $3.00/$4.50; 14.4K: $4.00/$6.50
services ———> telnet, rlogin, tn3270, XRemote
fees ———> $9/month minimum + $19 startup
email ———-> all-info@psi.com, world-dial-info@psi.com
voice ———-> 703-620-6651
fax ———-> 703-620-4586
ftp more info -> ftp.psi.com:/
off-peak ———> 8pm to 8am + weekends and holidays


<< PUCnet >>
name ———> PUCnet Computer Connections
dialup ———> 403-484-5640 (v.32 bis) 'guest'
area codes —> 403
local access —> AB: Edmonton and surrounding communities in the Extended
                Flat Rate Calling Area
long distance -> provided by user
services ———> shell, menu, ftp, telnet, archie, gopher, feeds, USENET
fees ———> Cdn$25/month (20 hours connect time) + Cdn$6.25/hr (ftp &
                telnet only) + $10 signup
email ———-> info@PUCnet.com (Mail responder) or pwilson@PUCnet.com
voice ———-> 403-448-1901
fax ———-> 403-484-7103
ftp more info -> n/a
```

```
<< realtime >>
name ------> RealTime Communications (wixer)
dialup ------> 512-459-4391 'new'
area codes --> 512
local access -> TX: Austin
long distance -> provided by user
services ----> shell, ftp, telnet, irc, gopher, feeds, SLIP, UUCP
fees ------> $75/year.  Monthly and quarterly rates available.
email ------> hosts@wixer.bga.com
voice ------> 512-451-0046 (11am-6pm Central Time, weekdays)
fax ------> 512-459-3858
ftp more info -> n/a


<< ssnet >>
name ------> Systems Solutions
dialup ------> contact for info
area codes --> 302
local access --> Wilminton, Delaware
long distance -> provided by user
services ----> shell, UUCP, SLIP, PPP, ftp, telnet, irc, gopher, archie,
               mud, etc.
fees ------> full service  $25/month $20/startup; personal slip/ppp
               $25/month + $2/hour, $20/startup; dedicated slip/ppp
               $150/month, $450/startup
email ------> sharris@marlin.ssnet.com
voice ------> (302) 378-1386, (800) 331-1386
ftp more info -> n/a


<< sugar >>
name ------> NeoSoft's Sugar Land Unix
dialup ------> 713-684-5900
area codes --> 504, 713
local access --> TX: Houston metro area; LA: New Orleans
long distance -> provided by user
services ----> bbs, shell, ftp, telnet, irc, feeds, UUCP
fees ------> $29.95/month
email ------> info@NeoSoft.com
voice ------> 713-438-4964
ftp more info -> n/a


<< teleport >>
name ------> Teleport
dialup ------> 503-220-0636 (2400) 503-220-1016 (v.32, v.32 bis) 'new'
area codes --> 503
local access --> OR: Portland, Beaverton, Hillsboro, Forest Grove, Gresham,
               Tigard, Lake Oswego, Oregon City, Tualatin, Wilsonville
long distance -> provided by user
services ----> shell, ftp, telnet, gopher, usenet, ppp, WAIS, irc, feeds,
               dns
fees ------> $10/month (1 hr/day limit)
email ------> info@teleport.com
voice ------> 503-223-4245
ftp more info -> teleport.com:/about


<< telerama >>
name ------> Telerama Public Access Internet
dialup ------> 412-481-5302 'new' (2400)
area codes --> 412
local access --> PA: Pittsburgh
long distance -> provided by user
services ----> telnet, ftp, irc, gopher, ClariNet/Usenet, shell/menu, uucp
fees ------> 66 cents/hour 2400bps; $1.32/hour 14.4K bps; $6 min/month
email ------> info@telerama.pgh.pa.us
voice ------> 412-481-3505
ftp more info -> telerama.pgh.pa.us:/info/general.info
```

```
<< tmn >>
name ———> The Meta Network
dialup ———> contact for numbers
area codes ——> 703, 202, 301, PDN
local access —> Washington, DC metro area
long distance -> SprintNet: $6.75/hr; FTS-2000; Acunet
services ———> Caucus conferencing, email, shell, ftp, telnet, bbs, feeds
fees ———> $20/month + $15 signup/first month
email ———-> info@tmn.com
voice ———> 703-243-6622
ftp more info -> n/a


<< UUNET-Canada >>
name ———> UUNET Canada, Inc.
dialup ———> contact for numbers
area codes ——> 416, 905, 519, 613, 514, 604, 403
local access —> ON: Toronto, Ottawa, Kitchener/Waterloo, London, Hamilton,
                QC: Montreal,   AB: Calgary,   BC: Vancouver
long distance -> provided by user
services ———> terminal access to telnet only, UUCP (e-mail/news),
                SLIP/PPP, shared or dedicated basis, from v.32bis to 56k+
fees ———> (All Cdn$ + GST) TAC: $6/hr, UUCP: $20/mo + $6/hr, IP/UUCP:
                $50/mo + $6/hr, ask for prices on other services
email ———-> info@uunet.ca
voice ———> 416-368-6621
fax ———-> 416-368-1350
ftp more info -> ftp.uunet.ca


<< uunorth >>
name ———> UUnorth
dialup ———> contact for numbers
area codes ——> 416, 519, 613
local access —> ON: Toronto
long distance -> provided by user
services ———> shell, ftp, telnet, gopher, feeds, IRC, feeds, SLIP, PPP
fees ———> (All Cdn$ + GST) $20 startup + $25 for 20 hours off-peak +
                $1.25/hr OR $40 for 40 hours up to 5/day + $2/hr OR $3/hr
email ———-> uunorth@uunorth.north.net
voice ———> 416-225-8649
fax ———-> 416-225-0525
ftp more info -> n/a


<< Vnet >>
name ———> Vnet Internet Access, Inc.
dialup ———> 704-347-8839, 919-406-1544, 919-851-1526 'new'
area codes ——> 704, 919
local access —> NC: Charlotte, RTP, Raleigh, Durham, Chappel Hill. Winston
                Salem/Greensboro
long distance -> Available for $3.95 per hour through Global Access. Contact
                Vnet offices for more information.
services ———> shell, ftp, telnet, hytelnet, irc, gopher, WWW, wais,
                usenet, clarinet, NNTP, DNS, SLIP/PPP, UUCP, POPmail
fees ———> $25/month individual. $12.50 a month for telnet-in-only.
                SLIP/PPP/UUCP starting at $25/month.
email ———-> info@char.vnet.net
voice ———> 704-374-0779
ftp more info -> n/a


<< well >>
name ———> The Whole Earth 'Lectronic Link
dialup ———> 415-332-6106 'newuser'
area codes ——> 415, PDN
local access —> Sausalito, CA
long distance -> Compuserve Packet Network: $4/hour
services ———> shell, ftp, telnet, bbs
fees ———> $15.00/month + $2.00/hr
```

```
email ——-> info@well.sf.ca.us
voice ——-> 415-332-4335
ftp more info -> n/a

<< wariat >>
name ——-> APK- Public Access UNI* Site
• dialup ——-> 216-481-9436  (V.32bis, SuperPEP on separate rotary)
area codes —> 216
local access -> OH: Cleveland
long distance -> provided by user
services ——-> shell, ftp, telnet, archie, irc, gopher, feeds,
                BBS(Uniboard1.10)
fees ——-> $15/20 hours, $35/monthly, $20 signup
email ——-> zbig@wariat.org
voice ——-> 216-481-9428
ftp more info -> n/a

<< world >>
name ——-> The World
dialup ——-> 617-739-9753 'new'
area codes —> 617, PDN
local access -> Boston, MA
long distance -> Compuserve Packet Network: $5.60/hour
services ——-> shell, ftp, telnet, irc
fees ——-> $5.00/month + $2.00/hr or $20/month for 20 hours
email ——-> office@world.std.com
voice ——-> 617-739-0202
ftp more info -> world.std.com:/world-info/description

<< wyvern >>
name ——-> Wyvern Technologies, Inc.
dialup ——-> (804) 627-1828 Norfolk, (804) 886-0662 (Peninsula)
area codes —> 804
local access -> VA: Norfolk, Virginia Beach, Portsmouth, Chesapeake, Newport
                News, Hampton, Williamsburg
long distance -> provided by user
services ——-> shell, menu, ftp, telnet, uucp feeds, irc, archie, gopher,
                UPI news, email, dns, archives
fees ——-> $15/month or $144/year, $10 startup
email ——-> system@wyvern.com
voice ——-> 804-622-4289
fax ——-> 804-622-7158
ftp more info -> n/a

<< xnet >>
name ——-> XNet Information Systems
dialup ——-> (708) 983-6435 V.32bis and TurboPEP
area codes —> 312, 708, 815
local access -> IL: Chicago, Naperville, Hoffman Estates
long distance -> provided by user
services ——-> shell, telnet, hytelnet, ftp, irc, gopher, www, wais,
                SLIP/PPP, dns, uucp feeds, bbs
fees ——-> $45/3 months or $75/6 months
email ——-> info@xnet.com
voice ——-> (708) 983-6064
ftp more info -> ftp.xnet.com:/xnet.info/
```

```
From: PDIAL -05-
Subject: What *Is* The Internet?
The Internet is a global cooperative network of university, corporate,
government, and private computers, all communicating with each other by
means of something called TCP/IP (Transmission Control Protocol/Internet
Protocol).  Computers directly on the Internet can exchange data quickly
and easily with any other computer on the Internet to download files, send
email, provide remote logins, etc.
```

Users can download files from publicly accessible archive sites (``anonymous FTP''); login into remote computers (telnet or rlogin); chat in real-time with other users around the world (Internet Relay Chat); or use the newest information retrieval tools to find a staggering variety of information (Wide Area Information Servers, Gopher, World Wide Web).

Computers directly on the Internet also exchange email directly and very quickly; email is usually delivered in seconds between Internet sites.

Sometimes the Internet is confused with other related networks or types of networking.

First, there are other ways to be ``connected to the Internet'' without being directly connected as a TCP/IP node. Some computers connect via UUCP or other means at regular intervals to an Internet site to exchange email and USENET newsgroups, for instance. Such a site can provide email (though not as quickly as a directly connected systems) and USENET access, but not Internet downloads, remote logins, etc.

``email'' (or ``Internet email'', ``netmail'') can be exchanged with a wide variety of systems connected directly and indirectly to the Internet. The email may travel solely over the Internet, or it may traverse other networks and systems.

``USENET'' is the collection of computers all over the world that exchange USENET news — thousands of ``newsgroups'' (like forums, or echos) on a wide range of topics. The newsgroup articles are distributed all over the world to USENET sites that wish to carry them (sometimes over the Internet, sometimes not), where people read and respond to them.

The ``NSFNET'' is one of the backbones of the Internet in the US. It is funded by the NSF, which restricts traffic over the NSFNET to ``open research and education in and among US research and instructional institutions, plus research arms of for-profit firms when engaged in open scholarly communication and research.'' Your Internet provider can give you more details about acceptable use, and alternatives should you need to use the Internet in other ways.

From: PDIAL -06-
Subject: What The PDIAL Is

This is the PDIAL, the Public Dialup Internet Access List.

It is a list of Internet service providers offering public access dialins and outgoing Internet access (ftp, telnet, etc.). Most of them provide email and USENET news and other services as well.

If one of these systems is not accessible to you and you need email or USENET access, but *don't* need ftp or telnet, you have many more public access systems from which to choose. Public access systems without ftp or telnet are *not* listed in this list, however. See the nixpub (alt.bbs, comp.misc) list and other BBS lists.

Some of these providers offer time-shared access to a shell or BBS program on a computer connected directly to the Internet, through which you can FTP or telnet to other systems on the Internet. Usually other services are provided as well. Generally, you need only a modem and terminal or terminal emulator to access these systems. Check for ``shell'', ``bbs'', or ``menu'' on the ``services'' line.

Other providers connect you directly to the Internet via SLIP or PPP when you dial in. For these you need a computer system capable of running the software to interface with the Internet, e.g., a Unix machine, PC, or Mac. Check for ``SLIP'', or ``PPP'' on the services line.

While I have included all sites for which I have complete information, this list is surely incomplete. If you have any additions or corrections please send them to me at one of the addresses listed in section -10-.

From: PDIAL -07-
Subject: How People Can Get The PDIAL (This List)

EMAIL:

From the Information Deli archive server (most up-to-date):
To receive the current edition of the PDIAL, send email containing the phrase "Send PDIAL" to "info-deli-server@netcom.com".

To be put on a list of people who receive future editions as they are published, send email containing the phrase "Subscribe PDIAL" to "info-deli-server@netcom.com".

To receive both the most recent and future editions, send both messages.

From time to time, I'll also be sending out news and happenings that relate to the PDIAL or The Information Deli. To receive the Info Deli News automatically, send email containing the phrase "Subscribe Info-Deli-News" to "info-deli-server@netcom.com".

From the news.answers FAQ archive:
Send email with the message "send usenet/news.answers/pdial" to "mail-server@rtfm.mit.edu". For help, send the message "help" to "mail-server@rtfm.mit.edu".

USENET:

The PDIAL list is posted semi-regularly to alt.internet.access.wanted, alt.bbs.lists, alt.online-service, ba.internet, and news.answers.

FTP ARCHIVE SITES (PDIAL and other useful information):

Information Deli FTP site:
ftp.netcom.com:/pub/info-deli/public-access/pdial [192.100.81.100]

As part of a collection of public access lists:
VFL.Paramax.COM:/pub/pubnet/pdial [128.126.220.104]
(used to be GVL.Unisys.COM)

From the Merit Network Information Center Internet information archive:
nic.merit.edu:/internet/providers/pdial [35.1.1.48]

As part of an Internet access compilation file:
liberty.uc.wlu.edu:/pub/lawlib/internet.access [137.113.10.35]

As part of the news.answers FAQ archive:
rtfm.mit.edu:/pub/usenet/news.answers/pdial [18.70.0.209]

From: PDIAL -08-
Subject: Appendix A: Other Valuable Resources
InterNIC Internet Help Desk

The US National Science Foundation has funded Information, Registration, and Directory services for the Internet, and they are available to all Internet users. The most useful branch for PDIAL readers is Information Services, which provides all sorts of information to help Internet users. Contact Information Services by:

```
voice:   800-444-4345 (US)
voice:   +1 (619) 455-4600
fax:     +1 (619) 455-4640
email:   mailserv@is.internic.net, put "SEND HELP" in body
email:   info@internic.net
gopher:  gopher gopher.internic.net / telnet gopher.internic.net
ftp:     is.internic.net
postal:  InterNIC Information Services
         General Atomics
         PO Box 85608
         San Diego, CA 92186-9784 USA
```

Internet Guide Books

Connecting To The Internet; Susan Estrada; O'Reilly & Associates; ISBN 1-56592-061-9 (A how-to on selecting the right IP provider, from dialup to dedicated.)

A DOS User's Guide to the Internet — E-mail, Netnews and File Transfer with UUCP; James Gardner; MKS; ISBN 0-13-106873-3 ("Internet" in the title is misleading — covers UUCP connections only.)

The Electronic Traveller — Exploring Alternative Online Systems; Elizabeth Powell Crowe; Windcrest/McGraw-Hill; ISBN 0-8306-4498-9. (A good tour of various personal IP and other types of providers, but some data is seriously out of date.)

Internet Basics; Steve Lambert, Walt How; Random House; ISBN 0-679-75023-1

The Internet Companion; Tracy LaQuey, Jeanne C. Ryer; Addison-Wesley; ISBN 0-201-62224-6

The Internet Companion Plus; Tracy LaQuey, Jeanne C. Ryer; Addison-Wesley; ISBN 0-201-62719-1

The Internet Complete Reference; Harley Hahn, Rick Stout; Osborne; ISBN 0-07-881980-6

The Internet Directory; Eric Brawn; Fawcett Columbine; ISBN 0-449-90898-4 (Phone book style listing of resources.)

The Internet for Dummies; John R. Levine, Carol Baroudi; IDG Books Worldwide; ISBN 1-56884-024-1 (Lots of useful information, but much of it is intermediate level, not "dummy".)

Internet: Getting Started; April Marine, Susan Kirkpatrick, Vivian Neou, Carol Ward; PTR Prentice Hall; ISBN 0-13-289596-X

The Internet Guide for New Users; Daniel P. Dern; McGraw-Hill; ISBN 0-07-016511-4 (Good, very thorough guide for new users.)

The Internet Navigator; Paul Glister; John Wiley & Sons; ISBN 0-471-59782-1 (Good, comprehensive guide for new users.)

The Internet Roadmap; Bennet Falk; Sybex; ISBN 0-7821-1365-6

Internet Starter Kit for the Macintosh With Disk; Adam C. Engst; Hayden Books; ISBN 1-568300646

The Mac Internet Tour Guide; Michael Fraase; Ventana Press; ISBN 1-56604-062-0

Navigating the Internet; Richard J. Smith, Mark Gibbs; SAMS Publishing; ISBN 0-672-30362-0

Welcome to... Internet — From Mystery to Mastery; Tom Badgett, Corey
Sandler; MIS:Press; ISBN 1-55828-308-0

The Whole Internet User's Guide & Catalog; Ed Krol; O'Reilly & Associates;
ISBN 1-56592-025-2 (Good all around guide.)

Zen & the Art of the Internet: A Beginner's Guide; Brendan P. Kehoe;
PTR Prentice Hall; ISBN 0-13-010778-6

Other BBS/Internet Provider Lists

FSLIST — The Forgotten Site List. USENET: alt.internet.access.wanted;
ftp: freedom.nmsu.edu:/pub/docs/fslist/ or login.qc.ca:/pub/fslist/

nixpub — public access Unixes. USENET: comp.bbs.mis, alt.bbs;
email: to <mail-server@bts.com>, body containing "get PUB nixpub.long";
ftp: VFL.Paramax.COM:/pub/pubnetc/nixpub.long

From: PDIAL -09-
Subject: Appendix B: Finding Public Data Network (PDN) Access Numbers

Here's how to get local access numbers or information for the various
PDNs. Generally, you can contact the site you're calling for help, too.

IMPORTANT NOTE: Unless noted otherwise, set your modem to 7E1 (7 data
bits, even parity, 1 stop bit) when dialing to look up access numbers
by modem as instructed below.

BT Tymnet
―――-

For information and local access numbers, call 800-937-2862 (voice) or
215-666-1770 (voice).
To look up access numbers by modem, dial a local access number, hit
<cr> and 'a', and enter "information" at the "please log in:" prompt.

Compuserve Packet Network
―――――――――-

You do NOT have to be a Compuserve member to use the CPN to dial other
services.

For information and local access numbers, call 800-848-8199 (voice).

To look up access numbers by modem, dial a local access number, hit
<cr> and enter "PHONES" at the "Host Name:" prompt.

PSINet
―――

For information, call 800-82PSI82 (voice) or 703-620-6651 (voice), or
send email to "all-info@psi.com". For a list of local access numbers
send email to "numbers-info@psi.com".

From: PDIAL -10-
Subject: Providers: Get Listed in PDIAL!

NEW SUBMISSION/CORRECTION PROCEDURES:

The PDIAL will be undergoing expansion in both breadth (how many and what
kinds of public access providers) and depth (how much information is

```
carried for each provider).  To collect the data, I will be emailing a
questionnaire to providers already on the PDIAL, and to any providers who
wish to be added.  Corrections can also be submitted via update
questionnaires.

 To be listed in the PDIAL, retrieve the PDIAL questionnaire by sending email
to <info-deli-server@netcom.com> containing the command "Send PDIAL-Q".  The
questionnaire will not be available until 15 Dec 1993, but requests received
before then will be queued and honored when it is available.

—
Peter Kaminski / The Information Deli

kaminski@netcom.com (preferred)
71053.2155@compuserve.com

End of PDIAL
************
```

FREENETS AND COMMUNITY NETS

Freenets and community nets are a cliché example of a good news/bad news situation. The good news is, new freenets and community nets start up every month, and you'll have no trouble finding one in your area. The bad news is, freenets and community nets disappear or change addresses with as great frequency—which is why this list gives only the names of those current as of March 1995; we don't list numbers. Instead, preceding the list is the name, address, and all access numbers for the National Public Telecomputing Network (NPTN), an organization that tracks the comings and goings of freenets and community nets. We recommend that you find a freenet or community net that you're interested in, then contact NPTN (via the Web, fax, or voice) for the most current access information for that net.

National Public Telecomputing Network
30680 Bainbridge Road
Solon, OH 44139
voice: 216-498-4050
fax: 216-498-4051
Web: **http://nptn.org/alt.online-service.freenet**

Alabama

Tennessee Valley Free-Net, Huntsville
Mobile Free-Net, Mobile
Tuscaloosa Free-Net, Tuscaloosa

Alaska

AnchorNet, Anchorage
FairNet, Fairbanks

Arizona

AzTeC, Tempe

Arkansas

Greater Pulaski County Free-Net, Little Rock

California

Los Angeles Free-Net, Los Angeles
SLONET, San Luis Obispo
California Online Resources for Education, Seal Beach
Northern California Regional Computing Network, Chico
Davis Community Network, Davis
Orange County Free-Net, Orange County
Sacramento Free-Net, Sacramento
Silicon Valley Public Access Link, San Jose
Santa Barbara RAIN, Santa Barbara
Redwood Free-Net, Ukiah

Colorado

Denver Free-Net, Denver

Connecticut

Danbury Area Free-Net, Danbury
CPBI – Free-Net, Hartford

Florida

SEFLIN Free-Net, Broward County
Alachua Free-Net, Gainesville
Tallahassee Free-Net, Tallahassee
Miami Free-Net, Miami
Naples Free-Net, Naples
Orlando Free-Net, Orlando
Palm Beach Free-Net, Palm Beach
Sarasota-Manatee Area Free-Net, Sarasota

MCNet, Stuart
Suncoast Free-Net, Tampa Bay

Georgia

Worth County-Sylvester Ga. Free-Net, Sylvester
404 Free-Net, Atlanta

Hawaii

The Aloha Free-Net Project, Honolulu
Maui Free-Net, Maui

Idaho

Panhandle Free-Net, Sandpoint

Illinois

Prairienet, Champaign-Urbana
Shawnee Free-Net, Carbondale
SWIF-NET, Edgemont

Indiana

Michiana Free-Net Society, Granger

Iowa

CedarNet, Cedar Falls
Iowa Knowledge Exchange, Des Moines
Fairfield Free-Net, Fairfield

Kentucky

Pennyrile Area Free-Net, Hopkinsville
Owensboro Free-Net, Owensboro

Louisiana

Baton Rouge Area Interactive Network, Baton Rouge
Acadiana Free-Net, Lafayette
Greater New Orleans Free-Net, New Orleans

Maine

Maine Community Access Network- Freeport

Maryland

Free State Free-Net, Baltimore
Community Service Network, Easton
Garrett Communiversity Central, McHenry

Massachusetts

UMASSK12, Amherst

Michigan

Greater Detroit Free-Net, Detroit
Genesee Free-Net, Flint
Education Central, Mount Pleasant
Almont Expression, Almont
Great Lakes Free-Net, Battle Creek
Huron Valley Free-Net, Ann Arbor
Grand Rapids Free-Net, Grand Rapids
Macatawa Area Free-Net, Holland
Capitol City Free-Net, Lansing

Minnesota

Twin Cities Free-Net, Minneapolis
Northfield Free-Net, Northfield

Mississippi

Magnolia Free-Net, Jackson
Meridian Area Free-Net, Meridian

Missouri

Columbia Online Information Network (COIN), Columbia
ORION, Springfield
Show-Me Free-Net, Cape Girardeau
KC Free-Net, Kansas City

Montana

Big Sky Telegraph, Dillon

Nebraska

Omaha Free-Net, Omaha

Nevada

Las Vegas International Free-Net, Las Vegas

New Hampshire

The Granite State Oracle, Manchester

New Mexico

New Mexico Free-Net, Albuquerque
Santa Fe Metaverse, Santa Fe

New York

Buffalo Free-Net, Buffalo
Capital Region Information Service, Albany
CASSYnet, Corning
Southern Tier Free-Net, Endicott
Rochester Free-Net, Rochester

North Carolina

Mountain Area Information Network, Asheville
Triangle Free-Net, Chapel Hill
Charlotte's Web, Charlotte
Forsyth County Free-Net, Winston-Salem

North Dakota

SENDIT, Fargo

Ohio

Tristate Online, Cincinnati
Cleveland Free-Net, Cleveland
Greater Columbus Free-Net, Columbus
Dayton Free-Net, Dayton

Lorain County Free-Net, Elyria
Youngstown Free-Net, Youngstown
SEORF, Athens
Learning Village Cleveland, Cleveland
Medina County Free-Net, Medina
Akron Regional Free-Net, Akron
Stark County Free-Net, Canton
Lima Free-Net, Lima
Richland Free-Net, Mansfield

Oklahoma

Ponca City/Pioneer Free-Net, Ponca City

Pennsylvania

Lehigh Valley Free-Net, Bethlehem
Erie County Free-Net, Erie
Pittsburgh Free-Net, Pittsburgh
Mercer County Free-Net, Sharon
Chester County Interlink, West Chester

Rhode Island

Ocean State Free-Net, Providence
South Carolina
MidNet, Columbia
Greenet, Greenville
GreenCo-NET, Greenwood

Tennessee

Jackson Area Free-Net, Jackson
Greater Knoxville Community Network, Knoxville

Texas

Rio Grande Free-Net, El Paso
Big Country Free-Net, Abilene
Austin Free-Net, Austin
North Texas Free-Net, Dallas

Tarrant County Free-Net, Fort Worth
Houston Civnet, Houston
West Texas Free-Net, San Angelo
San Antonio Free-Net, San Antonio

Vermont

Lamoille Net, Morrisville

Virginia

Central Virginia's Free-Net, Richmond
VaPEN, Richmond
SEVANET, Newport News
Blue Ridge Free-Net, Roanoke

Washington

Seattle Community Network, Seattle
Tri-Cities Free-Net, Tri-Cities
Kitsap Free-Net, Bremerton
Olympic Public Electronic Network (OPEN), Port Angeles
TINCAN, Spokane
Clark County Free-Net, Vancouver

Wisconsin

Chippewa Valley Free-Net, Eau Claire

AUSTRALIA

Victoria

Melbourne Free-Net, Melbourne

CANADA

Alberta

Calgary Free-Net, Calgary
Edmonton Free-Net, Edmonton
Praxis Free-Net, Medicine Hat

British Columbia

CIAO! Free-Net, Trail
Victoria Free-Net, Victoria
Campbell River Free-Net, Campbell River
Prince George Free-Net, Prince George
Vancouver Free-Net, Vancouver

Manitoba

Eastmanet, Pinawa
SEARDEN Free-Net, Sprague
Blue Sky Free-Net Of Manitoba, Winnipeg

New Brunswick

York Sunbury Community Server, Fredericton

Newfoundland

St. John's Free-Net, St. John's

Nova Scotia

Cape Breton Free-Net, Cape Breton
Chebucto Free-Net, Halifax

Ontario

National Capital Free-Net, Ottawa
North Shore Free-Net, Elliot Lake
Durham Free-Net, Oshawa
Niagara Free-Net, St. Catharines
Thunder Bay Free-Net, Thunder Bay
Toronto Free-Net, Toronto

Quebec

Free-Net du Montreal Metropolitan, Montreal

Saskatchewan

Moose Jaw Free-Net, Moose Jaw
Great Plains Free-Net, Regina
Saskatoon Free-Net, Saskatoon

FINLAND

Finland Free-Net, Helsinki

GERMANY

Bayreuth Free-Net, Bayreuth
Free-Net Erlangen-Nuernburg, Erlangen

IRELAND

Connect-Ireland, Dublin

ITALY

Venice Free-Net, Venice

NEW ZEALAND

Wellington Citynet, Wellington

PHILIPPINES

Philippine Public Telecomputing Network, Quezon City

SWEDEN

Medborgarnas Datanat, Norrkoping

Alphabetical Address and Country Code Lists

This appendix is a "for your convenience" listing of all the resources we mentioned throughout the book, in alphabetical order. It also gives you the contact number of the resources, whether it's an online address (in most cases), a modem number, or a telephone number. Finally, we've included the page number from the text on which the resource is mentioned so that you can quickly locate the discussion on it to assure yourself that this is the site you want to contact. At the end of this appendix is a list of country codes, which you'll need to help you decipher any international sources you are interested in contacting.

Resource Name	Contact Number	Page Number
Academe This Week	http://chronicle.merit.edu	262
Academe This Week (Chronicle of Higher Education)	gopher chronicle.merit.edu	300
Academic Physician and Scientist (Also listed as APS)	gopher aps.acad-phy-sci.com	300
Academic Position Network	gopher wcni.cis.umn.edu	300
ACM Sigmod	http://bunny.cs.uiuc.edu/jobs	261
Altera Corporation	http://www.careermosaic.com/cm/altera	270
Amdahl Corporation	http://www.amdahl.com/	270
America Online	Voice 800-827-6364	230, 312
American Accounting Association	http://www.rutgers.edu/accounting/raw/aaa/aaa.htm	239
American Astronomical Society	http://blackhole.aas.org/JobRegister/aas.jobs.html	262
American Marketing Association	http://www.mba.wfu.edu/b2b.html	262
American Mathematical Society	gopher e-math.ams.com	301
American Philosophical Association	http://www.oxy.edu/apa/apa.html	239
American Physiological Association	gopher gopher.uth.tmc.edu	301
AmeriCom Long Distance Area Decoder	http://www.xmission.com/~americom/aclookup.html	231
AMI: A Friendly Public Interface	gopher gopher.mountain.net	301
Andersen Consulting	http://www.ac.com/recruit/welcome.html	270
Architecture and Building: Net Resources	gopher una.hh.lib.umich.edu or http://www.uky.edu/artsource/bibliography/brown.html	239
Astronomy Resources on the Web	http://anarky/stsci/edu/astroweb/net-www.html	239
AT&T 800 Directory on the Internet	http://att.net/dir800	231
Auspex Systems	http://www.auspex.com/Welcome.html	271
AVADS-BBS	Modem: 800-366-3321	308
BBN Internet Services Corporation	http://www.helpwanted.com/bbnhome.html	271
Bionet	http://net.bio/ageinfo.tamu.edu:80/jobs.html	263
BIONET	gopher net.bio.net	301
BIOSCI	gopher net.bio.net	301
Broad	http://www.bus.msu.edu/news.htm	263
BTG Inc.	http://www.btg.com/jobs/jobmenu.html	271
Bureau of Labor Statistics	http://stats.bls.gov/blshome.html	220
Bureau of the Census	http://www.census.gov/	239
Business and Financial Information on the Web	http://www.wharton.upenn.edu/./netsites/businfo.html	226
Cambridge Scientific Computing, Inc.	http://www.camsci.com	271
CAPACCESS Career Center	Modem: 202-785-1523	308
Career Choices Page, Catapult	http://arthur.physics.wm.edu:80/~charette/choice.html	221

Resource Name	Contact Number	Page Number
Career Connections On-Line Information System (HEART)	telnet college.career.com or IP **198.207.167.3**	304
Career Link, Inc.	Modem: 602-973-2002	309
Career Magazine	**http://www.careermag.com/careermag/**	263
Career Mosaic	**http://www.service.com:80/cm/**	221, 226, 256
Career Taxi	**http://www.iquest.net/Career_Taxi/taxi.html**	257
Catapult	**http://www.wm.edu/catapult/catapult.html**	315
Chemical Bank	**http://www.careermosaic.com/cm/chemical-bank**	272
Chemistry Information	**http://www.chemie.fa-berlin.de/index_e.html**	240
CIA World Factbook	**http://www.ic.gov/94fact/fb94toc/fb94toc.html**	245
Cisco Systems	**http://cio.cisco.com/public/Employment.html**	272
CITE Job Bank	**gopher gopher.utexas.edu**	301
City Net	**http://www.city.net/**	245
ClariNet Communications Corp.	**http://www.clarinet.com/**	272
Clearinghouse for Subject-Oriented Resource Guides	**http://www.lib.umich.edu/chhome.html**	235
CLRnet	**http://www.clr.toronto.edu:1080/VIRTUALLIB/jobs.html**	263
Community of Science Web Server	**http://best.gdb.org/**	232
Compaq Computer Corporation	**http://www.iquest.net/Career_Taxi/compaq/Compaq.html**	273
CompuServe	Voice 800-848-8199 or 800-848-8990	230, 234, 312
Contract Employment Weekly (CE Weekly)	**http://www.ceweekly.wa.com**	257
Corporation for Public Broadcasting (CPB)	**http://www.cpb.org/home.html**	264
Country Studies/Area Handbooks	**http://lcweb.loc.gov/homepage/country.html**	246
CyberDyne CS	**http://www.demon.co.uk/cyberdyne/cyber.html**	257
DeLorme Mapping	Acess: **http://www.delorme.com./home.htm**	274
Delphi	Voice 800-695-4005	312
DICE National Network	Modem: 201-242-4166 214-782-0960 408-737-9339 515-280-3423 708-782-0960	309
Direct Marketing World's Job Center	**http://mainsail.com/jobsinfo.html**	258
Directory of Executive Recruiters	**http://www.careermag.com/careermag/**	221
ECCO BBS	Modem: 212-580-4510 312-404-8685 415-331-7227	310
Economic Bulletin Board	**gopher una.hh.lib.umich.edu**	239
EDGAR Dissemination Project	**http://town.hall.org/edgar/general.html**	226
Employment Board	Modem: 619-689-1348 or 619-993-9319	310

Resource Name	Contact Number	Page Number
Employment Edge Control	http://sensemedia.net/employment.edge	258
Employment Opportunities and Job Resources on the Internet	http://www.wpi.edu/~mfriley/jobguide.html	221
Engineering Meta-List	http:// epims1.gsfc.nasa.gov/engineering/engineering.html	236
E-Span's Interactive Employment Network (IEN)	http://www.espan.com	258
eWorld	http://www.eworld.com/Welcome.html or Voice 800-775-4556	274, 312
Federal Job Opportunity Board (FJOB)	telnet://fjob.mail.opm.gov or IP 198.78.46.10	306
FedWorld	http://www.fedworld.gov	259
FedWorld: The U.S. Government Bulletin Board	telnet:// fedworld.doc.gov or IP 192.239.92.201	306
Fidelity Investments	http://www.helpwanted.com/fidelhp.html	274
Financenet: U.S. Government Internet Service	http://www.financenet.gov	240
FirstStep	Modem: 404-642-0665	311
Forrester Research, Inc.	http://www.forrester.com/misc/employment.html	274
Franklin Search Group, Inc.	http://www.gate.net/bio-techjobs	264
Freenets U.S and Abroad	http://herald.usask.ca/~scottp/freewww.html	247
G-Web	http://www.cinenet.net/GWEB/index.html	265
GEnie	Voice 800-638-9636	313
GIS Jobs Clearinghouse	http://walleye.forestry.umn.edu:70/0/www/rsgisinfo/jobs.html	264
GNN Travel Centre	http://gnn.com/gnn/meta/travel	247
Gopher Jewels	gopher cwis.usc.edu	302
Great Organizations' Phone Books	gopher gopher.nd.edu	232
HeartMosaic	http://www.geo.net:8500/	260
Help-Wanted U.S.A.	http:/www.webcom.com/~career/hwusa.html or gopher://garnet.msen.com:906z/11/	314
Humbul Gateway	http://sable.ox.ac.uk/departments/humanities/international.html	236
Imaging Systems Laboratory (ISL)	http://www.cc.columbia.edu:80/~archpub/	240
Infomine Meta-List	http://lib-www.ucr.edu/rivera/california	236
Infonet Services Corporation	http://www.info.net/Public/infonet-toc.html	275
Informatrix	telnet:// informatrix.com or IP 204.213.232.3	306
Institute of Chartered Accountants of England and Wales, Accounting Information Service	http://www.ex.ac.uk/~BJSpaul/icaew/icaew.html	235
Integrated Computer Solutions, Inc.	http://www.ics.com	275
Intel	http://www.intel.com/intel/index.html	275
Interactive Employment Network	http://www.espan.com	222, 227
Interesting Business Sites on the Web	http://www.rpi.edu/~okeefe/business.html	229

Resource Name	Contact Number	Page Number
Intermetrics	http://www.inmet.com/index.html	276
International Career Employment Network (ICEN)	**gopher** or **INTLCENT@indiana.edu**	302
Internet Business Directory	**http://ibd.ar.com/**	228
Intuit, Inc.	**http://www.careermosaic.com/cm/intuit.html**	276
IPC Technologies, Inc.	**http://www.ipc.tech.com/~jobs/joblist.html**	275
Job Board	**http://www.io.org:80/~jwsmith/jobs.html**	265
Job Info at Yahoo	**http://mtmis1.mis.semi.harris.com/jobs.html**	315
Job Openings in the Federal Government	**gopher dartcms1.dartmouth.edu**	302
Job Web	**html://www.jobweb.com/jobweb.html**	261
Jobs in Education Research, Evaluation, and Measurement	**gopher vmsgopher.cva.edu**	302
JOBS-BBS	Modem: 503-281-6808	311
Labor Trends	**gopher gopher.enews.com**	222
Lexus/Nexus	Voice 800-227-4908	313
Library of Congress	**gopher marvel.loc.gov**	303
Martin Marietta Energy Systems, Oak Ridge, TN	**gopher1.ctd.ornl.gov**	303
Mathematics and Statistics Job Announcements	**http://math.umbc.edu/misc.html**	266
Medical Matrix: Guide to Internet Medical Resources	**http://kuhttp.cc.ukans.edu/cwis/units/medcntr/la/ homepag e.html**	236
MedSearch America	**http://www.medsearch.com** or **gopher gopher.medsearch.com**	266 **303**
Merit Gopher	**gopher nic.merit.edu**	237
Metricom	**http://www.metricom.com/Welcome.html**	276
Metropolitan Tuscon Electronic Communications Network (Metcom)	**gopher** or call 602-791-4241	303
Microsoft Network	Microsoft General Number only: 800-426-9400	313
Mother of all BBS	**http://www.cs.colorado.edu/cgi-bin/grepitp**	280
NASA	**http://www.gsfc.nasa.gov/**	241
National Center for the Workplace	**gopher uclink.berkeley.edu**	222
National Institute of Allergy and Infectious Diseases	**http://web.fie.com/web/fed/nih**	241
National Institutes of Health (NIH)	**gopher gopher.nih.gov**	241
National Science Foundation (NSF)	**gopher stis.nsf.gov**	241
National Semiconductors	**http://www.commerce.net/directories/participants/ ns/job.html**	277
NEC	**http// web.nec.com/index.html**	276
Netfind	Telnet to a host.	233
Netscape Communication Corporation	**http://www.netscape.com/help-wanted/index.html**	277
NeXT Computer	**http://www.next.com/HumanResources/**	277

Resource Name	Contact Number	Page Number
NISS	telnet://niss.ac.uk or IP **193.63.76.1**	306
Nonprofit/Fundraising Jobnet	**http://www.nando.net/philant/philant.html**	265
NPR Home Page (National Public Radio)	**http://www.npr.org/index.html**	266
NREL	**http://nrelinfo.nrel.gov:70/1s/people/jobs/data**	266
Online Career Center	**http://www.iquest.net/occ/** or **http://www.iquest.net/occ/HomePage.html**	223, 228, 260
Online Career Center (MSEN Inc.)	via **gopher Msen.com**	304
Online Opportunities	Modem: 610-873-7170	311
Open Market's Commercial Sites Index	**http://www.directory.net**	228
Opto-Link SPIE	**http://www.spie.org/web/employment/employ_home.html**	265
OS/2 Warp	Voice 800-426-4329 or **http://www.ibm.com**	313
Papyrus Media Careers Online	**http://www.Britain.EU.net/vendor/jobs/main.html**	260
PC Phone List	**http:// comp.sys.ibm.pc.harware.misc**	233
PeopleSoft	**http://www.peoplesoft.com/**	277
Peter's Page O' Jobs	**http://sahara.bu.edu:4021/Career/jobs.html**	316
Pharmacology	**http://pharminfo.com/**	241
Physics Jobs Announcements	**http://xxx.lanl.gov/announce/Jobs**	267
Primenet	**http://www.primenet.com/links/companies.html**	228
Prodigy	Voice 800-776-3449	314
Prudential Insurance and Financial	**http://www.helpwanted.com/prudent.html**	278
Purdue University OWL	**http://owl.trc.purdue.edu/**	242
Railroad-Related Internet Resources	**http://www-cse.ucsd.edu/users/bowdidge/railroad/rail-home.html**	248
Rocky Mountain Region Manufacturers Information Service	**http://129.72.1761** or **http://129.72.176.1/man-docs/man-query-info-sys.html**	229
SAGE (System Administrator's Guild)	**http://www.usenix.org/about_sage.html**	267
Santa Cruz Operation (SCO)	**http://www.sco.com/Company/Jobs/jobs.html**	278
Skill Search	**http://www.internet-is.com:80/skillsearch**	314
Starlink News Items	**http://ast.leeds.ac.uk./news.html**	267
Supernet Int'l	telnet:// **supernet.ans.net** or Telnet://**hpcwire.ans.net**	307
Symatec	**http://www.careermosaic.com/cm/symantec/**	278
Tangram Enterprise Solutions	**http://www.tesi.com/employ.htm**	278
The Internet Access Company, Inc.	**http://www.tiac.net/staff/open.html**	278
The Job Board	**http://www.fsu.edu/Jobs.html**	260
The Monster Board	**http://ageninfo.tamu.edu/jobs.html**	261
The Resume File	Modem: 805-575-6521	311
The Virtual Hospital	**http://www2.osaka-med.ac.jp/iowa/virtualhospital.html**	242
Thomas	**http://thomas.loc.gov**	242

Resource Name	Contact Number	Page Number
TKO Personnel, Inc.	http://www.internet-is.com/tko/	268
Toll-Free Airline Phone Numbers	gopher cs4sun.cs.ttu.edu	248
Toll-Free Numbers for Health Information	http://nhic-nt.health.org/html/gen/html/gen.ex/ tollfree?descriptor='800'	243
Transaction Information Systems, Inc.	http://www.tisny.com/tis/hotjobs.html	279
TRW	http://www.helpwanted.com/trwhp.html	279
U.S. Geological Survey	http://info.er.usgs.gov/network/science/earth/index.html	244
U.S. Industry Outlook	gopher umslvma.umsl.edu	223
U.S. Institute of Management	http:// starbase.ingress.com.ioma	244
Union Bank	http://www.careermosaic.com/cm/union_bank/ub1.html	279
US West	http://www.careermosaic.com/cm/uswest	279
Veterinary Job Opportunities	http://www.ovcnet.voguelph.ca/jobs.ovc/list.html	268
Virtual Reference Desk	http://www.gnn.com/gnn/wic/refbook.ll.html	237
VT2 (successor to Virtual Tourist)	http://wings.buffalo.edu/world/vt2	249
White House Information	http://www.whitehouse.gov	244
Who's Online	http://www.ictp.trieste.it/Canessa/entries/entries.html	233
Whole Internet Catalog	http://nearnet.gnn.com/wic/newrescat.toc.html	238
World Wide Web Virtual Library	http://info.cern.ch/hypertext/DataSources/bySubject/ Overview.html	238
World Wide Web Yellow Pages	http://www.yellow.com	229
X500 World Directory	Gopher umich.edu	234
Yahoo	http://akebono.stanford.edu/yahoo/	238
Yahoo List	http://akebono.stanford.edu/yahoo/regional_information/	250
Yahoo List of Organizations and Associations	http://akebono.stanford.edu/yahoo/economy/ organization/professional/	234
Young Scientists Network	http://snorri.chem.washington.edu:80/ysnarchive	269
Your Software Solutions	http://helpwanted.com/	280
Zycad Job Page	http://www.zycad.com:80/jobs/	269

GLOBAL NEWSGROUPS

Resource	Description	Page Number
ab.jobs	Jobs in Alberta, Canada	282
atl.jobs	Atlanta-based jobs	286
Atl.resumes	Atlanta resumes	287
aus.jobs	Jobs in Australia and New Zealand	282
Austin.jobs	Jobs in Austin, Texas	287
az.jobs	Jobs in Arizona	287

Resource	Description	Page Number
ba.jobs.contract	San Francisco Bay area contract jobs	288
ba.jobs.misc	Miscellaneous positions in San Francisco Bay area	288
ba.jobs.offered	Positions offered in the San Francisco Bay area	288
balt.jobs	Jobs available in the Baltimore-Washington D.C. area.	289
bionet.jobs	This is a listing of a wide variety of jobs in the biological sciences.	296
bionet.jobs.wanted	People who are seeking work and or research opportunities in biology and related professions.	297
Bionet.women-in-bio	Biology discussion group for women.	297
biz.jobs.offered	List of commercial postings.	297
bln.jobs	Berlin jobs	282
can.jobs	Jobs available in Canada	283
chi.jobs	Chigago jobs	289
cmh.jobs	The jobs ranged from technical to managerial for entire United States.	289
conn.jobs.offered	Connecticut jobs	289
dc.jobs	Jobs in Washington D.C. and the surrounding area.	289
de.markt.jobs	Jobs in Germany	283
de.mrkt.jobs.d	A discussion group about jobs in Germany	283
dfw.jobs	Dallas/ Fort Worth jobs	290
dk.jobs	Jobs in Denmark	284
dod.jobs	Department of Defense jobs, and more	298
fl.jobs	Jobs available in Florida	290
fr.jobs.demandes	Jobs wanted in France	284
fr.jobs.offres	Jobs in France	284
hepnet.jobs	high energy and nuclear physics	298
houston.jobs.offered	Positions available in Houston, Texas.	290
houston.jobs.wanted	Positions wanted in Houston, Texas	291
hsv.jobs	Positions in the health services industry.	299
ia.jobs	Jobs in Iowa	291
il.jobs.misc	Positions available in Illinois.	291
Il.jobs.offered	Illinois jobs	291
il.jobs.resumes	Resumes of people seeking employment in Illinois.	292
in.jobs	Indiana jobs	292
kw.jobs	Kitchener-Waterloo, Ontario, Canada jobs	284
la.jobs	Los Angeles jobs	292
la.wanted.jobs	Los Angeles jobs wanted	292
mi.jobs	Michigan job listings	292
milw.jobs	Milwaukee, Wisconsin jobs	293
misc.jobs.entry	Entry-level jobs listing	281
misc.jobs.misc	A general discussion group about jobs and job searching	280
misc.jobs.offered	A listing of jobs available worldwide	281
misc.jobs.resume	Postings of electronic resumes in ASCII format	281
ne.jobs	Jobs available in the New England region	294

Resource	Description	Page Number
nm.jobs	Jobs in New Mexico, primarily in Albuquerque	294
nyc.jobs.contract	Contract jobs in New York City	294
nyc.jobs.misc	Discussion group of jobs and work in New York City	294
nyc.jobs.offered	Jobs in New York City	294
nyc.jobs.wanted	Jobs wanted in New York City	295
ont.jobs	Jobs in Ontario, Canada	284
pgh.jobs.offered	Jobs in Pittsburgh, Pennsylvania	295
pgh.jobs.wanted	Jobs wanted in Pittsburgh, Pennslyvania	295
prg.jobs	programming jobs	299
sdnet.jobs	Jobs in San Diego with overlap to Orange County	295
seattle.jobs.offered		295
seattle.jobs.wanted	Jobs wanted in Seattle	296
tor.jobs	Jobs in Toronto and Ontario, Canada	285
triangle.jobs	Jobs in the Raleigh, North Carolina area.	296
uk.jobs.offered	Jobs in the United Kingdom	285
uk.jobs.wanted	Jobs wanted in the United Kingdom	285
vmsnet.employment	Moderated job list of DEC VAX/VMS and DECNET computer systems users.	299
za.ads.jobs	Jobs available in South Africa	286

ALPHABETICAL COUNTRY CODE LIST

Code	Country	Code	Country
AD	Andorra	BD	Bangladesh
AE	United Arab Emirates	BE	Belgium
AF	Afghanistan	BF	Burkina Faso
AG	Antigua and Barbuda	BG	Bulgaria
AI	Anguilla	BH	Bahrain
AL	Albania	BI	Burundi
AM	Armenia	BJ	Benin
AN	Netherland Antilles	BM	Bermuda
AO	Angola	BN	Brunei Darussalam
AQ	Antarctica	BO	Bolivia
AR	Argentina	BR	Brazil
AS	American Samoa	BS	Bahamas
AT	Austria	BT	Buthan
AU	Australia	BV	Bouvet Island
AW	Aruba	BW	Botswana
AZ	Azerbaidjan	BY	Belarus
BA	Bosnia-Herzegovina	BZ	Belize
BB	Barbados	CA	Canada

Code	Country	Code	Country
CC	Cocos (Keeling) Isl.	GP	Guadeloupe (French)
CF	Central African Rep.	GQ	Equatorial Guinea
CG	Congo	GF	Guyana (French)
CH	Switzerland	GM	Gambia
CI	Ivory Coast	GN	Guinea
CK	Cook Islands	GR	Greece
CL	Chile	GT	Guatemala
CM	Cameroon	GU	Guam (US)
CN	China	GW	Guinea Bissau
CO	Colombia	GY	Guyana
CR	Costa Rica	HK	Hong Kong
CS	Czechoslovakia	HM	Heard and McDonald Islands
CU	Cuba	HN	Honduras
CV	Cape Verde	HR	Croatia
CX	Christmas Island	HT	Haiti
CY	Cyprus	HU	Hungary
CZ	Czech Republic	ID	Indonesia
DE	Germany	IE	Ireland
DJ	Djibouti	IL	Israel
DK	Denmark	IN	India
DM	Dominica	IO	British Indian O. Terr.
DO	Dominican Republic	IQ	Iraq
DZ	Algeria	IR	Iran
EC	Ecuador	IS	Iceland
EE	Estonia	IT	Italy
EG	Egypt	JM	Jamaica
EH	Western Sahara	JO	Jordan
ES	Spain	JP	Japan
ET	Ethiopia	KE	Kenya
FI	Finland	KG	Kirgistan
FJ	Fiji	KH	Cambodia
FK	Falkland Islands (Malvinas)	KI	Kiribati
FM	Micronesia	KM	Comoros
FO	Faroe Islands	KN	St.Kitts Nevis Anguilla
FR	France	KP	Korea (North)
FX	France (European Ter.)	KR	Korea (South)
GA	Gabon	KW	Kuwait
GB	Great Britain (UK)	KY	Cayman Islands
GD	Grenada	KZ	Kazachstan
GE	Georgia	LA	Laos
GH	Ghana	LB	Lebanon
GI	Gibraltar	LC	Saint Lucia
GL	Greenland	LI	Liechtenstein

Code	Country
LK	Sri Lanka
LR	Liberia
LS	Lesotho
LT	Lithuania
LU	Luxembourg
LV	Latvia
LY	Libya
MA	Morocco
MC	Monaco
MD	Moldavia
MG	Madagascar
MH	Marshall Islands
ML	Mali
MM	Myanmar
MN	Mongolia
MO	Macau
MP	Northern Mariana Isl.
MQ	Martinique (Fr.)
MR	Mauritania
MS	Montserrat
MT	Malta
MU	Mauritius
MV	Maldives
MW	Malawi
MX	Mexico
MY	Malaysia
MZ	Mozambique
NA	Namibia
NC	New Caledonia (Fr.)
NE	Niger
NF	Norfolk Island
NG	Nigeria
NI	Nicaragua
NL	Netherlands
NO	Norway
NP	Nepal
NR	Nauru
NT	Neutral Zone
NU	Niue
NZ	New Zealand
OM	Oman
PA	Panama
PE	Peru

Code	Country
PF	Polynesia (French)
PG	Papua New Guinea
PH	Philippines
PK	Pakistan
PL	Poland
PM	St. Pierre and Miquelon
PN	Pitcairn
PT	Portugal
PR	Puerto Rico (US)
PW	Palau
PY	Paraguay
QA	Qatar
RE	Reunion (French)
RO	Romania
RU	Russian Federation
RW	Rwanda
SA	Saudi Arabia
SB	Solomon Islands
SC	Seychelles
SD	Sudan
SE	Sweden
SG	Singapore
SH	St. Helena
SI	Slovenia
SJ	Svalbard and Jan Mayen Islands
SK	Slovak Republic
SL	Sierra Leone
SM	San Marino
SN	Senegal
SO	Somalia
SR	Suriname
ST	St. Tome and Principe
SU	Soviet Union
SV	El Salvador
SY	Syria
SZ	Swaziland
TC	Turks and Caicos Islands
TD	Chad
TF	French Southern Terr.
TG	Togo
TH	Thailand
TJ	Tadjikistan
TK	Tokelau

Code	Country	Code	Country
TM	Turkmenistan	VA	Vatican City State
TN	Tunisia	VC	St.Vincent and Grenadines
TO	Tonga	VE	Venezuela
TP	East Timor	VG	Virgin Islands (British)
TR	Turkey	VI	Virgin Islands (US)
TT	Trinidad and Tobago	VN	Vietnam
TV	Tuvalu	VU	Vanuatu
TW	Taiwan	WF	Wallis and Futuna Islands
TZ	Tanzania	WS	Samoa
UA	Ukraine	YE	Yemen
UG	Uganda	YU	Yugoslavia
UK	United Kingdom	ZA	South Africa
UM	US Minor outlying Islands	ZM	Zambia
US	United States	ZR	Zaire
UY	Uruguay	ZW	Zimbabwe
UZ	Uzbekistan		

Resources

This appendix contains information about software, data-bases, associations, and books/directories that will help you in your job search. You will also find information about privacy and encryption software, plus a list of associations and online sites with a privacy emphasis.

===== SOFTWARE AND CD-ROMs FOR THE JOB HUNT

Database America

800-223-7777
100 Paragon Drive
Montvale, NJ 07645
Format:PC/Windows/CD-ROM

Database America has two excellent products available for job seekers. USA Businesses lists more than 10 million U.S.-based companies, and Phone is a database of all White Pages and Yellow Pages in the United States. You can purchase the data-bases as diskettes or as CD-ROMs. As of this writing, the cost is $79 each or $129 when purchased together.

Federal Occupation and Career Information System

National Technical Information Service
5285 Port Royal Road
Springfield, VA 22161
Format: PC

The National Technical Information Service provides the software for the Federal Occupation and Career Information System for a cost of $55. Career guidance information is available on the software, but the real bonus is the listing of the occupations and government agencies. This information is duplicated online at FEDIX, but if you want to save online time, this is a good option.

Information USA

Infobusinesses
887 South Orem Blvd.
Orem, UT 84058
800-657-5300
Format: PC/CD-ROM

This is software created by Mathew Lesko. Information USA contains several powerful databases of potential help to the job seeker. Primary among them is the Federal Domestic Assistance Catalog which lists all grants available to residents. Also helpful are the vast files on the U.S. government databases, which could be of help for finding professional information. And if you get too bogged down in your job search, you can use the "great American gripe" portion of the software to send in a complaint to your favorite government agency. PC and CD-ROM, also $49.95.

Job Hunt

Scope International
P.O. Box 25252
Charlotte, NC 28229
800-843-5627
Format: PC with hard drive

Job Hunt (version 5) gives information on more than 6,000 leading companies. Searchable by industry, growth rate, state, and more. According to the purveyors of this product, it also contains files for creating mailing lists, a telephone helper that will dial stored phone numbers, and a word processor. As of this writing, the cost was $49.95.

Job Hunter, Resumate

RESUmate, Inc.
P.O. Box 7438
Ann Arbor, MI 48107
800-530-9310
Format: PC/Windows

Job Hunter is software that allows the individual job seeker to create a database of up to 200 names of contacts. The database you create is then searchable by many different criteria. A mailing label program is also included. Resumate is a product aimed more toward employers trying to set up a resume database system. Job Hunter costs $49.95 for the DOS version and $59.95 for the Windows version.

Marketplace Business

Marketplace Information Systems
Three University Office Park
Waltham, MA 02154
800-590-0065
Format: CD-ROM for Windows or Macintosh

This product may convince you to move to CD-ROM. Over 10 million companies along with SIC codes are available. According to the company, many job seekers purchase this product to look for companies that hire in their industry, particularly engineers. SIC codes are listed (all 476 pages) and are searchable by keyword. You can also print labels from this database. Cost, $849.

Perfect Resume

Permax, Inc.
P.O. Box 826
Woodstock, NY
800-223-6460
Format: PC/Windows/CD-ROM

The Perfect Resume program helps people get over any writer's block they may have in getting started on their resume. The interactive program leads you through the writing process and lets you sample other resumes along the way. DOS version costs $39.95, Windows is $49.95, and CD-ROM is $59.95.

You're Hired, and Quick and
Easy Federal Government Jobs Kit

> Datatech
> 6360 Flank Drive #300
> Harrisburg, PA 17112
> 800-556-7526
> Format: PC/Windows

The You're Hired software helps job seekers through the resume process. There are a resume builder, a format section, a contacts manager, an interview assistant, and a cover letter writer included in the package. The interview assistant looks like a good way to practice interviewing. Also available through Datatech is the Quick and Easy Federal Government Jobs Kit, which is a must-have for anyone who wants to work for the government. The software will take the headaches out of filling out those interminable application forms. Well worth the price. Both products sell individually for $49.95 plus shipping.

═══ NAVIGATION SOFTWARE FOR COMMERCIAL ONLINE SERVICES

Navigation software is designed to help users of commercial online services save time and money online. Instead of logging on, and, for example, reading through every bulletin board message you're interested in or reading email messages online, navigation software logs on for you and collects what you ask it to, then pops it into an offline area for you to read at your leisure.

Be aware, however, that this software can come and go—you'll need to keep up to date on the latest time-saving software available in your favorite commercial online service. To do this, call the service's toll-free number and ask customer support for information on navigation software. If you're online, you can leave a message for the sysop in the customer support section.

America Online

America Online, according to our last check, has redesigned its navigation software to include some built-in offline features, most notably something called Flash Session, which is available through its email utility at no extra charge. When in AOL's email utility, look for the menu option Flash Session. It allows you to compose email offline, and then send it when you get back online. See directions within AOL.

CompuServe

NavCis is the popular navigation software available for CompuServe. It checks messages, lets you compose email offline, and compiles bulletin board postings for you. NavCis is available for downloading online. You can find it through a keyword search of *NavCis* on CompuServe, or you can call 303-661-0345 to order. (This information was correct at press time, but may have changed when you read this.)

Delphi

Delphi currently has two navigation software offerings: D-Lite and Rainbow. Both cost from $39.00 to $79.00, depending on which version you buy. The main function of these products is to allow you to compose mail and messages offline. Use the keywords *D-Lite* and *Rainbow* in Delphi to find information about the software.

EWorld

EWorld is another service that has built an offline navigation system into its basic system. EWorld's is called Automatic Courier, and is free to its subscribers. Automatic Courier will collect newsclips for you and place them in folders (to read offline later), let you create offline mail and bulletin board messages, and let you ignore mail.

To access Automatic Courier, just go to the File menu and click on it. You will see Automatic Courier listed as an option.

GEnie

GEnie's popular navigator is Alladin. Alladin will gather news, bulletin board messages, and email for you, and allow you to read the material offline. Alladin is available by typing in the keyword *Aladdin* at GEnie's keyword search function. You also can download Alladin online, the cost of which varies, depending on which version you need. Expect to pay about $30 to $50.

Prodigy

Prodigy has three navigation software products available. Email connection and Bulletin Board are both available online for $14.95. To find them, perform a keyword search with the title you're interested in, and download them. Both products allow users to compose and read messages offline.

The Journalist is a product available by ordering it online. The Journalist creates news clippings from information culled from Prodigy and lets you read it offline. Again, find The Journalist by searching for the product name in a keyword search. It costs about $29.00.

Databases

Here are some selected databases for you to check into. Most of these charge a fee in addition to online time—sometimes a significant amount. It is likely that pricing and other information may have changed by the time you read this book.

Access

1900 W. 47th Pl. Suite 215
Shawnee Mission, KS 66205
913-432-0700
913-432-9451 FAX

Pricing is as follows: $25 initial three-month listing, $20/each additional three months; $25/initial six-month listing if you graduated from high school or college within the past six months. The fee is refunded when you find a job through Access. Employers in many industries use this database, including law, manufacturing, and health care. You can update your resume for free.

AIA Referral Network

American Institute of Architects
1735 New York Ave NW
Washington DC 20006
800-242-6381

Available to AIA members/student members. Call/write for fee and resume format information.

Career Database

104 Mt. Suburn Street 5th Floor
P.O. Box 2341
Cambridge, MA 02238
508-487-2238

Resume database. Annual fee for membership.

College Recruitment Database

Contact ETSI
1200 Quince Orchard Blvd.
Gaithersburg, MD 20878
800-638-8094
301-590-2300

This is a resume retrieval service that provides essential data about 13,000 graduating, undergraduate, and graduate students. All colleges and universities can participate in this service. Have your college contact ETSI so that you can list your electronic resume here.

CONNEXION

Peterson's Connexion Services
202 Carnegie Center
P.O. Box 2123
Princeton, NJ 08543
800-338-3282

or

Connexion
On line service
800-638-9094

An International database of job listings.

DIRECTLINK for the disABLED

Direct Link for the Disabled, Inc.
P.O. Box 1036
Solvang, CA 93464
805-688-1603

This service will inform you about placement services and job training programs for people with disabilities. Contact Direct Link representatives to tell them about the nature of your disability, where you live, and that you are specifically looking for job placement information.

4-Sights Network

16625 Grand River
Detroit, MI 48227
313-272-3900 Free

This is part of a national computer system for people who are blind or visually impaired. It requires the use of a computer modem.

Human Resource Information Network

ETSI, 1200 Quince Orchard Blvd.,
Gaithersburg, MD 20878
800-638-8094
301-590-2300 Contact for costs.

Among the databases on this service is the Job Ads USA database which lists well over 15,000 private sector job openings gleaned from more than 100 newspapers. Users can search for jobs by job title, job abstract, geographic location, date advertised, and more. (Note that the cost of this database can be prohibitive. Call the phone numbers listed for price quotes.)

Job Bank USA

> 1420 Spring Hill Rd.
> McLean, VA 22102
> 800-296-1872
> Fee

The good thing about this database is that your resume is never distributed without your approval. The cost is reasonable (under $100.00) and you can update your resume at any time.

kiNexus

> Information Kinetics, Inc.,
> 640 N. LaSalle St., Suite 560
> Chicago IL 60610
> 800-828-0422
> 312-642-7560
> Annual fee

This is an online resume database service for college students and graduates with up to five years work experience. After completing your resume, the information is put into the kiNexus computer. You can request the higher-cost confidential option and a number will be assigned. Free if you are a student at one of the 1,500+ universities that subscribe to this service. Check with your school's placement office.

SkillSearch

> 104 Woodmont Blvd #306
> Nashville, TN 37205
> 800-252-5665
> 615-383-4743 FAX

Alumni networking database. Call for details about which alumni qualify.

BOOKS FOR THE JOB SEEKER

Many of the books listed here are directories that you will be able to find in a good library or bookstore, but many are also available online through commercial online services such as CompuServe and America Online.

AMA's Executive Employment Guide

American Management
135 W. 50th St.
New York, NY 10020

AMBA's MBA Employment Guide

Association of MBA
227 Commerce St.
East Haven, CT 06512
204-467-8870

America's Corporate Families and International Affiliates

Dun's Marketing Services
3 Sylvan Way
Parsippany, NJ 07054
201-526-0651

Association Yellow Book

Monitor Publishing Co.
104 Fifth Ave,
2nd Floor
New York, NY 10011
212-627-4140

Business Organizations, Agencies, and Publications Directory

Gale Research Inc.
645 Griswold
835 Penobscot Bldg.
Detroit, MI 48226
800-877-4253

Business Publications Rates & Data

Standard Rates & Data Service, Inc.
3004 Glenview Rd.
Wilmette, IL 60091
708-256-6067

Career & Job Fair Finder

College Placement Council Inc.
62 Highland Ave.
Bethlehem, PA 18017
215-868-1421

Chemical Industry Directory

State Mutual Book and Periodical Service
521 Fifth Ave.
New York, NY 10017
212-682-5844

Community Jobs
(opportunities at nonprofit organizations)

1516 P Street, NW.
Washington, DC 20005

Corporate Technology Directory

Corp-Tech
12 Alfred St., Suite 200
Woburn, MA 01801
617-932-3939

Directory of Executive Recruiters

Kennedy Publications
Templeton Rd.
Fitzwilliam, NH 03447
800-531-0007
603-585-6544

Directory of Public High Technology Corporations

American Investor, Inc.
311 Bainbridge St.
Philadelphia, PA 19147
215-925-2761

Directories in Print

Gale Research Inc.
645 Griswold
835 Penobscot Bldg.
Detroit, MI 48226
800-877-4253

Directory of Corporate Affiliations

Reed Reference Publishing
P.O. Box 31
New Providence, NJ 07974
800-323-6772

Directory of Leading Private Companies

Reed Reference Publishing
P.O. Box 31
New Providence, NJ 07974
800-323-6772

Directory of Top Computer Executives

Applied Computer Research
P.O. Box 9280
Phoenix, AZ 85068
602-995-5929

Dun & Bradstreet Million Dollar Directory

Dun's Marketing Services
3 Sylvan Way
Parsippany, NJ 07054
800-526-0651

Lists major public and private U.S. corporations with a net worth of $500,000 or more.

Dun & Bradstreet Reference Book of Corporate Managements

Dun's Marketing Services
3 Sylvan Way
Parsippany, NJ 07054
800-526-0651

Dun's Business Rankings

Dun's Marketing Services
3 Sylvan Way
Parsippany, NJ 07054
800-526-0651

Dun's Career Guide

Dun & Bradstreet Information Services
3 Sylvan Way
Parsipanny, NJ 07054
800-526-0651
201-455-0900

Features companies with more than 1,000 employees in fields in a variety of technical and professional areas.

Dun's Directory of Service Companies

Dun's Marketing Services
3 Sylvan Way
Parsippany NJ 07054
800-526-0651

Dun's Guide to Healthcare Companies

Dun's Marketing Service
3 Sylvan Way
Parsippany, NJ 07054
201-605-6000

Dun's Regional Business Directory

Dun's Marketing Services
3 Sylvan Way
Parsippany, NJ 07054
800-526-0651

Encyclopedia of Associations: Regional, State, and Local Organizations

Gale Research Inc.
835 Penobscot Bldg.
Detroit, MI 48226
800-877-4253

This directory describes nonprofit organizations with interstate, state, city, or local scope and interest, including professional associations for most occupations.

Federal Career Opportunities

Federal Research Service, Inc.
370 West Maple Avenue
Vienna, VA 22180
703-281-0200

Federal Jobs Digest

325 Pennsylvania Ave., S.E.
Washington, DC 20003
914-762-5111

Hospital Phone Book

Reed Reference Publishing
121 Chanlon Rd.
New Providence, RI 07974
800-521-8110

International Directory of Corporate Affiliations

Reed Reference Publishing
P.O. Box 31
New Providence, NJ 07974
800-323-6772

Job Hunter's Sourcebook

Gale Research Inc.
835 Penobscot Bldg.
Detroit, MI 48226
800-877-4253

Job Seeker's Guide to 1,000 Top Employers

Gale Research Inc.
835 Penobscot Bldg.
Detroit, MI 48226
800-877-4253

This directory tells you who to contact for job information at 1,000 private and public firms from all industries throughout the country.

Macmillan Directory of International Advertisers and Agencies

National Register Publishing Co.
3004 Glenview Rd.
Wilmette, IL 60091
800-323-6772

Macmillan Directory of Leading Private Companies

Reed Reference Publishing
P.O. Box 31
New Providence, NJ 07974
800-323-6772

Moody's Industry Review

Moody's Investors Service, Inc.
99 Church St.
New York, NY 10007
212-533-0300

Annual reference includes information on 4,000 leading businesses.

National Trade and Professional Associations of the United States

Columbia Books
1212 New York Ave., NW, Suite 330
Washington , DC 20005
202-898-0662

Peterson's Job Opportunities for Business and Liberal Arts Graduates

P.O. Box 2123
Princeton, NJ 08543
609-243-9111

Peterson's Job Opportunities for Engineering, Science, and Computer Graduates

P.O. Box 2123
Princeton, NJ 08543
609-243-9111

Standard & Poor's Register of Corporations, Directors, and Executives

Standard & Poor's Corp.
25 Broadway
New York, NY 10004
212-208-8702

Lists more than 45,000 corporations.

Telecommunications Directory

Gale Research Inc.
835 Penobscot Bldg.
Detroit, MI 48226
800-877-4253

The Almanac of American Employers

Corporate Jobs Outlook
P.O. Drawer 100
Boerne, TX 78006
210-755-8810

The Electronic Resume Revolution

John Wiley & Sons, Inc.
605 Third Ave.
New York, NY 10158-0012
800-225-5945 Orders
212-850-6000

The Guide to American Directories

B. Klein Publications, Inc.
P.O. Box 8503
Coral Springs, FL 33075
305-752-1708

Lists 330 directories of some 400 topics.

The National Directory of Internships

National Society for Experiential Education
3509 Haworth Dr., Suite 207
Raleigh, NC 27609-7229
919-787-3263

Lists internship opportunities.

Thomas' Register of American Manufacturers

Thomas Publishing Co.
1 Pennsylvania Plaza
New York, NY 10110
212-695-0500

Lists product manufacturers.

Personnel Executives Contactbook

Gale Research, Inc.
835 Penobscot Bldg.
Detroit MI 48226-4094
800-877-4253

This is the best reference for identifying personnel directors at over 30,000 U.S. companies.

Vocational Careers Sourcebook

Gale Research, Inc.
835 Penobscot Bldg.
Detroit, MI 48226
800-877-4253

Ward's Business Directory of U.S. Private and Public Companies

Gale Research, Inc.
835 Penobscot Bldg.
Detroit, MI 48226
800-877-4253

ASSOCIATIONS

You will discover that many associations are going online in order to deliver their messages to a wider audience. If you find an association you like, ask if they have an online resume service or database and if they have plans to go online (if they're not already online). If you don't see an association here that fits your profession, check online or in the *Encyclopedia of Associations.*

Academy of Motion Picture Arts & Sciences

8949 Wilshire Blvd.
Beverly Hills, CA 90211
213-859-9619

American Association of Advertising Agencies

666 Third Ave. 13th Floor
New York, NY 10017-4565
212-682-2500

American Association of Finance & Accounting

5757 Wilshire Blvd., Suite 447
Los Angeles, CA 90056
213-852-1311

Resume database service for accounting/financial.

American Bankers Association

1120 Connecticut Ave., NW
Washington, DC 20036
202-663-4000

American Association of Engineering Societies

1111 19th St., NW. Suite 608
Washington, DC 20036
202-296-2237

American Institute of Biological Sciences (AIBS)

730 11th Street NW
Washington, DC 2001-4584
202-628-1500
800-992-AIBS

American Nurses Association

2420 Pershing Rd.
Kansas City, MO 64108
816-474-5720

American Public Health Association

1015 15th Street NW
Washington, DC 2005
202-7898-5600

Health Placement Services

American Nurses Association
2420 Pershing Rd.
Kansas City, MO 64108
816-474-5720

American Pharmaceutical Association

2215 Constitution Ave. NW
Washington, DC 20037
202-628-4410

American Society of Design Engineers

P.O. Box 931
Arlington Heights, IL 60006
708-259-7120
708-225-6517 fax

Artists in Print

665 3rd
San Francisco, CA 94107
415-243-8244

Job referral for graphic artists.

Association of Computer Professionals

230 Park Ave., Suite 460
New York, NY 10169
212-599-3019

Association for Women in Computing

P.O. Box 21100
St. Paul, MN 55123
612-681-9371

Bank Executives Network

300 S High St.
West Chester, PA 19382
215-431-1900

Database service to banks of active job seekers.

Electronic Industries Association

1722 I Street NW, Suite 300
Washington, DC 20006
202-457-4900

Graphic Artists Guild

11 W 20th St.
8th Floor
New York, NY 10011
212-463-7730

Information Technology Association of America

1616 N. Ft. Meyer Dr., Suite 1300
Arlington, VA 22209
703-522-5055

National Association of Personal Financial Advisors

1130 W. Lake Cook Rd.
Buffalo Grove, IL 60089
800-366-2732

National Computer Graphics Association

2722 Merrilee Dr.
Reston, VA 22031
703-698-9600

National Education Association

1201 Sixteenth St., NW
Washington, DC 20036
202-822-7200

Newspaper Association Job Bank

111600 Sunrise Valley Dr.
Reston, VA 22091
703-648-1072
800-562-2672

Newspaper positions.

National Federation of the Blind

1800 Johnson Street
Baltimore, MD 21230
410-659-9314 for information about programs
800-638-7518 for information about the J.O.B. program
410-752-5011 bulletin board system

The National Federation of the Blind has an excellent array of materials and programs to help any resident who is legally blind. Available are adaptive devices for computers, job opportunities, and a vast network of blind professionals in various professions. Free audiocassettes and job information. Especially helpful in assisting blind people to get online.

National Lawyers Guild

55 6th Ave.
New York, NY 10013
212-966-5000

National Society of Professional Engineers

1420 King St.
Alexandria, VA 22314
703-684-2800

Public Relations Society of America

33 Irving Place
New York, NY 10003
212-995-2266
212-995-0476 Job Hunt Line
212-995-0757 fax

The National Association of Legal Assistants

1601 S. Main St., Suite 300
Tulsa, OK 74119
918-587-6828

Women in Information Processing

Lock Box 39173
Washington, DC 20016
202-328-6161

Women in Sales Association

Eight Madison Avenue
P.O. Box M
Valhalla, NY 10595
914-946-3802

PRIVACY PROTECTION

Because job hunting is a confidential endeavor, many people worry that using the online services for this purpose will expose their efforts, thereby potentially jeopardizing their current positions. If this is a concern for you, read this section to learn about programs that can help keep your private business private.

Anonymous Remailer Information

An anonymous remailer is a free computer service that takes your regular email and makes it anonymous. Often, remailers also encrypt your messages with PGP, the current popular encryption software. (Read the next section on PGP to learn how to access it.)

Remailers work by stripping out your personal information from your email and posts before it goes to the intended recipient. When the recipient gets the anonymous email, he or she also gets a set of instructions telling how to reach you.

System administrators who operate remailers carefully monitor use of these services. They do not allow their servers to be used for sending nasty notes or other marginal information. Keep your use on the up and up, or you'll find yourself booted off the system.

The cost of most remailers is very reasonable, and each comes with a specific set of instructions for use. For a current list of remailers, see:

http://www.cs.berkeley.edu/~raph/remailer-list.html

This site is a gold mine of information on remailers, with links to the remailers and download locations included. Be aware, though, that remailer sites come and go with greater frequency than most Internet sites, so keep up to date on this information.

PGP: Pretty Good Privacy

PGP is software that is a "freely redistributable public key cryptosystem." This means that the software doesn't cost anything for you, and it's widely available on the Internet for you to download. This software encrypts, or scrambles, messages so that they cannot be read by people unless they have your "key."

Phillip Zimmerman, who created PGP, views encrypting email very much like using an envelope for regular mail. Why send your email out there to be read by anyone, when you can put it in an envelope? For a job seeker worried about security, an email envelope isn't a bad idea.

If you work on a MS-DOS, Amiga, Atari ST, or UNIX system, you can use PGP. The complete documentation for PGP is available at:

http://www.pegasus.esprit.ec.org/people/arne/pgp.html

This lengthy documentation will tell you how to get PGP and how to use it.

It is against the law in some countries to download PGP from a U.S. or Canadian site if you are within the borders of any other country. But there are sites around the world from which you can download PGP, which you can find in the list at the above address. Or try this address:

http://www.ma ntis.co.uk/pgp/pgp.html

Other Privacy Information Available

An excellent book is available on this topic titled *The Computer Privacy Handbook: A Practical Guide to E-Mail Encryption, Data Protection, and PGP Privacy Software.* Contact

abacard@well.com

for more details on the book, which was just about to be published at this writing.

Some of the following information was excerpted from *An Online Guide to Privacy Resources.* This excellent online guide is available in its entirety at:

http://epic.digicash.com/epic

or

http://cpsr.org/cpsr/privacy/epic/privacy_resources_faq.html

Usenet News Groups

alt.privacy.anon-server

If you read the PGP documentation and still have questions about what to do or how to use it, ask your questions on this Usenet group. There are several world-class encryption and remailer experts who frequent this group and will be able to answer your questions.

Sci.crypt

Unmoderated technical discussion of encryption. Another good place to visit with those PGP questions.

Privacy Organizations

Electronic Privacy Information Center (EPIC)

666 Pennsylvania Ave, SE
Suite 301
Washington, DC 20003
202-544-9240
Marc Rotenberg, Director

EPIC was established in 1994 to focus public attention on emerging privacy issues relating to the National Information

Infrastructure, such as the Clipper Chip, the Digital Telephony proposal, medical records privacy, and the sale of consumer data. EPIC conducts litigation, sponsors conferences, produces reports, publishes the EPIC Alert and leads campaigns on privacy issues.

Email: **info@epic.org** or
http://epic.digicash.com/epic

Privacy International

Privacy International c/o EPIC
666 Penn. Ave, SE, Suite 301
Washington, DC 20003
Director General: Simon Davies

An international human rights group based in London, England with offices in Washington, DC and Sydney, Australia. PI has members in over 40 countries and has led campaigns against privacy violations in numerous countries including Australia, New Zealand, and the Philippines. PI publishes the International Privacy Bulletin and sponsors international conferences on privacy issues.

Email: **pi@epic.org** or
gopher://cpsr.org/cpsr/privacy/privacy_international/

US Privacy Council (USPC)

P.O. Box 15060
Washington, DC 20003
Voice: 202- 829-3660

A coalition of U.S. privacy groups and individuals founded in 1991 to deal with privacy issues. USPC works in Washington monitoring legislation and the activities of government agencies, and works closely with other groups on privacy issues including National ID cards, reforming credit reporting, caller ID, and international issues.

Email: **privtime@access.digex.net**

Privacy Rights Clearinghouse

5998 Alcala Park
San Diego, CA 92110
Voice: 619-260-4806
800-773-7748 (in CA only)

A California-based organization formed in 1992. This is an expecially good place for job seekers to visit, as Beth Givens has put together many fact sheets dealing specifically with job search issues such as interview questions and background checking. The 800 number is a hotline to help educate consumers about their rights.
Email: **prc@teetot.acusd.edu** or
http://www.manymedia.com/prc/

Computer Professionals for Social Responsibility

P.O. Box 717
Palo Alto, CA 94301
Voice: 415- 322-3778
Managing Director: Kathleen Kells

A national organization of people concerned about the impact of technology on society. CPSR sponsors an annual conference, maintains numerous mailing lists on computer-related issues, a large Internet site of information, and publishes a quarterly newsletter. It has 24 local chapters across the U.S. and several international affiliates. CPSR sponsors working groups on civil liberties, working in the computer industry, and others.
Contact: **cpsr-info@cpsr.org** or **http://cpsr.org/cpsr**

Internet Society

12020 Sunrise Valley Drive
Suite 270
Reston, VA 22091
Voice: 703-648-9888
Executive Director: Anthony Rutkowski

This group is dedicated to fostering evolution of the Internet and its use. It sponsors a yearly conference, publishes an excellent quarterly newsletter, and works with standards committees to develop Internet standards for networking and privacy.
Email: **isoc@isoc.org** or **http://info.isoc.org/**

Electronic Frontier Foundation

1667 K St. NW, Suite 801
Washington, DC. 20006-1605
Voice: 202-347-5400
Director: Andrew Taubman

Formed in 1990, this group maintains an Internet site, publishes an electronic newsletter, and lobbies in Washington.
Email: **info@eff.org** or **http://cpsr.org/cpsr</a>**

Index